THE UPPER CLOTH REVOLT IN SOUTH TRAVANCORE

THE UPPER CLOTH REVOLT IN SOUTH TRAVANCORE

Theological Interpretation of a Subaltern Movement

VIJU WILSON

MANOHAR
2025

First published 2021

Reprinted 2022, 2023, 2024, 2025

ISBN 978-81-949912-3-6

Published by
Ajay Jain *for*
Manohar Publishers & Distributors
4753/23 Ansari Road, Daryaganj
New Delhi 110002

Typeset by
Ravi Shanker
Delhi 110095

Printed at
Replika Press Pvt. Ltd.

Contents

Preface

The historical event, which contributed to the defining moment in the upward social mobility of a subaltern community, has to be remembered in the present for two reasons. First, it provides them confidence to challenge the forces that threaten the further advancement of their community life, and thus enlarge the space of empowerment in society. The memory of liberating historical movement primarily motivates the subalterns to initiate bold steps towards their wholistic liberation. Second, the liberating historical event of a subaltern community is a potential source of motivation for other subalterns who continue to be disempowered in different aspects of social life. The memory of such events cannot be neutral because they are the products of 'taking side' with values of justice, equality and freedom. It demands the empowered subalterns to actualize the value of solidarity with those who are disempowered in life. Every liberating movement can speak to the contemporary world if they are meaningfully interpreted in the context.

The Upper Cloth Revolt in South Travancore, a liberating movement of Nadars, in the nineteenth century, stands as a model movement for the subaltern communities in India. It contains the stories of resistance, assertion of rights and liberative ventures. It tells the subalterns that they can speak out. They remain powerless if they don't speak and act upon what they believe to be egalitarian. Of course, if the subalterns speak against subjugation, they have to endure the consequences: both physical and psychological. However, they carry the seeds of resistance which may germinate new life for the future generation. The movements of resistance are the expressions of yearning for a new hope of liberated life. The liberating potential of subalterns gets visibility when the movements of resistance occur among them. The upward mobility of subalterns depends on how they respond to the life-negating forces and realities which perpetuate their backwardness. The Upper Cloth Revolt informs us that subalterns can endure the pain of resistance and achieve liberation from the forces of oppression and marginalization.

Every liberating historical movement has some unique features. In the Upper Cloth Revolt, it was Nadar women who challenged the existing social restriction on the dress code of the time and took assertive steps to assert their right to wear 'upper cloth', the symbol of dignity. In this movement, the dignity of women defined the status of a community in the caste-ridden patriarchal society. The issue of women became the substance of a community's journey of struggle towards liberation. Both men and women jointly countered the social disabilities and faced the consequences of resistance. In fact, women brought out the liberating potential of a community. Religion functioned as a source of liberation behind this movement. The internalization of the liberative values of Christian faith led to the emergence of a movement which defined the destiny of a subaltern community. It reminds one that faith values become meaningful if they engage with broken life realities and initiate the process of healing the wounded bodies.

The liberating historical events can be interpreted from different perspectives. In this volume, an attempt is made to interpret the Upper Cloth Revolt in south Travancore from the theological perspective. Religious faith has visible or invisible role in many historical events. In the Upper Cloth Revolt, Christian faith influenced the Nadars, particularly women, to question their social disabilities. It gives scope for the theological interpretation of this movement. This perspectival reading is enriched by the subaltern consciousness and discourses. A new meaning of faith is contextually evolved through the interpretation of an historical event. A historical episode in the life of a subaltern community became a 'text' of liberation which needs to be interpreted. On the one hand it makes the Christian faith historically connected to the life of people and brings forth new theological discourses for faith-praxis; on the other hand it empowers the subalterns to initiate a liberating process for enlarging their space in society.

This book was originally a doctoral dissertation submitted to the Senate of Serampore College (University). I express my gratitude to the authorities for granting permission to publish it. As a research scholar I worked under the supervision of late Rev. Dr. (habil.) James Massey, a well known Indian scholar and theologian and a former member of National Commission for Minorities. I am grateful to him for his resourceful guidance that shaped my thinking and perspective throughout the work. Apart from him, the person whose scholarship and guidance I immensely received all through my work was Sr. Dr. Shalini Mulackal, Professor of Christian Theology, Vidyajyoti College of Theology, New Delhi. She critically looked at the manuscript and offered comments and suggestions. I sincerely thank her for the time and energy she spent on this work. My gratitude also goes to Bishop Dr. J.W. Gladstone and Prof. R.N. Yesudas who gave initial comments on my research topic. This volume has immensely benefited from the resources available in United Theological College Archives, Bangalore; Central Archives, Thiruvananthapuram, Kerala; Archives Directorate, Thiruvananthapuram; Vidyajyoti College of Theology, New Delhi and Centre for Dalit/Subaltern Studies, New Delhi. I am also grateful to Rev. Dr. Ravi Tiwari, Rev. Dr. H. Vanlalauva and Rev. Dr. P.G. George and Rev. Dr. Santanu K. Patro for their support and encouragement throughout my research programme at South Asia Theological Research Institute (SATHRI), Serampore, West Bengal. I also remember with gratitude Mr. Imti Jamir and Mr. Nungsang Jamir at Centre for Dalit/Subaltern Studies for their sincere support and love during my research work. This work would not have been possible without the financial and prayer support of my family: P. Wilson and P. Suseela, my parents; Sonia, my wife; Sia and Vihann, my children. Thank you for your love and encouragement. This work comes to the readers in the form of a book because of the academic interest shown by Manohar Publishers & Distributors and their editorial team, New Delhi. I am thankful to them. Above all, I am thankful to God for enabling me to complete this work, which I hope, may speak to the contemporary world, and initiate new studies on the liberating movements of subalterns.

Union Biblical Seminary, Pune VIJU WILSON

Abbreviations

AICS	Academy of Integrated Christian Studies
ATC	Asian Trading Corporation
ATTWI	Association of Theologically Trained Women of India
BTESSC	Board of Theological Education Senate of Serampore College
CCA	Christian Conference of Asia
CDS	Centre for Dalit/Subaltern Studies
CLC	Christian Literature Centre
CLS	Christian Literature Society
CMS	Church Missionary Society
CSS	Christava Sahitya Samithi
CWMA	Council for World Mission Archive
ETC	Eastern Theological College
GLTC	Gurukul Lutheran Theological College
GTC	Gossner Theological College
HRPT	Historical Research and Publications Trust
ICHR	Indian Church History Review
ISPCK	Indian Society for Promoting Christian Knowledge
KUTS	Kerala United Theological Seminary
LMS	London Missionary Society
OBC	Other Backward Classes
PTCA	Programme for Theology and Cultures in Asia
SATHRI	South Asia Theological Research Institute
SC	Scheduled Caste
SCEPTRE	Senate Centre for Extension and Pastoral Theological Research
SPCK	Society for Promoting Christian Knowledge
TSC	Tribal Study Centre
UELCI	United Evangelical Lutheran Churches in India

UTC	United Theological College
UTCA	United Theological College Archives
WSC	Women Study Centre

Glossary

aṭiyan	your slave
chāla	house of a Cheraman
cheri	house of a Pariah
chitaravadham	kill in a cruel manner without any reason
chōru	rice
dēśavāḻi	chieftain with less than a hundred Nair soldiers
dharmmabhūmi	land of charity
ēṭam	space/place/room
hiraṇyagarbhaṁ	ritual conducted in relation to the succession of a new king
illaṁ or *mana* or *manakkal*	house of a Nambudiri Brahmin
janmi	landlord
janmaṁ	hereditary and tax-free land
kārikkādi	dirty gruel
kōvilakaṁ or *koṭṭaraṁ*	king's palace
kudi or *pura*	home of a blacksmith, goldsmith, or carpenter, weaver, or toddy drawer
kudiyān	tenant
kuppāyam	a kind of shirt
mādam	hut
mannappedi	fear of Manna (Manna fear)
murajapaṁ	customary prayer
nāduvāḻi	chieftain with minimum hundred Nair soldiers
parappēdikkālam	period of paraya fear
ponnu tamburān	golden god
prāyaśchitam	penitence
pulappedi	pulaya fear

sarkkār paṭṭaṁ — government land
satyaparikṣa — trial by ordeal
śri padmanābha dasā — servant of Sri Padmanabha
tān — oneself/he/she/it
taṉṯē — one's/his/her
taṉṯēṭam — courage, capacity, competency, arrogance, pride, etc.
taṉṯēṭakkāran — courageous man
taṉṯēṭakkāri — courageous woman
taṉṯēṭi — courageous person
tiru manassu — sacred mind
tulabhāraṁ — ritual conducted in relation to the succession of a new king
tūkku — ordeal by balance
ūḻiaṁ — gratuitous service (Service without payment)
upanayana — investiture of sacred thread for royal family members
ūttupura — free inn
viruti — supplying things free of cost
vīṭu or *bhavanam* — house of a Nair

Introduction

Subaltern Movements and Religious Faith

A New Reading

Our world comprises diverse cultures, ideologies, traditions, and religions, each is valid and relevant in the context in which it developed. If a religious tradition is introduced in a particular historical setting, which is alien to it, it is probable that an encounter between the existing one and the new one will take place. This may lead to a meaningful interaction resulting in the assimilation of certain characteristics of both faiths.[1] In Christianity, such encounters have resulted in the emergence of various interpretations and the development of contextual doctrinal formulations. They are different expressions of faith, which attempt to make it intelligible and meaningful in a particular sociocultural context. Any attempt of universalizing the Christian faith through the lens of a particular culture is invalidated. No cultural heritage or social location can comprehensively contain or communicate its message universally. Every historical context has a significant role in making the faith relevant. Yet something will be missed out of new interpretations, thanks to contextual diversity. There have been many attempts to interpret Christianity in the light of the cultural and historical resources/realities of different communities.

Along with cultural factors, historical events/realities play an important role in the contextual articulations of faith and they are one of the main sources of theologizing.[2] Indeed, theology is the result of the interaction between faith and history/ historical events. This interface is not a single occurrence but a process, faith encountering the human realities, and vice-versa. Since there is no fixed interpretation of faith relevant to every context, the understanding of faith continuously gets shaped when it is read by the historical experiences of people. The faith which is articulated without the backing of history cannot respond to the life situations of people.[3] Therefore, faith has to be interpreted with historical consciousness. For instance, it is very much evident in the Bible that the historical experiences of the people of Israel, the people of God in the Biblical stories, shaped their faith expressions – how did they understand and experience God in their lives. The contextual liberation theologies, the interpretations of Christian faith from liberation point of view, are also articulated in the light of historical experiences of oppressed communities in different contexts. They underscore the role of history/historical events in interpreting the faith.

It is important to note that some historical events decided the future of certain communities who had gone through various forms of oppression and marginalization in Indian society. They shaped people's understanding of their faith, giving them dignity, identity and subjecthood. In a dehumanizing caste setting painful historical events have motivated subalterns to claim their space in society. Such historical events can serve as sources of developing new theologies (new interpretations of faith) in local context. For instance, the Upper Cloth Revolt in South Travancore[4] a liberating historical event which facilitated the social mobility of Nadars, and a potential source for developing new expressions of Christianity.

In the Travancore Kingdom,[5] society had imposed restrictions on the dress code of the low castes.[6] Women of high caste origin, who claimed superior identity, wore a piece of cloth over their breasts and shoulders, called the 'Upper Cloth',[7] but women of low caste were not allowed to wear it. The cloth was a symbol of respect and selfhood of women[8] in the social milieu of Travancore State in the nineteenth century. The restriction on upper cloth had legal support, and was strictly implemented by the government machinery. By denying this privilege, the lower-caste women were dishonoured and humiliated in all aspects of life. In fact, their womanhood became subject to public mockery in a male-centred and upper-caste controlled society.

The restriction on wearing upper cloth had community dimension as well. Physical and sexual atrocities of upper caste men against the low caste women have multiple implications. True, the deep-seated gender prejudices of upper-caste men existed, but the rule was not just to control and subjugate the women; it was primarily to humiliate their community. Social restrictions and physical violence against low caste women have to be basically understood as community issues. The physical and psychological aggression of upper caste men against subaltern women was an attempt to perpetuate the hegemony of upper castes and to remind the lower castes of their powerlessness.[9] It was very much true in the Travancore society where the human body, especially those belonging to the lower caste, was controlled by caste rules. Within the framework of caste, the body and dignity of low caste women were also controlled and defined by the upper caste men. By controlling the selfhood of low caste women the upper caste men were actually controlling the low caste communities. By not allowing Nadar women to wear the upper cloth,[10] a symbol of dignity, upper caste men not only trampled on the dignity of Nadar women but also subjugated the Nadars as a community. But the Nadars, who had accepted the Christian faith, were not ready to accept the humiliation. They encouraged their women to cover their bodies.[11] The dignity of Nadar women was the dignity of the Nadar community. Hence, in Upper Cloth Revolt, Nadar women were encouraged to break this restriction on their customary dress code.[12]

Nadar women, particularly the Christians among them, appeared in public with the upper cloth and in doing so challenged the hegemony of the upper castes. This revolt later was known as the Upper Cloth Revolt.[13] It was a struggle to restore their dignity and basic right to cover their bosom. This movement not only gave a new direction in the social and religious life of Nadars but also created a platform for initiating other movements against social inequalities in Travancore.[14] The Christian faith had an important role in initiating the revolt. It was a movement in which the Nadars encountered their subalternized life with a new religious faith. The Biblical faith had taught them that every human being is created in the image and likeness of God with equal rights and dignity. The missionaries helped them to understand their faith contextually. Thus, claiming the privilege of wearing upper cloth became a location for the praxis of a new faith. Throughout the revolt, the upper cloth remained as a social symbol through which Nadars encountered the Divine. It was the symbol which united them and made them assertive.

The Christian faith element of the Upper Cloth Revolt has, however, been eclipsed though there have been very few attempts to interpret historical events from the Christian point of view. The role of women is also important – it was Nadar women who had become the agents of resistance and change. They took bold steps to cover themselves in their society with its rigid caste rules on dress. Indeed, they felt they had become revolutionary tools in the hands of God. The Upper Cloth Revolt was the movement of a subaltern community, which can be interpreted from different perspectives. My study attempts to narrate the contemporary significance of this movement in terms of gender and caste from a Christian perspective informed by subaltern methodological and conceptual reflections.

Historical Events

Though some once-subaltern groups are now economically and politically advanced, a majority are still under the stigma of caste and other social and cultural prejudices. Economic and political empowerment has not improved the 'social standing' of subalterns in the eyes of the so-called upper castes. In order to escape caste and its purity-pollution apparatus many subalterns had embraced the Christian faith, but they continue to face different forms of violence and exclusion. They resist oppression and affirm their selfhood in everyday life. They should be encouraged to initiate liberating historical movements for asserting life and to interpret their religious faith in the light of those movements. It is also to be noted that the patriarchal subjugation makes women in the subaltern communities more vulnerable and victimized. Their historical experience of pain and historical events of assertion against life-negating forces can also become a source of interpreting the faith. The interpretation of subaltern historical movements like Upper Cloth Revolt can motivate subaltern communities in general and subaltern women in particular to confront dehumanizing forces in today's society and to develop new interpretations and expressions of their faith out of their historical experiences. In this narrative, focus is given on the interpretation of Christian faith in the light of the historical experiences of a subaltern community in Upper Cloth Revolt and vice versa.

The attempt to interpret liberating historical events such as the Upper Cloth Revolt is significant in many ways. Some of them are as follows:

(1) Interpreting the Upper Cloth Revolt from a subaltern perspective will enhance the morale of other subaltern communities and subaltern women to fight against their social disabilities. The Upper Cloth Revolt is a model social movement for the empowerment of subalterns today. The empowerment of subalterns is possible only through their own initiative and agency. In any subaltern movement, the subalterns should be both leaders and subjects. They need to emerge with a subversive energy. Interpreting the experiences of the Nadars in this revolt can encourage other subaltern communities who are in a journey of liberation.

(2) The distinctiveness of the Upper Cloth Revolt was the agency of subaltern women. Nadar women were motivated to challenge the hegemony of men and assert their selfhood and dignity. This was the first step for the advancement of women, particularly subaltern women, in a caste-ridden society. Caste society is patriarchal in nature too. In order to gather strength for affirming selfhood and dignity in a caste-man dominated society, women need to look back to historical events like the Upper Cloth Revolt in which their mothers stood for reclaiming value and dignity of womanhood. The nature and substance of the Upper Cloth Revolt will encourage subaltern women to exercise their agency. It can also contribute to the feminist theological discourse and methodology for enabling the women, particularly the subalterns, to break their silence in the Church and society.

(3) The struggle of one subaltern community does not end with

a full or partial social advancement or with liberation from bondage. The struggle has to be continued by identifying with the struggles of other downtrodden groups who are not able to break the barriers of social progress. At the same time, memories of past experiences help the communities know the historical condition of their existence and religious faith. They also persuade the respective communities to resist the hegemonic tendencies which may sneak into the community life. In this sense, theological interpretation (interpreting in relation to Christian faith) of Upper Cloth Revolt facilitates the Nadar Christian community to know the historical dimension of their faith and to celebrate their faith by participating in the struggles of other subaltern communities.

(4) The history of subaltern communities is the history of struggle and suffering. The experiences of the subaltern communities during their resistance are resources to be articulated from different perspectives. The theological articulation of the Upper Cloth Revolt gives a framework for the subaltern communities to develop their own local interpretations of faith based on historical struggle. Local expressions of faith through historical experiences can speak to the people more meaningfully than the interpretations of faith through the prism of philosophies and ideologies alien to them.

Methodology: Through the Subaltern Lens

Every discipline has its own methodology to develop new ideas and interpret concepts and realities. Methodology is basically about the process of knowledge construction or formation. It gives guidelines to construct new knowledge or add new data to the existing knowledge. It refers to the procedures and rules used in an inquiry or research also. Besides, methodology implies a perspective. The question that is implicit here is how do we do this? It does not mean that there is only one way to do theology. Classical and contextual-liberation theologies have been developed with different methodologies. Subaltern methodology attempts to develop new interpretations of faith from the perspective of the downtrodden. It is informed by historical experiences, culture and religious traditions of those people.

Methodologically, in this work, I have attempted to construct a new interpretation of the Christian faith in the light of a historical event. The Upper Cloth Revolt in South Travancore is taken as a historical event for methodological exploration.

In the words of Veena Das, 'Subalterns are not morphological categories, but represent a perspective.'[15] This means that subaltern life is itself a perspective. It represents values, questions, voices, cultures and traditions different from those dominant in society. It embodies a perspective which is non-hegemonic and egalitarian, and demands a perspectival change: from hegemonic to non-hegemonic. The existence of subalterns points to the need to see realities different from the conventional perception. Often the subaltern life stories are not even articulated from the perspective of what they have experienced and sensed.

Subaltern consciousness and initiative occurs at the margins. The potential of this consciousness depends on the specific context in which it is expressed.[16] It may not be in the well-articulated form of the dominant outlook, e.g. in written form, with its own value and space, and does not get much recognition in the dominant academic discourse. It is interpreted in a negative sense as 'capricious, emotional and fickle.'[17] But subalterns always have a perspective, even if not articulated as discourse. The perspective is egalitarian and therefore it appears resistant to the dominant.

The subalterns can take action without the support of the dominant. Their critical consciousness leads to bold initiatives. Dipesh Chakrabarty says,

> the central aim of the Subaltern Studies in India is to understand the consciousness that informed and still informs (political) actions taken by the subaltern classes on their own, independently of any elite initiatives. It is only by giving this 'consciousness' a central place in historical analysis that we see the subaltern as the 'maker' of history. . . . However, this does not mean that we place this consciousness outside the history, as the charge of 'idealism' implies.[18]

According to V.V. Thomas, 'By subaltern perspective, we mean an attempt to bring into focus the subjectivity of the subalterns in developing their history. It is a methodology through which the subalterns do not just become the objects of history-writing but the very subjects themselves.'[19]

One has to be aware that the subaltern woman's perspective is different from subaltern perspective in general. Not only is it shaped by caste discrimination and its mechanism, it is in addition a realization of gender stereotypes. A wounded self subjected to patriarchal conditioning[20] has more to say than cumulative subalternity.

I have endeavoured to develop a new theological articulation based on the historical struggle of a subaltern community. The basic premise is that a theological articulation of the experiences of subaltern community should be constructed only from their perspective.[21] The subaltern view is nothing but looking through the spectacles of subaltern experience from below. It is a look from the life-realities of subalterns, through their historical experience. In this I am theoretically and conceptually informed by the methodology of Dalit theology.

Arvind P. Nirmal argues that Dalit Christian theology is based on the *pain-pathos* of Dalits. A genuine Dalit theology can only be produced by Dalits because its content is fed by Dalit historical sufferings, aspirations, and hope. In order to avoid the invasion of dominant ideologies, concepts, and world views into the Dalit spectrum, Nirmal stands for the exclusive character of Dalit theology – a theology by the Dalits, of the Dalits and for the Dalits. In his methological approach, Nirmal places historical Dalit consciousness as the primary datum of the theology of Dalits. For him, this consciousness, characterized by *pain-pathos*, should shape the theology which aims at the liberation of Dalits, the 'glorious liberty of the Children of God'.[22]

While insisting on methological exclusivism, Nirmal also opens the doors of Dalit theology to non-Dalits. 'Many people ask me if I rule out the possibility of Dalit theology being done by non-Dalits. The answer to such a question must be a complex one. I would maintain that there are three different modes of knowing. They are pathetic knowing, the empathetic knowing and the sympathetic knowing.'[23] These three modes of knowledge point to the three levels of knowing the sufferings of Dalits. Sathianathan Clarke views pathetic knowing, empathetic knowing and sympathetic knowing in 'concentric circles'. Pathetic knowledge represents the *pain-pathos* of Dalits, the core of Dalit theology. Empathetic knowledge is a circle around pathetic knowledge. It is the knowledge of the other people in similar conditions, victims of caste and patriarchy. Sympathetic knowledge is the third circle which represents people who do not have any experience of suffering from a caste position. They can have solidarity with the Dalits in their journey of struggle towards liberation.[24]

Sathianathan Clarke observes that methological exclusivism aims to protect subjugated Dalit resources as the starting point of Dalit reflectivity. It helps to preserve Dalit subjectivity as the *loci* and *foci* of Dalit theology. The inclusive character of Dalit theology resulted from 'the interrelatedness of theological knowledge and the inclusive character of the Christian community'. Non-Dalits can intentionally engage in Dalit theology provided the *pain-pathos* of Dalits is recognized as unique.[25]

M.E. Prabhakar observes that methodologically, Dalit theology is from 'below', the bottom-up experience of the Dalits. It is sourced by the languages, stories of sufferings and triumphs and the popular wisdom of Dalits who are made to live at the lower rungs of society. Its point of departure is the liberation of Dalits from the bondage of caste.[26] It affirms that the critique of caste, which maintains inequality in the Church and in society, should be theological.[27]

According to James Massey, 'beside the text (Biblical text) there are three main requirements for the formation of a living form of theology: life context, history, and language'.[28] For him, a Dalit theology is holistic and based on the Christ event of redemption: liberation/salvation of Dalits from the oppressive structures and the liberation of oppressors.[29] He also views that re-construction of Dalit history is the first step towards theology from a Dalit perspective.[30] His emphasis on the reconstruction of Dalit history is based on the premise that only the past history of Dalits can tell about the past identity of Dalits. Only now are they reduced to a degraded life.[31]

After examining the different stages of the development of Dalit theology and methodology, Sathianathan Clarke sees 'Resistancehyphenated liberation activity' as the approach of Dalit theology.[32] As a counter theology, Dalit theology upholds a hermeneutics of suspicion which rejects, refutes and deconstructs dominant theories, concepts and interpretations.[33] It is not simply a counter theology without aspiration, self-narration, and alternate discourse.[34] He suggests that Dalit theology has to explore the possibilities of the 'co-mingling of Dalit religious worldviews and Christian symbolic resources'.[35]

According to Sathianathan Clarke, the 'theological method ought to start with an affirmation and exposition of the mundane and expressed world of the Dalits'.[36] It helps to understand both the subjection and the subjectivity of Dalits.[37] Subjectivity should be analysed within the framework of context.[38] In *Dalits and Christianity: Subaltern Religion and Liberation Theology in India*, the *drum* is pictured as the main symbol with which Dalits, 'express' and 'experience' their relationship with the Divine and with one another. The religious experience centered on *drum* led to the interpretation of Christ as *drum*.[39] He attempted to interpret Christ through the eyes of Dalit (Paraiyar) conceptual world using their religious symbols.[40]

In the context of the gap between academic Dalit theology and the praxis of the Church, Peniel Rajkumar explores the healing stories in the synoptic Gospels as an alternative paradigm to boost the potential of Dalit theology. For him, a reason for the gap is the content of Dalit theology, which does not lead the Church in praxis. In his methodology, he places the healing stories in the synoptic Gospels to re-think Dalit agency and to re-signify the Dalit resistance, which are the content of Dalit praxis. At the same time, with critical self-reflectivity, he offers the synoptic healing stories as tools to re-perceive Dalit theology as a concrete and context-specific expression of Christian faith.[41]

The *pain-pathos* of people involved in the Upper Cloth Revolt is the point of departure for a new theological articulation, articulation from the 'bottom-up' experiences of those involved in the struggle. As a symbol through which the Nadar men and women expressed their resistance against oppression and experienced the guidance of Divine to fight against social restriction, the Upper Cloth stands as a symbol of the affirmation of a dignified life and a confirmation of the Divine in the journey of their struggle. In the theological interpretation of Upper Cloth Revolt, Biblical stories are juxtaposed with those of Nadars in the revolt. The subaltern identity of Nadars also qualifies this event to be interpreted from a subaltern perspective.

This book is mainly based on literary research. Subaltern experiences centered on Upper Cloth Revolt are narrated in different sources. Government records, reports of missionaries and books written after a few years of the event are used as primary sources to extract the historical experiences of the Nadars. The Christian faith was involved in these experiences, and Biblical sources are also used in this direction. Secondary sources are used to fill in the narrative. Interviews with J.W. Gladstone[42] and R.N. Yesudas[43] have given resourceful insights to this work. Methodological insights were gained from select liberation theologies such as Gustavo Gutierrez's *Theology of Liberation*, *Black Theology*, *Minjung Theology*, Kazoh Kitamori's *Theology of the Pain of God*, Eleasar S. Fernandez's *Theology of Struggle*, *Dalit Theology and Indian Feminist Theology*. They provide enough guidance on the use of history in developing new theological interpretations and supply resources to build up new theological expressions out of the subaltern experiences involved in the Upper Cloth Revolt.

I have attempted in this volume to understand and interpret the Upper Cloth Revolt theologically. Therefore, its scope is limited to the framework of theological study: reading from the Christian theological point of view. I acknowledge the limitation of this endeavour. I have given sufficient focus to furnish the historical details of the event. Some terminologies in this volume such as 'Subaltern', 'Nadars', 'Upper Cloth Revolt', 'Theological articulation', 'Liberation Theologies/Theologians' now need clarification.

'Subaltern' is originally a military term which literally means 'subordinate'. In its adjectival form, it means 'of lower status'.[44] It was Antonio Gramsci, an Italian Marxist leader and philosopher, who first popularized the term, all non-hegemonic peoples or working class/proletariat, 'subaltern'.[45] The Subaltern Studies Group, who introduced the expression 'subaltern' in the Indian academic circle, uses it as 'of inferior rank'. For them, the expression 'subaltern' stands for any category/group which has the status 'of inferior rank' in a particular realm.[46]

Sathianathan Clarke in *Dalits and Christianity: Subaltern Religion and Liberation Theology in India*, situates Dalits in the subaltern space. He takes departure from the generalization of subaltern class to the identification of subalternity with a particular community. He focused on the caste dimension of subalternity, and argues that if caste is the determining factor for subalternity in Indian context, it is Dalits who deserve to be called as subalterns.[47] But James Massey proposes Dalit-Bahujan (Dalits-Tribals-OBCs and religious minorities of lower caste origin) as subalterns in the Indian context. He argues that majority of the Indian population has a history of discriminations and disabilities inflicted by the caste. They are victims of the caste system historically. Dalit-Bahujan shares the common 'inferior status' which has been imposed on them by dominant caste groups.[48] In this volume, subaltern is interpreted not in terms of class category or general classification of people with 'inferior rank',[49] but as Dalit-Bahujan, the historical victims of caste, which has space for the communities presently categorized as Other Backward Classes (OBC) who were and now are discriminated and treated as of 'inferior status' in one or the other form. At the same time, I am aware of the politically and economically dominant communities within the OBC category.

The Nadars were a non-landowning working-class community in Travancore in the nineteenth century. Traditionally, they were involved in cultivating and climbing of palmyra trees and making jaggery out of palmyra olives and sap.[50] This industrious and hard working group was socially degraded and economically exploited. They lived in a state of fear, and were despised when the British arrived in Travancore.[51] The missionary sources found that the Nadars had become 'timid', 'deceitful' and 'ignorant' because of oppression.[52] In fact, the Nadars lived a life of struggle, pain and humiliation. They were categorized as a lower (inferior, subordinated) caste even though they do not fall in the category of 'caste' in the strict sense of the Hindu caste order. They were subordinate in all aspects of life. They had to be submissive to the ruling castes.

It is also to be noted that Nadar women were subalterns within the subaltern community. Their subalternity was the result of the interplay of caste and patriarchy.

Col. John Munro, the Dewan of Travancore, issued a proclamation in 1812, permitting low caste women converted to Christianity to cover themselves. In 1814, Christian women of low caste origin were given permission to wear the *kuppāyam,*[53] the dress worn by Syrian Christian and Muslim women. They were strictly prohibited to wear the upper cloth worn by the upper caste women.[54] But the Nadar women appeared not only with *kuppāyam* but also with upper cloth. This caused resentment among upper caste people, particularly the Nairs. They took the law into their hands and unleashed violence against Nadar women and men for violating caste regulations.[55] What gradually developed into a violent revolt later known as Upper Cloth Revolt, recurring now and again for nearly four decades. Finally, it ended with the royal proclamation on 26 July 1859. It was a turning point for the social empowerment of the Nadar community, particularly the dignity of its women.[56]

In this volume, 'theological articulation' implies interpreting the Upper Cloth Revolt in terms of gender and theology. The subaltern experiences centered on Upper Cloth Revolt have been interpreted in the light of Christian faith and vice-versa.

Liberation theologies are theological expressions of Christian faith emerged out of oppressive human experiences in respective contexts. Liberation is the focus and the poor/oppressed people are the locus in liberation theologies. Liberation theology, Black theology, Theology of Struggle, Minjung theology, Dalit theology, Feminist theology, all fall into this category. Liberation is central to these theologies. Liberation theologians are those who interpret the Christian faith with a liberation thrust. They articulate new expressions of faith out of the oppressed historical and contextual experiences of people. Gustavo Gutierrez,[57] Kazoh Kitamori,[58] James H. Cone,[59] Kim Young-Bock,[60] Eleasar S. Fernandez,[61] Arvind P. Nirmal,[62] James Massey,[63] etc., have articulated new expressions of faith in their contexts. Indian Feminist theology too falls under the category of Liberation theology, aiming for the liberation of women from the oppressive patriarchal culture and caste system. Gabriele Dietrich,[64] Aruna Gnanadason,[65] Presanna Kumari,[66] Shalini Mulackal,[67] etc., belong to this theological stream.

Much has been written on this revolt – *The Land of Charity,*[68] *A History of Travancore from Earliest Times,*[69] *Church History of Travancore,*[70] *The Travancore State Manual Vol. I,*[71] *A Hundred Years in Travancore 1806-1906,*[72] *A Survey of Kerala History,*[73] *Protestant Christianity and People's Movements in Kerala,*[74] *Conversion and Social Equality in India,*[75] *A History of the London Missionary Society in South Travancore 1806-1959,*[76] *A Forgotten History,*[77] *Liberation of the Oppressed: A Continuous Struggle,*[78] etc., are a few such. These works do not narrate the Upper Cloth Revolt exclusively. Some narrate it in a representative form as part of describing either London Mission Society work or the history of Nadars, or social movements in Travancore. R.N. Yesudas' *A People's Revolt in Travancore*[79] is an attempt to recount the movement in a comprehensive way, but does not make it relevant to other subaltern communities in contemporary society. *Converting Women*[80] is another work which attempts to study the sexual dimension of restricted clothing in south India in the nineteenth century. In this study, the symbol of upper cloth and its restriction for the women of lower caste origin is also examined. None of the existing works deal directly with the event from a theological point of view and interpret it to motivate subaltern communities, particularly subaltern women. The present volume is an initial attempt in this regard. It also furnishes a systematic historical narration of this revolt.

Subaltern Studies[81] is a collection of edited works which attempted to understand South Asian History and Society from subaltern perspective, bringing out the subaltern agency hidden in the dominant historiography. A group of scholars such as Ranajit Guha, Partha Chatterjee, Gyanendra Pandey, David Arnold, David Hardiman, Dipesh Chakrabarty, Gautam Bhadra, etc., edited this multi-volume work. *Understanding Subaltern History: Theoretical Tools*[82] is another useful resource in the area of subaltern studies. It furnishes theoretical tools to dig out the subaltern action neglected in dominant historical narratives. It also gives methodological hints to develop a subaltern perspective.

Dalit Pentecostalism[83] brings out the 'forgotten' agency, voice and contribution of Dalits towards the origin and development of Pentecostal movement in Kerala. *Religion and Politics from Subaltern Perspective*[84] is an engagement with the pertinent issues of Dalits and other marginalized sections in society from a subaltern perspective. It highlights social struggles of marginalized people groups in terms of political systems and dynamics in India. *Towards Justice and Peace: A Subaltern Initiative*[85] is a subaltern search for retrieving peace and justice in the lives of Dalits and tribals. It attempts to understand the role of religions to create and maintain a just social order in which Dalits and tribals can celebrate peace and justice.

Caste-Class Victims and Their Assertion for Justice[86] is a resource manual for a subaltern expression of theology. It identifies the victims of the caste-class system, the subalterns in Indian context and gives guidelines for new expressions of faith from a subaltern perspective. *Dalits and Christianity: Subaltern Religion and Liberation Theology in India*[87] interprets Dalit experience centered on their religious symbols like the drum from a subaltern perspective. *Wisdom of the Weak*[88] offers methological foundations, sources, etc., for subaltern theologizing. *Adivasi Theology: Towards a Relevant Christian Theology for the Jharkhandi Adivasis*[89] is a subaltern theological reading of Jharkhandi Adivasi context to construct a relevant Adivasi theology. *Dalit Bible Commentary*[90] is a first attempt to interpret the Bible from a Dalit/subaltern perspective in India. It is a contextual liberative interpretation of Bible through the eyes of Dalit/subalterns. The multi-volume commentary written by different authors under the leadership of James Massey provides methological reflections for subaltern theologizing. It also supplies resources to build new theological expressions relevant to the subaltern communities in India. The works on subaltern and subaltern theologizing stand as resources to get subaltern perspectival insights for the present volume to develop a theological expression of Upper Cloth Revolt from a subaltern perspective.

This volume is structured in the following way. After this introductory chapter, the first chapter is an attempt to understand the historical context. The second chapter narrates the different episodes of Upper Cloth Revolt in detail, the third surveying different contextual theologies to understand the interaction between faith and history. In the fourth chapter, an effort is made to bring out a theological expression of the Upper Cloth Revolt. The concluding chapter explains how the interpretation of liberating historical events can speak to subaltern communities, particularly the subaltern women, in their struggle for liberation, selfhood, and empowerment.

NOTES

1. D.S. Amalorpavadass, 'Theological Reflections on Inculturation', *Indian Theological Studies* 29/3-4 (1990): 217-72 at 229-30; James Massey, *Dalit Bible Commentary, Old Testament*, vol 2, *Exodus* (New Delhi: Centre for Dalit/Subaltern Studies, 2010), pp. 19-27 & 42-81.
2. A process of developing new interpretations of religious faith. Theology is basically an interpretation of what we hold as divine. Here, religious faith refers to the Christian faith.
3. M.M. Thomas, 'Foreword', in R.H.S. Boyd, *An Introduction to Indian Christian Theology* (Delhi: ISPCK, 1991), p. v; K.C. Abraham, 'Third World Theologies', *CTC Bulletin*, vol. XI, nos. 2&3 (May-December 1992): 4-12 at 5; James Massey, 'Ingredients for a Dalit Theology', in *Towards a Dalit Theology*, ed. M.E. Prabhakar (Delhi: ISPCK, 1989), p. 60.
4. South Travancore consisted of present Kanyakumari District in Tamil Nadu and the southern part of the Thiruvananthapuram District in Kerala.
5. Travancore was one of the Princely States in the present Kerala State.
6. In the strict sense of the caste mechanism, the people of 'lower caste' origin in Travancore are outside the caste system. They are not 'caste' people.
7. The 'Upper Cloth' had a social symbolism.
8. In patriarchal society, the selfhood of women is determined by men. Men decide the amount of freedom and respect women should get in society. In the case of the caste-ridden patriarchal society of Travancore in the nineteenth century, 'restricted freedom' was not equally distributed to the women of all castes. Since caste was the measuring rod of status and freedom, women of low caste origin were more vulnerable, and subjected to inhuman regulations.
9. Maria Mies, 'Class Struggles and Women's Struggles in Rural India', in *Women: The Last Colony*, ed. Maria Mies et al. (New Delhi: Kali

for Women, 1988), p. 138; Prathama Banerjee, 'Caste and History Writing', in *Dalit Assertion in Society, Literature and History,* ed. Imtiaz Ahmad and Shashi Bhushan Upadhyay (New Delhi: Orient Black-Swan, 2010), p. 229; Bama, 'Dalit Christian Women Today: Their Struggles and Prospects for Future', *Jeevadhara*, vol. XLI, no. 241 (January 2011), pp. 35-44 at 36-7; A. Maria Arul Raja, *Dalit Bible Commentary, Old Testament*, vol. 1, *Genesis* (New Delhi: CDS, 2012), p. 38.

10. Though no woman of low caste was allowed to wear upper cloth, it was the Nadar men and women who opposed the restriction in public.
11. Both Hindu and Christian Nadar women were not allowed to cover their bosom. But the Nadar Christian women were allowed to wear a *kuppayam*. Detailed description in this regard is given in the second chapter of this böok.
12. Though the Nadar men encouraged their women to appear with an upper cloth, it cannot be assumed that both men and women were equal in Nadar community. Nadar community was also patriarchal in nature. Nadar women did not enjoy equal status with their men within the community. Like any other women in the Travancore society, Nadar women were also victims of patriarchy within the community. Still their space and freedom within the community are restricted by patriarchal outlook.
13. It was Nadar Christian women who initiated the violation of the restriction and later their Hindu counterparts followed.
14. Dick Kooiman, *Conversion and Social Equality in India* (New Delhi: Manohar, 1989), 205f.
15. Veena Das, 'Subaltern as Perspective', in *Subaltern Studies*, vol. VI, ed. Ranajit Guha (New Delhi: Oxford University Press, 1999), p. 324.
16. Ibid., p. 320.
17. Ibid., p. 321.
18. Dipesh Chakrabarty, 'Invitation to a Dialogue', in *Subaltern Studies* vol. IV, ed. Ranajit Guha (New Delhi: Oxford University Press, 1985), p. 374.
19. V.V. Thomas, *Dalit Pentecostalism* (Bangalore: ATC, 2008), p. 14.
20. Nadar women in the present volume were/are not only victims of caste but also of patriarchal ideology and culture within and outside their community.
21. Subaltern includes women also.
22. Arvind P. Nirmal, 'A Dialogue with Dalit Literature', in *Towards a Dalit Theology*, ed. M.E. Prabhakar (Delhi: ISPCK, 1989), pp. 76-9.

23. Arvind P. Nirmal, 'Doing Theology from a Dalit Perspective', in *A Reader in Dalit Theology*, ed. Arvind P. Nirmal (Madras: Gurukul, 1991), pp. 141-2.
24. Sathianathan Clarke, 'Dalit Theology: An Introductory and Interpretative Theological Exposition', in *Dalit Theology in the Twenty-first Century*, ed. Sathianathan Clarke, Deenabandhu Manchala and Philip Vinod Peacock (New Delhi: Oxford University Press, 2010), p. 22.
25. Ibid., pp. 20-2.
26. M.E. Prabhakar, 'The Search for a Dalit Theology', in *Towards a Dalit Theology*, ed. M.E. Prabhakar (Delhi: ISPCK, 1989), p. 44.
27. M.E. Prabhakar, 'Introduction', in *Towards a Dalit Theology*, ibid., p. 2.
28. James Massey, 'Ingredients for a Dalit Theology,' in *Indigenous People,* ed. James Massey (Delhi: ISPCK, 1994), p. 340.
29. James Massey, *Introducing Dalit Theology* (New Delhi: Centre for Dalit Studies, 2004), p. 27.
30. James Massey, 'Vision, Nature and Method of Dalit Theology', in *Dalit-Tribal Theological Interface*, ed. James Massey and Shimreingam Shimray (Jorhat: TSC/WSC and New Delhi: CDS, 2007), p. 56.
31. Ibid., p. 69.
32. Sathianathan Clarke, 'Dalit Theology: An Introductory and Interpretative Theological Exposition', p. 23.
33. Ibid., p. 24.
34. Ibid., p. 29.
35. Ibid., p. 31.
36. Sathianathan Clarke, *Dalits and Christianity*, p. 33.
37. Ibid., p. 63.
38. Ibid., p. 64.
39. Ibid., pp. 185-90.
40. Ibid., p. 99.
41. Peniel Rajkumar, *Dalit Theology and Dalit Liberation* (Burlington: ASHGATE, 2010), pp. 127, 177 & 183.
42. Bishop J.W. Gladstone, Professor of Church History, is former Moderator of Church of South India and former Principal of Kerala United Theological Seminary, Kannamoola, Thiruvananthapuram, Kerala.
43. Prof. R.N. Yesudas, Professor of History, is former Director of the Institute of Distance Education and Dean of Social Sciences, University of Kerala, Thiruvananthapuram.
44. Catherine Soanes and Angus Stevenson, eds., *Concise Oxford English*

Dictionary, Indian Edition (New Delhi: Oxford University Press, 2007), p. 1434.

45. Antonio Gramsci, *Selections from the Prison Notebooks of Antonio Gramsci*, ed. and translated by Quintin Hoare and Geoffrey Nowell Smith (Chennai: Orient Longman, 1996), p. xiv.
46. Ranajit Guha, 'Preface', in *Subaltern Studies*, vol. I, ed. Ranajit Guha (New Delhi: Oxford University Press, 1994), p. vii.
47. Clarke, *Dalits and Christianity*, p. 7.
48. James Massey, *Caste-Class Victims and Their Assertion for Justice* (New Delhi: Centre for Dalit/Subaltern Studies, 2013) pp. 14-15; James Massey, 'Subaltern People and the Rise of their Movements', in *A Vision of Mission in the New Millennium*, ed. Thomas Malipurathu and L. Stanislaus (Mumbai: St. Paul's, 2001), pp. 27-9.
49. Antonio Gramsci interpreted the 'subaltern' in relation to political and economic realities. The subaltern study group applied 'subaltern' to any group/person who experience 'inferior rank' in any aspect of societal life. Both interpretations on 'subaltern' are critically analyzed in the second chapter. 'Subaltern' is understood mainly in terms of the victimhood of caste in this volume.
50. J.W. Gladstone, *Protestant Christianity and People's Movements in Kerala* (Trivandrum: The Seminary Publications, KUTS, 1984), p. 27.
51. Joy Gnanadason, *A Forgotten History* (Madras: GLTC, 1994), p. 27.
52. Kooiman, *Conversion and Social Equality in India*, p. 15.
53. A sort of a shirt.
54. C.M. Agur, *Church History of Travancore* (Madras: S.P.S. Press, 1903; New Delhi: Asian Educational Service, 1990), pp. 779-80; R.N. Yesudas, *Col. John Munro in Travancore* (Trivandrum: Kerala Historical Society, 1977), pp. 53-4.
55. C.M. Agur, *Church History of Travancore*, p. 779.
56. Ibid., p. 829 ff; R.N. Yesudas, *The History of the London Missionary Society in Travancore 1806*-1908 (Trivandrum: Kerala Historical Society, 1980), pp. 259-61; V. Nagam Aiya, *The Travancore State Manual,* vol. I (Trivandrum: Government Press, 1906), pp. 526-31.
57. Gustavo Gutierrez, *A Theology of Liberation: History, Politics and Salvation* (New York: Orbis Books, 1973).
58. Kazoh Kitamori, *Theology of the Pain of* God (London: SCM Press, 1966).
59. James H. Cone, *A Black Theology of Liberation* (Maryknoll: Orbis Books, 1986).

60. Kim Yong-Bock, *Messiah and Minjung* (Hong Kong: Christian Conference of Asia, 1992).
61. Eleazar S Fernandez, *Toward a Theology of Struggle* (Maryknoll: Orbis Books, 1994).
62. Arvind P. Nirmal, 'A Dialogue with Dalit Literature', in *Towards a Dalit Theology*, ed. M.E. Prabhakar (Delhi: ISPCK, 1989); Arvind P. Nirmal, 'Doing Theology from a Dalit Perspective', in *A Reader in Dalit Theology*, ed. Arvind P. Nirmal (Madras: Gurukul/UELCI, 1991); Arvind P. Nirmal, 'Towards a Christian Dalit Theology', in *A Reader in Dalit Theology*, ed. Arvind P. Nirmal (Madras: Gurukul/UELCI, 1991), etc.
63. James Massey, *Towards Dalit Hermeneutics: Re-reading the Text, the History and the Literature* (Delhi: ISPCK, 1994); James Massey, ed., *Indigenous People: Dalits Issues in Today's Theological Debate* (Delhi: ISPCK, 1994); James Massey, *Dalit Bible Commentary, Old Testament*, vol. 2, *Exodus* (New Delhi: Centre for Dalit/Subaltern Studies, 2010); James Massey and T.K. John, eds., *Rethinking Theology in India* (New Delhi: Manohar and CDS, 2013), etc.
64. Gabriele Dietrich, *New Things on Earth* (New Delhi: ISPCK, 1999); Gabriele Dietrich, 'The Origins of the Bible Revisted-Reconstructing Women's History', in *Theology of Humanhood: Women's Perspectives*, ed. Aruna Gnanadason (Delhi: ISPCK, 1986), etc.
65. Aruna Gnanadason, ed., *Towards a Theology of Humanhood: Women's Perspectives* (Delhi: ISPCK, 1986); Aruna Gnanadason, 'We Will Pour Our Oilment on the Feet of the Church: The Ecumenical Movement and the Ordination of Women', in *Feminist Hermeneutics*, ed. Lalrinawmi Ralte and Evangeline Anderson Rajkumar (Delhi: ISPCK, 2002); Aruna Gnanadason, 'Feminist Methodology', in *Confronting Life: Theology out of the Context*, ed. M.P. Joseph (Delhi: ISPCK, 1995), etc.
66. Presanna Kumari Samuel, ed., *Reader in Feminist Theology* (Madras: Gurukul, 1993); Prasanna Kumari, *Dalit Women's Experiences: A Theological imperative for Indian Feminist Theology* (Chennai: Gurukul Lutheran Theological College, 2009), etc.
67. Shalini Mulackal, *Dalit Bible Commentary, Old Testament*, vol. 6, *Esther, Ruth and Judith* (New Delhi: Centre for Dalit/Subaltern Studies, 2011); Shalini Mulackal, 'Women: Theology and Feminist Movements in India', in *Rethinking Theology in India*, ed. James Massey and T.K. John (New Delhi: Manohar and CDS, 2013); Shalini Mulackal, 'Dalit Belief Systems and Rituals', in *Theology for a New*

Community, ed. T.K. John and James Massey (New Delhi: Centre for Dalit/Subaltern Studies, 2013), etc.

68. Samuel Mateer, *The Land of Charity* (London: John Snow and Co., 1871).
69. P. Shungoonny Menon, *A History of Travancore from Earliest Times* (Madras: Higginbotham and Co., 1878).
70. C.M. Agur, *Church History of Travancore* (Madras: S.P.S. Press, 1903; New Delhi: Asian Educational Service, 1990).
71. V. Nagam Aiya, *The Travancore State Manual*, vol. I (Trivandrum: Government Press, 1906).
72. I.H. Hacker, *A Hundred Years in Travancore 1806-1906* (London: H.R. Allenson Limited, 1908).
73. A. Sreedhara Menon, *A Survey of Kerala History* (Kottayam: National Book Stall, 1970).
74. J.W Gladstone, *Protestant Christianity and People's Movements in Kerala* (Trivandrum: The Seminary Publications, KUTS, 1984).
75. Kooiman, *Conversion and Social Equality in India* (New Delhi: Manohar, 1989).
76. John A. Jacob, *A History of the London Missionary Society in South Travancore 1806-1959* (Nagarcoil: The Diocesan Press, 1990).
77. Joy Gnanadason, *A Forgotten History* (Madras: GLTC, 1994).
78. D. Peter and Ivy Peter, *Liberation of the Oppressed A Continuous Struggle* (Nagarcoil: Kanyakumari Institute of Development Studies, 2009).
79. R.N. Yesudas, *A People's Revolt in Travancore* (Trivandrum: Kerala Historical Society, 1975).
80. Eliza F. Kent, *Converting Women* (New York: Oxford University Press, 2004).
81. Ranajit Guha, ed., *Subaltern Studies*, vol. I (New Delhi: Oxford University Press, 1982); idem., *Subaltern Studies*, vol. II (New Delhi: Oxford University Press, 1983); idem., *Subaltern Studies*, vol. III (New Delhi: Oxford University Press, 1984); idem., *Subaltern Studies*, vol. IV (New Delhi: Oxford University Press, 1985); idem., *Subaltern Studies*, vol. V (New Delhi: Oxford University Press, 1987); idem., *Subaltern Studies* vol. VI (New Delhi: Oxford University Press, 1989); Partha Chatterjee and Gyanendra Pandey, eds., *Subaltern Studies*, vol. VII (New Delhi: Oxford University Press, 1992); David Arnold and David Hardiman, eds., *Subaltern Studies*, vol. VIII (New Delhi: Oxford University Press, 1994); Shahid Amin and Dipesh Chakrabarty, eds., *Subaltern Studies*, vol. IX (New Delhi: Oxford University Press, 1996); Gautam Bhadra, Gyan Prakash and Susie Tharu, eds.,

Subaltern Studies, vol. X (New Delhi: Oxford University Press, 1999); Partha Chatterjee and Pradeep Jeganathan, eds., *Subaltern Studies*, vol. XI (New Delhi: Permanent Black and Ravi Dayal Publisher, 2000).

82. V.V. Thomas, *Understanding Subaltern History: Theoretical Tools* (Bangalore: BTESSC/SATHRI, 2006).
83. V.V. Thomas, *Dalit Pentecostalism* (Bangalore: ATC, 2008).
84. Thomas Kadankavil, ed., *Religion and Politics from Subaltern Perspective* (Bangalore: Dharmaram Publications, 1999).
85. Monodeep Daniel and Yangkahao Vashum, eds., *Towards Justice and Peace: A Subaltern Initiative* (Jorhat: ETC, Nagpur: CNI Desk on Dalit and Tribal Concerns and New Delhi: CDS, 2010)
86. James Massey, *Caste-Class Victims and Their Assertion for Justice* (New Delhi: CDS, 2013).
87. Sathianathan Clarke, *Dalits and Christianity: Subaltern Religion and Liberation Theology in India* (New Delhi: Oxford University Press, 1998).
88. Anthoniraj Thumma, *Wisdom of the Weak* (Delhi: ISPCK, 2000).
89. Christ Sumit Abhay Kerketta, *Adivasi Theology: Towards a Relevant Christian Theology for the Jharkhandi Adivasis* (Ranchi: ATCR/GTC, 2009).
90. Monodeep Daniel, *Dalit Bible Commentary: New Testament*, vol. 1 (New Delhi: CDS, 2008); Maria Goretti, Monodeep Daniel and A Maria Arul Raja, *Dalit Bible Commentary: New Testament*, vol. 2 (New Delhi: CDS, 2009); James Massey, *Dalit Bible Commentary: New Testament*, vol. 3 (New Delhi: CDS, 2007); Raj Irudaya, *Dalit Bible Commentary: New Testament*, vol. 4 (New Delhi: CDS, 2009); James Massey, *Dalit Bible Commentary: New Testament*, vol. 5 (New Delhi: CDS, 2008); James Massey and Monodeep Daniel, *Dalit Bible Commentary: New Testament*, vol. 6 (New Delhi: CDS, 2008); Monodeep Daniel, *Dalit Bible Commentary: New Testament*, vol. 7 (New Delhi: CDS, 2008); Busi Sunil Bhanu, Monodeep Daniel and Indukuri John Mohan Razu, *Dalit Bible Commentary: New Testament*, vol. 8 (New Delhi: CDS, 2009); Sunil M. Caleb, Monodeep Daniel, Philip Vinod Peacock and James Massey, *Dalit Bible Commentary: New Testament*, vol. 9 (New Delhi: CDS, 2008); A Maria Arul Raja, *Dalit Bible Commentary: New Testament*, vol. 10 (New Delhi: CDS, 2009); A Maria Arul Raja, *Dalit Bible Commentary: Old Testament,* vol. 1 (New Delhi: CDS, 2012); James Massey, *Dalit Bible Commentary: Old Testament,* vol. 2 (New Delhi: CDS, 2010); Monodeep Daniel, *Dalit Bible Commentary: Old Testament,* vol. 3 (New Delhi: CDS, 2010);

I. John Mohan Razu, *Dalit Bible Commentary: Old Testament,* vol. 4 (New Delhi: CDS, 2011); Monodeep Daniel & James Massey, *Dalit Bible Commentary: Old Testament,* vol. 5 (New Delhi: CDS, 2012); Shalini Mulackal, *Dalit Bible Commentary: Old Testament,* vol. 6 (New Delhi: CDS, 2011); I. John Mohan Razu, *Dalit Bible Commentary: Old Testament,* vol. 7 (New Delhi: CDS, 2012); James Massey, *Dalit Bible Commentary: Old Testament,* vol. 8 (New Delhi: CDS, 2011); Monodeep Daniel, *Dalit Bible Commentary: Old Testament,* vol. 18 (New Delhi: CDS, 2012), A. Maria Arul Raja, *Dalit Bible Commentary: Old Testament,* vol. 11 (New Delhi: CDS, 2012); James Massey, *Dalit Bible Commentary: Old Testament,* vol. 17 (New Delhi: CDS, 2012); James Massey and I. John Mohan Razu, *Dalit Bible Commentary: Old Testament,* vol. 9 (New Delhi: CDS, 2012); James Massey, *Dalit Bible Commentary: Old Testament,* vol. 10 (New Delhi: CDS, 2013); I. John Mohan Razu, *Dalit Bible Commentary: Old Testament,* vol. 13 (New Delhi: CDS, 2013).

CHAPTER 1

Travancore in Historical Context

The previous chapter narrated the need to interpret liberating historical events from a subaltern perspective and the possible methodology in such academic endeavour. This chapter explains the historical context of Travancore in the nineteenth century, which witnessed the different episodes of the Upper Cloth Revolt. Reform movements, revolutions and people's voices against unjust social structures are the result of the chemistry of contextual realities in respective societies. Travancore society also witnessed the reactions against the oppressive social realities.

A Brief Geographical Sketch of Travancore

The Princely State of Travancore, the Princely State of Cochin and British Malabar were three major geographical divisions of the present Kerala state in the later part of eighteenth and in the beginning of nineteenth century. It has been argued that the Chera Kingdom or Chera Mandalam, which once ruled a major segment of South India, was the mother country of Travancore. It was blessed and protected by natural boundaries which saved it from potential foreign invasions. It was a long and narrow strip of terrain situated between the Malabar Coast and the Western Ghats. Its boundaries can be summarized: an eastern side covered with high mountains; southern and western parts bordered by the Indian Ocean; a northern part mostly encircled with back-waters, rivers and lakes. Though geographical features kept Travancore in an isolated position, it was extremely difficult for the armies of those days, which mainly consisted of horses and elephants, to march towards Travancore easily.[1]

Travancore was blessed with hill slopes, valleys, low ground, lakes, streams, and rivers. Rice was cultivated in the fields, and varieties of fruit trees were grown on the hill slopes. Different kinds of grains and edible roots were also grown. There were many inland lakes which local people called 'back waters'. These 'back waters' helped to provide water transport between north and south. Native people mainly depended on these canals and backwaters for transportation. A major road also ran in parallel with the coastline. Travancore always had a pleasant climate thanks to cool breeze from the sea, the south-west monsoon, and the north-east monsoon. Towns and villages were mainly located in close proximity to the coast. Trivandrum was the capital, where the Maharaja resided. The headquarters of the native government, chief courts and other administrative offices were also located in the capital.[2] As a kingdom blessed with natural beauty and resources, Travancore was a destination for travellers through the centuries. However, the benefit of the natural gifts of Travancore was limited to the ruling class and upper caste landlords. The major portion of the land, particularly agricultural fields, was largely owned by upper castes. The people of lower caste origin were landless workers who had to work in those fields. This beautiful kingdom was also unfortunately known for the notoriety of rigid social customs and practices rooted in the caste system, which will be discussed later on.

The Origin of Travancore: The Myth

The mythical origin of Travancore is ascribed to Parashurama, the sixth incarnation of Vishnu, as his gift to the Brahmins. According to the myth, Parashurama appeared as a great warrior and destroyed all the Kshatriyas for their cruel rule. He fought and defeated his enemies twenty-one times. He then withdrew to a mountain and engaged in rigorous penance. Varuna, the sea-god, pleased with him, granted him land as far as he could throw his battle axe. He hurled the axe from Gokarnam to Cape Comorin, and the land of Kerala emerged from the sea. Then he brought in Brahmins from the north and distributed the land to them. After making all arrangements for their comfort, he disappeared.[3] This account was often used to legitimize the superiority of Brahmins in society, and the relation between the Brahmins and the Shudras, brought from different locations to serve the Brahmins.[4] It is also believed that after creating Kerala and settling Brahmins in sixty-four gramams,

Parashurama ordained several Brahmin heads and consecrated many temples. He invited a Soma Kshatria called Bhanu Vicrama and his three brothers, and made Bhanu Vicrama king of the new land between Cape Comorin and Gokarnam.[5] The Brahmins called Travancore as *dharmmabhūmi*. Predictably, this creation account reflects the future course of the socio-economic and religious relations between different communities in Travancore society. It placed Brahmins on the top of the hierarchy, and gave religious validity to Brahmanic and upper caste domination. Brahmins became the original landowners and the religious authority that consecrated kings. The lower castes became the servants of Brahmins and other upper castes. The Brahmins and upper castes appropriated this legend to subjugate the subaltern communities. Indeed, a legend became a tool of oppression. From a subaltern perspective, the creation story of Kerala is a legend of oppression.

Travancore Society

Travancore society in the nineteenth century was a caste-oriented society. Its social life functioned within the framework of caste. People were defined and valued by caste. Various customs and practices related to caste were strictly practised, with political support.

The Reality of Caste

Caste was an observable fact in the Indian subcontinent, a hierarchical division of people, norms of purity-pollution, and Hindu understandings of *Karma-Samsara* and *Dharma* which existed throughout.[6] Everyone was born to a particular caste. Upward mobility of a lower caste into a superior one was impossible. The influence of caste can be sensed in the Census Report of Travancore in 1891: 'The institution (Caste) has taken a firm hold on the popular mind. It is impossible to uproot it as an evil in society. It is still stronger as a social than as a religious institution.'[7] Caste remained firm in society as a link that retained the Hindu religious system.[8] The religious and the social dimensions of caste had been unnoticeably blurred: even change of religion did not give a casteless identity.[9] What can be observed is that this was a reality in Travancore society, but a life-line for the upper castes.

Casteless Society of Ancient Kerala

It is argued that ancient Kerala, which consisted of Travancore kingdom, was a casteless society. Caste was introduced by the Aryans or the Brahmins who came from the North.[10] After the seventh century, a process of social stratification began in ancient Kerala. Thus there were Kshatriyas in seventh century and Shudras in ninth century. In the eighth century a large group of Brahmins, who later came to be known as Nambudiri Brahmins, migrated to Kerala from the Deccan. They were able to bring society under their social and religious dominance and implement their caste system before the eleventh century. They named kings or chieftains as Kshatriyas; cultivators, who took the land on lease, were Shudras.[11] Those involved in manual labour were inferior, or out-castes, subject to many social and religious disabilities. In the social scale, there were also sub-castes within each major caste. Certain restrictions and privileges were even practised between sub-castes.[12] By the nineteenth century, social relationships in Travancore were completely based on caste, and low castes and slaves who constituted a majority of the population were in a state of complete subjugation to the high castes.[13] With the introduction of caste, ancient Kerala became a land where people were forced to live in 'graded inequality'.[14] This implies that before the arrival of Brahmins with their caste mechanism, the people of Travancore had lived without restriction and discrimination.

Major People Groups

In the nineteenth century, Travancore society was mainly based on caste. In South Travancore, the higher castes were the Nambudiri Brahmins and next to them the Nairs, one of the Shudra[15] communities. The lower castes[16] were the Nadars and the Ezhavas. The slave castes were the Pariahs and the Pulayas.[17] There were also hill people or aborigines or tribals or adivasis called Kanikars.

The Brahmins were classified into two categories: the Nambudiri or Malayali Brahmins and the foreign Brahmins who settled in Travancore. Though they were foreigners they held higher positions in Travancore society than in any other part of India. They were wealthy and led comfortable lives in all possible ways. Many of them engaged in the performance of religious rituals and ceremonies in temples. Their religious vocation gave them reverence, respect, and power in society. Strict followers of caste rules and ceremonial purity, they were inaccessible to lower castes, and even to Europeans. They were perfectly free from all social and religious disabilities. They were exempt from capital punishment for any offence, and protected with various rules and regulations.[18]

The Nairs occupied the next position. Religiously, they were Shudras, the lowest of the Hindu caste order. Considered polluted in north India, the Nairs were regarded as a high caste in Travancore because there were other groups below them in terms of status, wealth, and standard of living. Though they were middle class, they were the actual ruling class. They owned large portions of land and possessed many slaves. They occupied most government offices. They were wealthy merchants, farmers and skilled artisans of the country. But they were forbidden to perform religious ceremonies. Polyandry and other social customs existed among them. They were shrewd, unscrupulous, arrogant, and oppressive to the people of lower caste. It is argued that the royal family members were from this caste.[19]

The Ezhavas and the Nadars[20] were the two main lower castes in Travancore. The former were more in the north and the latter in south Travancore. Both communities faced more or less same social and religious disabilities. Their condition was humiliating and degrading. Both were involved in toddy production. Their women were not permitted to cover the upper part of the body, and had to carry water pots on the head, but not on the hip. They could not carry umbrellas, or wear shoes or gold ornaments. The Ezhavas and the Nadars were not allowed to have proper housing, and could not milk cows or use ordinary language. Often they were forced to do unpaid work for the government and upper-caste landlords for long hours without rest.[21]

Below the lower castes, there was another division in the Travancore society: the slaves. The Pulayas and the Pariahs were the principal slave groups, their proximity sufficient to pollute the high castes. They lived in very deplorable conditions. However, they were the backbone of agriculture. Engaged most of their time in the rice fields, they were subjected to hard work, and lacked food. In the drought season they used to work with empty stomachs, and had to depend on roots and fruits from the forest.[22]

Tribal people in South Travancore were called Kanikars. They lived in a wretched condition without proper food, dress or other basic facilities. They lived in small huts in the forests. Though they were cut off from the mainstream, the government officials and others exploited them for various purposes such as the digging of elephant pits. They were not even paid for their work. They were charged higher prices for the articles which they purchased in the markets.[23] Meanwhile, irrespective of caste, women were subject to male domination in domestic and public spheres. Their role and space were defined by men. The mobility of upper caste women was also controlled by patriarchal norms on the pretext of culture and religious practice. Besides the burden of domestic work, lower caste women also had to work along with their men in the fields of upper caste landlords. Their mobility, dress, voice, thinking, were controlled not only by men of their own respective community and but also men of upper castes. The Upper Cloth Revolt encouraged many subaltern communities to raise their voice against this state of affairs. This social structure made the subaltern communities timid, subservient, and feckless in social life.

Polluted by Touch and Presence

'Hindu society was not based on inequality but on graded inequality.'[24] This is evident in the various restrictions imposed on the low castes and on slaves.[25] These restrictions were made and practiced based on the concept of purity-pollution. One of the restrictions was maintaining a fixed distance between different castes in social relations.[26] In the past, two kinds of pollution existed in Kerala:

atmospheric pollution and pollution by touch. Atmospheric pollution was caused by the approach of Nayadi, Pulayan, Kanisan, Mukkuvan (fishermen) towards high-caste individuals less than 72 feet, 64 feet, 36 feet and 24 feet respectively. The upper castes were considered polluted if the fixed distance was violated by the lower castes. Muslims, Syrian Christians, and foreign Hindus[27] were allowed to approach, but not touch a Brahmin or an upper caste man.

In Travancore, except Brahmins, certain fixed distances and manners were prescribed to all castes to avoid pollution. For instance, a Nair was allowed to approach a Brahmin but not to touch him. The Ezhavas and Nadars had to stand at a distance of 36 steps from a Brahmin. A Pulayan was not allowed to approach a Brahmin closer than 96 steps. The Nadars and Ezhavas were permitted to approach a Nair up to 12 steps. A Pulayan had to keep 66 steps away from a Nair. A Syrian Christian was allowed to touch a Nair. But it was not acceptable everywhere in the country. A Nair would not eat with a Syrian Christian. The Pulayas and Pariahs used to approach other castes within the stipulated distance, but never allowed to touch. The shadow of these slave castes too were considered polluting.[28] In the practice of social-cum-ritual pollution, while the Brahmins and the upper castes experienced more pollution than other communities; the lower castes inflicted the same by violating the norms of purity-pollution. It was the subversive power of subalterns, though they were not conscious of it.

The rules of purity-pollution were applied to the Europeans also. In Travancore, in the 1800 Europeans were prohibited to travel on the main roads. The capital of Travancore, where more Brahmins lived, was inaccessible to the Europeans for many years. The high castes used to sit and talk with the Europeans, but never dined with them.[29] Europeans were considered polluted because of their lifestyle: eating meat, mingling with low castes and slaves, etc.[30] For years European officials like the Resident were met by the King or the Queen outside the capital, to avoid the danger of pollution.[31] Since Christians were considered polluted, Churches were not allowed to be constructed near roads used for religious processions.[32]

The normal method of purification was bathing in a pond or river. But if a Brahmin was touched by a Pulayan, the former used to bathe and change his sacred thread, and read the sacred books. If a Nair was touched by a Pulayan, he had to have a bath.[33] The restrictions of purity-pollution were strictly applied to maintain the superiority of high castes, particularly the Brahmins. It was strange that the touch of low castes and slaves were considered as polluting but not the food grain cultivated and touched by them. It was their laborious work which sustained the Travancore kingdom. Society judged that a subaltern's approach was a source of pollution, but not his/her labour.

Pulappedi and Mannappedi

Pulappedi (Pulaya Fear) and *mannappedi* (Manna Fear) were two scandalous social customs which prevailed in Travancore. According to these dreadful customs, Pulayas and Mannans, two untouchable outcastes, could touch Nair women during the month of February and March. If a Pulaya or Mannan man met a Nair woman unaccompanied by a man, she would be considered polluted, and would lose her caste. The assumption was that since, as a privilege, Pulaya or Mannan could touch Nair woman in a particular season he must have used the opportunity to molest her. In order to avoid the dishonour, Nair women observed *pulappedi* or *mannappedi.* During those months, out of the fear of touch, they used to keep away from Pulaya or Mannan men. They would not even look at a Pulaya or Mannan man during the time of *pulappedi* and *mannappedi.* In South Travancore, it was called *parappēdikkālam* (the Period of Paraya Fear). Interestingly, these Pulaya, Pariah, and Mannan men used to try their best to touch Nair women. If they could not do so during the day, they would try it secretly at night. But even if there was no witness, women used to announce the touch instantly, and would leave home and take refuge in the house of one of the low castes, hiding from her caste people who might kill her. In order to escape from her caste people, often she would allow herself to be sold as a slave to the foreigners.[34] The victims of these customs were poor slaves and high caste women. Slaves were objects of fear. No protection was given to women in the patriarchal society where men of high caste enjoyed immunity from the pollution of the touch of low caste or slave. It underlines the interplay of caste and gender in the victimization of women. Though molesting a woman is not the morality of subalterns, the behavior of Pulaya, Paraya and Mannan men has to be understood as the contextual sign of subaltern resistance to the molest of subaltern women by the upper caste men.

Caste Disabilities

The institution of caste denied the basic rights of the people of low caste origin. It perpetuated, as B.R. Ambedkar articulated, 'graded inequality'[35] in society. In Travancore, it decided what type of house lower castes could construct and what material should be used for such construction. The Nadars and Ezhavas were not allowed to have houses with more than one storey. They were forbidden to carry umbrella. They were asked to go barefooted. They were not allowed to milk cows. They had to use language in a different manner. Their women were restricted to wear gold ornaments, and were not allowed to cover their bosoms with an upper cloth.[36]

Low castes had to donate money to high caste landlords on special occasions such as marriages. All castes were not allowed to do business in the markets. There was even restriction for the business of all commodities by all castes. All lower caste converts to Christianity had to perform *ūḻiaṁ* duties (free service to local government and landlords) except on Sundays. The low castes were not permitted to reside in tiled houses. Even non-Hindus were forced to supply provisions to the temples.[37] All men except Brahmins were prohibited to wear anything above the waist.[38] Except Brahmin women all were required to go bare-breasted[39] before the men of superior castes.[40] So caste disabilities blocked the advancement of subalterns in Travancore.

Burden of Tax and Wage Free Labour

Travancore was known for oppressive taxes and unpaid services to which the low castes and slaves were subjected. There was not less than 110 different taxes which prevailed in Travancore. A poll tax was imposed on slaves, low castes and Syrian Christians. It was paid not only for the living but also for the dead. The Nadars had to pay a tax for toddy. There was a certain fee charged on low caste marriages also. Special occasions were used to squeeze the earnings of the poor. There was a tax for huts or houses of the poor low castes and slaves. Handlooms, oil-mills, bows, boats and nets, and hunting were also taxed. Taxes were extracted from goldsmiths, fishermen, drummers and bearers. People were forced to give money during the time of festivals, the end of the year, various anniversaries, and other occasions such as royal marriages and birthdays. Though some of the taxes were abolished, government officials used to exploit the ignorance of poor people and continuously collected taxes from them. In short, nothing was untaxed in Travancore.[41]

Unpaid labour, known as *ūḻiaṁ*, was another yoke in the life of the low castes. They had to be available on demand for government work on roads and public buildings, acquiring provisions for festivals and temples and for government officials on tour, guarding government properties, cutting and transporting timber, carrying salt, supplying firewood, etc. They were exploited physically for these burdensome tasks, and were sent home unpaid. Poor Nairs and Syrian Christians were also used occasionally. The poor labourers usually did not get the small amount allotted for some works. Out of fear, they used to work without complaint, as they could not disobey the landlords. Many low-caste families were assigned to do *ūḻiaṁ* services to high caste families.[42] Women were also not excluded from taxes and *ūḻiaṁ* services, but the high castes were excluded from *ūḻiaṁ* services and from the oppressive taxes. Thus was ensured a luxurious life for the high castes and the ruling class.

Slavery

Slavery was one of the evil systems which chained thousands of people to the lowest of the low in the social hierarchy of Travancore. Slaves, both men and women, were mainly drawn from the slave castes/outcastes such as the Pallans, the Pariahs, the Kuravars and the Pulayars.[43] The slaves were bought and sold like cattle. They were forced to work hard in the most difficult and unhealthy situations. They were not given sufficient food or medical aid. They lived in a miserable environment, and their clothing was scanty. They were sold in such a way that husband and wife, parent and children would be separated in different directions. They were offered as gifts to their master's friends or to temples, and even mortgaged along with the land on which they lived and worked. When they were sold or transferred, one of the clauses in the deed or agreement was 'you may sell him or kill him', or 'tie and beat, but do not destroy their legs or eyes'. The caste tyranny did not allow them to be courageous and raise their voice. They could not own anything except humiliation and an 'empty stomach'. They were beaten and confined in stocks or cages for even minor faults. If they were late for work, they were tied and whipped.[44]

The price of a slave varied from place to place. In 1852, the normal price of a slave was Rs. 6, but it was Rs. 18 in the place called Mallapalli. In some places it was six to fourteen rupees. Slaves were owned by government and individuals in Travancore. There were 164,864 slaves in 1836 and 165,000 in 1843. In the final proclamation of the abolition of slavery 136,000 slaves, both government and private, were liberated.[45] Though slavery was abolished in British India in 1843, with the pressure from Madras Government and the relentless persuasion of missionaries, the Maharaja of Travancore issued the final proclamation of the abolition of slavery only in June 1855. This proclamation did not liberate them in the true sense. They could not enjoy the expected outcome of the proclamation.[46] In fact, Travancore was built on the sweat and blood of the slave class in agriculture. The women slaves were exploited physically and sexually. It is the caste system which perpetuated slavery in Travancore because all slaves had come from the untouchable communities. S/he became a slave because s/he was born in a slave community.

Discriminatory Language

In Travancore, language had caste colour and flavour. The people of lower caste origin were not allowed to use certain words and phrases which were exclusively high caste in usage. The persons of inferior castes had to use the language in most servile and humiliating way which would please the ears of the persons of high castes. The lower caste person and a slave should not address himself or herself as 'I' but *aṭiyan*, 'your slave'. S/he must not say his/her rice as *chōru* but *kārikkādi*, 'dirty gruel'. His/her house was called *mādam*, a 'hut'. His/her children were called 'monkeys' or 'calves'. Moreover, while speaking to high caste person, s/he had to keep his/her hand over the mouth so that his/her breath might not pollute the addressee.[47]

In the Malabar[48] the word for house was based on the caste of the inhabitant. While the house of a Pariah was called *cheri*, Cheraman lived in a *chāla*.[49] *Pura* or *kudi* was the home of blacksmiths, goldsmiths, carpenters, weavers and toddy drawers. Nairs resided in *vīṭu* or *bhavanam*. Nambudiri Brahmins lived in an *illaṁ* or *mana* or *manakkal*. The king's palace was called *kōvilakaṁ* or *koṭṭaraṁ*. In front of Nambudiri Brahmins, persons of inferior castes could not speak of their houses. They used to name their homes 'dung heaps'.[50] It is interesting to note that royal food was addressed as 'nectar'; royal birth as 'incarnation'; and a royal birthday as 'holy day'. The Maharaja was addressed as *ponnu tamburān* (golden god) or *tiru manassu* (Sacred Mind) or 'the Maharaja themselves'. Royal family members were never called by their proper names but by the star under which they were born, or as Senior or Junior Prince/Queen.[51] The discriminative usage of the language proves the deep-seated caste psyche of the Travancore society in the nineteenth century. Language orientation made the people of lower caste origin psychologically more timid and submissive. In a social context where education was denied to the lower castes, it is possible that they would not have even understood the difference between the words in regular use and the root cause of the use of different words by different communities. But movements like the Upper Cloth Revolt prove that the subalterns were not completely unconscious of the caste dimension of the use of language. It reflects the contradictory consciousness of subalterns: resistance and submission.

Human Trafficking and Sacrifice

Though prohibited by law, human trade was prevalent in the Travancore kingdom. People were sold and bought, mostly during famines. Except Brahmins, people of all castes were sold and purchased. Children of high castes were also sold. Slaves and their children were the main victims of the human trade. People were sold in distant regions such as Malabar.[52] Human sacrifices were also performed: landlords were advised to conduct them to please deities or for success in new ventures and slaves were offered as sacrifices.[53] Clearly, outcastes and slaves were the primary victims of the heinous practices in society.

The Caste Councils

In South Travancore there was a council of Shudras called National Council of the *Pidagaikars*. They were more powerful than the government, and exercised considerable authority over the people, particularly the low castes and slaves. They would meet annually at Suchindram during the time of the famous Car Festival, the main agenda being to discuss and evaluate the matters related to caste and religion. They used to examine if members of their castes and other castes strictly had observed the customs and manners of their respective caste. They also examined whether any individual or caste violated his/her caste conduct. Most importantly, they observed and deliberated whether any low caste imitated the dress code, food, speech and life-style of higher castes. Severe punishment was given to the violators of caste rules and customs. The council acted as a court, and had given even capital punishment, and pressurized the rulers to do things in their favour. Even the rulers of the state were afraid of the council and used to consult with them in many civil and religious matters. But Col. Munro, the Resident, abolished the council which created terror in the minds of the people, especially the low castes in South Travancore.[54] In the name of caste, everything was allowed. The high castes decided the lifestyle of subalterns: what they should wear and how they should behave. The high caste council functioned almost like the *khap* panchayats today, though the latter is limited to the affairs of their respective community.

Caste and Brahmins

The creation story in the *Purushasukta* of the *Rigveda*, places Brahmins on the top of the creation order. According to this hymn, four orders of the society – Brahmin, Kshatriya, Vaishya and Shudra – originated from the sacrifice of the primeval being. They emanated from the four parts of the Creator: the mouth, the arms, the thighs and the feet respectively. The position of each organ probably denoted the status of each order (caste) in the hierarchy.[55] The social superiority of the Brahmin was accepted in Travancore too. The Census Report of Travancore in 1875 says, 'His tenants . . . bow down to him not simply as a landlord but as their royal liege and benefactor, their suzerain master, their household deity, their very God on earth. . . . His person is holy; his directions are commands; his movements are processions; his meal is nectar. He is the holiest of human beings. He is the representative of God on earth.'[56] In South Travancore, the position and privileges of Nambudiri Brahmins were enjoyed by the Pottis who were considered inferior Brahmins.[57] Caste created a situation in which everyone was created for the service of Brahmins. No system could question or control them. They lived on 'privileges,' not on 'restrictions'. The government and social system supported their social needs.

Low Castes and Religion

In Travancore, there were separate temples for upper castes and lower castes. Compared to the temples of upper castes, the lower castes had no well-constructed or maintained temples. The Brahmin temples were not accessible to the 'impure' castes. They could not even touch the outer walls of the temples. They were not allowed to hear or read the sacred texts. Though the presence of lower castes was considered polluted, their offerings in the form of money were not polluted. They used to make their offerings from a specific distance. In some temples, they were allowed to approach a bit closer for worship and amusement on certain festival days, but common worship was not possible.[58]

The lower castes worshipped Bhadrakali, Sastavu, Veerabhadran, etc. They also venerated the spirits of their ancestors. They had their own places of worship such as *kavu*. They also worshipped in sacred groves. They believed that epidemics and sudden illness were the result of divine wrath, and offered animal or bird sacrifices to Bhadrakali, Madan, Marutha and Pey.[59] The slave castes had no permanent place of worship. They mainly worshipped Madan, Mallan, Karumkali, Chavus, and Bhuthams.[60] In a nutshell, the lower castes were not considered as part of Hindu religion in the true sense of its expression. They had no religious identity or dignity in the eyes of Brahmins and upper castes. The caste system not only limited the social space of subalterns but also the religious space. The dominant religion neither recognized them nor allowed them to opt out of it. The negation of religious space later contributed to the large-scale conversion of subalterns into Christianity, which gave them a new space and identity.

Political Situation

The Travancore Kingdom was under British rule, with its own native sovereign and administrative system. The political relation of Travancore and the British Government was based on the treaty of 1795, modified in 1805. The treaty, signed in the context of the impending attack of Tipu Sultan, was termed a 'treaty of subsidiary and defensive alliance'. Travancore had to pay Rs. 6 lakh as annual subsidy or tribute, and in turn the British army would protect their kingdom from any external aggression. But in the modification of the treaty in 1805, more pro-British clauses were included. The annual subsidy was increased up to Rs. 8 lakh; no European would be allowed to stay in the country without the permission of the British Government; advice of the British administration would have to be taken for important matters related to the civil administration. Also, the treaty gave power to the British Government to interfere in the internal affairs of Travancore if there was failure in the payment of tribute and in the administration of justice.[61] The king was not happy with the modified treaty, but finally agreed to the new version and Travancore virtually came under the control of British rule.[62] But the native government was not able to meet all conditions of the treaty, and the payment of subsidy fell in arrears. Gradually, conflict developed between the king, the Resident and the Dewan, and this led to the famous Travancore rebellion against the British in 1809.[63] Though the rebellion was controlled by the

British forces, the political atmosphere of Travancore continued with conflict between the British Resident and the Maharaja. Often it badly affected the attempts of innovative reforms which might have improved the condition of low castes and slaves.

The Travancore Kings

It is traditionally believed and claimed that the Travancore dynasty was descended from Veera Keralen, one of the sons of Cheraman Perumal, the ruler of ancient Kerala.[64] As a kingdom Travancore came into existence around the ninth century.[65] It is argued that Travancore rulers were not Shudras but Soma Kshatriyas.[66] The kingdom began to take shape in the fourteenth century and reached its present stage by conquering and absorbing the neighbouring states, in the later part of eighteenth century. King Martanda Varma is regarded as the maker of modern Travancore. He subdued most of the neighbouring kingdoms and expanded the boundaries of his kingdom.[67] The rulers were devout Hindus and took interest in religious ceremonies and festivals. They generously donated to the construction and maintenance of temples and religious places. Their prime concern was the welfare of Brahmins and the observance of caste laws prescribed in Hindu scriptures and Dharma Shastras.[68]

The kings of Travancore like all rulers in the country were protectors of the institution of caste. They strictly followed the caste laws in delivering justice and protected the privileges of high castes. For instance, Brahmins were exempted from tax and were given legal protection. They were treated with high social and religious honour. The Travancore kings were ideal Hindu kings who lived and ruled according to the Hindu *Shastras*, particularly the laws of Manu.[69] Often the religiosity of kings was misused by Brahmins, and influenced the policies of the government.[70] Under the ideal Hindu king, both men and women of low caste and slave caste origin were even deprived of their basic status as human beings. They were not protected by the king in their attempts at social advancement. This is evident in the approach of the Travancore king and queen during the period of Upper Cloth Revolt.

Śri Padmanābha Dāsa: The Religious Identity of Travancore Kings

Travancore was purely a Hindu state with a conservative social and religious outlook. The religious identity of the country was legitimately established when King Martanda Varma dedicated the state to Sri Padmanabha, the local designation of Vishnu, on 17 January 1750.[71] After this, Travancore kings came to be known as the regents of Sri Padmanabha. After annexing small neighbouring kingdoms and freeing the kingdom from external aggressions, King Martanda Varma, along with his heir apparent, the royal family members and the Prime Minister, went to Sri Padmanabha Swamy Temple. In the presence of all priests he laid down his sword in front of the deity and declared that he would be the vassal or agent of the deity from now on. On that day he adopted the title, *śri padmanābha dāsa*, the servant of Sri Padmanabha. His successors also continued to adopt this title and ruled the nation with great reverence to the deity. After this event, the people of Travancore began to consider the sovereign as sacred. Speaking against the king was considered a sin. The dedication of the state to the deity and adoption of the title *śri padmanābha dāsa* was a political strategy of legitimation. In this strategy, while religion protected the king from internal political turmoil or opposition, his political decisions supported religious motives.

The Government Machinery

The unjust government machinery was fully controlled by the upper castes. Bribery was rampant in the police, the courts and government offices.[72] Corrupt officials extorted money from the poor and treated them badly for even small crimes.[73] The concerns of upper caste people were dealt with respect and kindness. No lower caste person used to go with impunity if s/he was accused. The complaints of lower castes did not get proper attention either in the police or in government offices. The officials and police used to delay the cases of poor people against the high castes. They never used to get justice from the local officers.[74] Even the British Resident had no faith in the police system of the kingdom.

The government often neglected public works and used the machinery for conducting festivals and other religious functions. In the name of forced labour for the government, officials oppressed the poor and used them for personal needs.[75] Every government official from the Dewan to the peon was in friendship or alliance with the higher castes.[76] It is not surprising that General Cullen, the British Resident, was also under the counsel of Brahmins and other high castes.[77] In such a situation, the subalterns could expect only an unjust administrative system which made them objects in the hands of the upper castes. For them, the administrative system virtually functioned as a seat of caste nepotism. Moreover, women and subalterns were completely excluded from administrative jobs. The influence of upper castes in administration was the main obstacle for the empowerment of subalterns who had been victimized for centuries.

Education and Public Employment

The notion of purity-pollution barred the lower castes and the Syrian Christians from employment in government service. In Travancore, the civil duties were always connected with religious functions. The government officials had to attend not only the public concerns and office work but also the administration and management of temples and free inns for Brahmins. Therefore, Christians and lower caste people were excluded from government services. The basic assumption was that if appointed, they would pollute the officials of higher castes and temple premises where most of the offices were located. Though a few Syrian Christians were appointed into government service during the time of Col. Munro, they were given employment in inferior sections, and were placed under British officials.[78]

Lower-caste children, Christians and Hindus, were not admitted to most of the government schools. Government spent money for the education of higher castes. The inferior status of their caste did not allow the lower castes even to approach the school and get education. In some government schools, Syrian Christian boys were not allowed to be seated near the high-caste Hindu boys.[79] The women irrespective of caste and religion, except royal family members, kept away from formal education and employment. In fact, the government and its various departments functioned within the framework of caste, patriarchy and religion, and completely ignored the lower caste women and people of non-Hindu traditions. However, education initiated by missionaries among the subalterns contributed to the social advancement of lower castes in Travancore.

The Judicial System

Travancore had a judicial system based on the principles of Dharmashastra. The Brahmins interpreted the sacred law and pronounced the judgements, their word was considered law.[80] In the nineteenth century new laws were framed partly based on Dharmashastra and partly on the rules and regulations in the British territories.[81] But for the subalterns, 'native courts at that time were centres of injustice and oppression'.[82] Judges were compulsorily appointed from Brahmin and Nair castes.[83] Access of the lower castes to the courts was either restricted or prohibited. They could not easily approach courts in the temple premises. Moreover, the court officials never tolerated the approach of low caste witnesses for fear that they would be polluted. If a low caste person happened to be a witness, the court official would go to him/her, but not too close, and take down the evidence with the help of an intermediary such as a peon or any person whose approach would not pollute the official. Often neither the question nor the answer would be audible to the people involved in the process. If an inferior caste individual wanted to submit a petition, s/he was made to stand and wait outside the court for a day or two.[84]

Cruel punishments existed in Travancore. The death penalty was given for crimes such as theft, killing of cows, etc. Blowing up from the mouth of a mortar, impaling, hanging spread for days (*chitaravadham*), maiming, crushing to death under an elephant's feet, whipping, severe fines, confiscation of property, selling as a slave, banishment from the country, were common punishments. These punishments were mainly given to lower castes. Women criminals were punished by shaving their head, and then banishing them from the country.[85]

Trial by ordeal (*satyaparikṣa*) was based on the caste of the accused. Ordeal by balance (*tūkku)* was for the Brahmins, by fire for the Kshatriyas and by poison for the Shudras, to prove the innocence of the accused. There was no such ordeal for the low castes.[86]

The Economic Life

The economy of Travancore was based on agriculture, revenue from land, and various kinds of taxes. It was controlled and manipulated by the upper castes and ruling class. The low castes were victims with no role and space, except offering the labour, in the economic system of the county. Caste played a crucial role in the ownership of land. The state revenue was indiscriminately used for religious ceremonies and for feeding the Brahmins.

Ownership of Land

In Travancore, land was mainly in the hands of Brahmins. The possession of land by the Brahmins had a legendary and historical background. According to the creation myth, Parashurama divided the land among the Nambudiri Brahmins. It is argued that before the ninth century, most of the land was owned and cultivated by the non-Brahmins.[87] After the Chera-Chola war in eleventh century, the Nambudiri Brahmins were able to accumulate extensive land. As trustees of the temples, they manipulated temple properties and amassed huge amount of property and resources. Petty non-Brahmin landlords and tenants were convinced to transfer their lands to the control of Brahmins and temple managements which enjoyed immunity from confiscation and devastation. Thus the Brahmins became landlords by manipulating the immunity enjoyed by the temples and by cheating petty tenants in the erstwhile Kerala territory.[88] The Brahmins, the non-cultivating owners leased out the land to the non-cultivating tenants, mainly the Nairs. The lessee cultivated it with the help of both men and women of low and slave castes and gave a fixed rent to the landlord.[89] With this system, Nairs became the supervisors of the land owned by the Brahmins.[90] This continued in the nineteenth century. Since caste factor was involved in the possession of land, lower castes continued as landless people in Travancore. They had to toil in the land to increase the wealth of landlords.[91] Since, the Travancore economic system was mainly based on land the lower castes had to depend on land lords for their livelihood and obey them at any cost. This was the predicament of subalterns: the necessity of survival leads them to be submissive rather than resistive.

The Janmi System

The *janmi*[92] system, an exploitative economic system, prevailed in Travancore for many centuries. In the beginning of *janmi* system, the landlords functioned as chieftains in respective areas and supplied provisions and soldiers to the Raja. According to wealth and the possession of land, they were assigned areas to govern in subjection to the king. The *dēśavāḻi* had less than a hundred Nair soldiers and the *nāduvāḻi* had a minimum of hundred Nair soldiers. They cultivated their lands through slaves or leased out them to tenants (*kudiyān*). The feudal lords exploited the tenants and extracted heavy levies. They controlled the lower-caste workers and tenants with personal militias. The tenants and workers had to give taxes of various kinds and to get permission from the landlords for certain privileges. They even had to give gifts to chieftains on special occasions such as weddings and festivals.[93]

There were three types of land: *janmaṁ,* impure *janmaṁ* and *sarkkār paṭṭaṁ.*[94] *Janmaṁ* was hereditary and tax-free land mostly in the hands of Brahmins. 'Impure' *janmaṁ* was land alienated to other castes. It was subjected to tax. It was non-Brahmanic land.[95] It was mainly owned by non-Brahmin upper castes. *sarkkār paṭṭaṁ* was government land given to tenants with certain conditions for a fixed tenure. A majority of *sarkkār paṭṭaṁ* was held by the Nairs. In all these lands low and slave castes carried out the cultivation.[96] In the beginning of *janmi* system Brahmins owned the land and Nairs supervised it, but with the provision of the *sarkkār paṭṭaṁ*, Nairs also began to own the land. The system survived on the sweat and blood of both men and women of lower caste and slave caste origin.

The Expensive Rituals

The native government spent large sums of money on religious rituals and festivals. *hiraṇyagarbhaṁ, tulabhāraṁ* (both related to the succession of king), *murajapaṁ* (conducted once in six years for the prosperity for the nation), *upanayana* (investiture of sacred thread for royal family members), etc., were performed as state rituals. They were expensive, and spent from the state exchequer. They were considered essential to the well-being of the king and his subjects.[97] More than fifty thousand people used to attend *murajapaṁ* (customary prayer) ceremony. Government used to make all arrangements for the participants. Gifts were also distributed to the participants. Brahmins were the main beneficiaries of this ritual, they were fed and given royal treatment for weeks.[98] *Hiraṇyagarbhaṁ* was another expensive ritual conducted in relation to the succession of a new king. Once Rs. 120,000 was spent only to purchase gold needed for this ceremony. All Brahmins who attended the ceremony were distributed gold.[99] *Tulabhāraṁ* was yet another expensive ritual conducted by the state. It was estimated that Rs. 1,21,598 spent for purchasing gold for conducting this ritual in the last part of nineteenth century.[100] In one *upanayana* ceremony Rs. 18,000 was spent.[101] These expensive rituals were justified with religious reasons.[102] The government had money for conducting religious rituals and festivals but not for the upliftment of poor sections of the society. The upper castes monetarily benefitted from these ceremonies. The state exchequer was also exhausted because of these costly rites. Moreover, the subalterns had no role or participation in these ceremonies though it was claimed that they were conducted for the wellbeing of all subjects.

As Hinduism was the state religion, festivals and ceremonies in major temples were conducted at the expense of the state. It was estimated that government spent around Rs. 33,000 annually for the maintenance of temples at Suchindram. Apart from the temples in Travancore, government maintained many temples in different parts of the then India.[103] It was calculated that one-fifth of the state income had been spent for maintaining Hindu temples and for supporting Brahmin priests.[104] While huge amount of money was spent for the management of religious institutions, the lower castes and slaves lived in sheer poverty and without basic amenities. They were not even allowed to enter those temples managed with state revenue comprised of their income also. While the dominant religion manifests itself through grand festivals, rituals and huge architecture, the subaltern religion revolves around the survival needs of people. The state sponsored religions are always controlled by the dominant and ignore the life of subalterns.

Ūttupura (Free Inn)

Ūttupura or free inns were one of the evil institutions in Travancore. They were made to feed the Brahmins at the expense of the government. Brahmins were given free meals at *ūttupuras* constructed throughout the country. They were given boiled rice, curry, chutney, curd, milk, fruits, etc. At the main *ūttupura* near Padmanabha Swamy Temple in Trivandrum, residents could eat throughout the day. It was estimated that annually Rs. 3 lakh were spent for these free inns.[105] Needless to say, there was no *ūttupuras* to feed the low castes and slaves in the society. In the age of economic liberalization, *ūttupura* is replaced by liberal economic institutions which empower the upper castes economically. New *ūttupuras* in the form of welfare measures, subsidies and canteens have been opened to pacify the subalterns who have no share in the economic growth. The dominant always reap the benefits in any economic system.

Royal Expenditure

Though Travancore was protected under British rule, it was an independent kingdom with its own ruler and administrative system. But it was always under the surveillance of a Resident, the representative of British rule in India. The uncontrolled expenditure of the king and royal family members was often unchecked. They used to spend enormous amounts of money on religious vows and ceremonies. In 1843, the king donated Surat Rs. 1 lakh to Sri Padmanabha Swamy Temple. It was argued that he donated this huge sum of money in the context of his conflict with the Resident. During this period, palace expenditure was also increased. The annual purchase of ornaments and dress went up to Rs. 3 lakh. Valuable jewels were offered to the deity. Costly buildings were constructed. In 1845 Rs. 34 lakh were spent on vows and religious ceremonies from the palace treasury.[106] The indiscriminate expenditure of the king and royal family used to exhaust the state treasury, and this in turn added burden in the form of taxes upon the people. The most affected people were the low castes and slaves.

Religious Communities in Travancore

Major religious traditions existed within the social matrix of Travancore. Hinduism enjoyed the royal patronage and the status of 'official religion'. Majority of Travancoreans were Hindus. In 1816, Hindus constituted 82.7 per cent of the total population.

Apart from Hinduism other religious traditions also existed in Travancore. Christianity is traditionally believed to have come to Malabar in AD 52 through St. Thomas. The early Christians were called St. Thomas Christians or Syrian Christians. From the very beginning, they functioned as a caste due to the 72 privileges granted by the kings of the periods of their migrations in the fourth and ninth centuries. They observed the Hindu apparatus of purity-pollution and considered themselves equal to the Nairs. In all areas of social life, they were influenced by the Hindu caste practices and customs. At the same time many of them were ignorant of their faith, and were economically poor. In fact, they were happy with the social position and did not bother to put their faith into practice in the caste-ridden society. They were not hesitant to follow the caste rules and practices even though they contradicted their faith tenets.[107] Later, Syrian Christians faced many social and religious disabilities such as *ūḻiaṁ* duties (gratuitous services), supplying provisions to *ūttupura* (free inn for Brahmins), treating them equal with low caste converts, considering their approach to temples as pollution, exclusion from government services, inaccessible to all schools, all streets or public wells, ill-treatment from government officials, discrimination in schools, etc.[108] Before the coming of Protestant missionaries, there were also Roman Catholic converts from fishing communities such as Mukkuva and Parava. They were not treated equal with Syrian Christians.[109]

The Muslims were concentrated in British Malabar. In 1857, Muslims constituted 5-6 per cent of the population in Travancore. There were seven classes of Muslims in Travancore. Apart from a few of Arab or Afghan ancestry, the majority were converts from different Hindu castes or children of mixed marriages. They were called Lubbays. In south, most of them were descendants of proselytes. They were completely ignorant of their faith and tradition. The Muslims were industrious and engaged in trade and agriculture. There were no nobles among them. Many of them were poor and lived in miserable condition. Their high priest was called *Tangal*. The Muslims were also influenced by Hindu religious practices. Many superstitions prevailed among them. They too practised purity-pollution norms.[110]

There were very few Buddhists, Jews, Sikhs, Jains and Zoroastrians. It is evident from the Census of 1901: Buddhists-227, Jews-151, Sikhs-15, Zoroastrians-2 and only one Jain. Once there had been a strong Buddhist influence in South Travancore as attested by Buddha *viharas*/temples in places like Karunagapalli, Pallipuram, Pallikal, etc. A Buddha statue was discovered from the famous Pallikal temple. In 1881, the same temple was converted and dedicated to Goddess Bhagavati.[111] It is believed that Nagaraja temple, the famous Hindu temple at Nagarcoil in the southern part of Travancore, was originally a Jain temple. The Jain temple (Chitharal Rock Temple) at Chitharal in Kanyakumari district proves the presence of Jains in Travancore.[112] Though different faith traditions existed in Travancore, they were not patronized as equal with Hindu religion. The followers of other religious traditions were treated within the framework of caste. The subalterns had very limited or no space in all religious traditions. The religious space of women in those religious traditions was also restricted. The status of women, irrespective of religious traditions, was more or less same. It is important to note that major religious traditions with egalitarian ideology could not escape from the snares of the caste system and patriarchy. It continues even today. Caste and gender still determine the space of subalterns in the religions of the dominant.

Christians and the Government

Christianity had its presence in Travancore long before the dawn of nineteenth century. Early Christians were called Syrian Christians or St. Thomas Christians. They were not enthusiastic in missionary activities as the Protestant missionaries had undertaken. By the end of fifteenth century, Roman Catholic missionaries came, and after three centuries of work they could add thousands of converts, mostly from fishing communities, to their faith. They also could bring a large section of the Syrian Christians into their fold. But in South Travancore, the Syrian Church was not much known, and the presence of Roman Catholic Church was limited entirely to the fishermen communities.[113] In 1816, Christians constituted 12.37 per cent of the total population. It rose to 20.60 per cent in 1891. The Christian population was mainly divided among major denominations such as Jacobite or St. Thomas Syrian Church, Roman Catholic Church of both Latin and Syrian rites, Protestant Missions, mainly London Missionary Society (LMS) in the south and Church Missionary Society (CMS) in the north etc.[114]

It is claimed that enlightened and large-hearted rulers of Travancore followed a tolerant religious policy which protected Christianity for many centuries and helped to establish Protestant missions in the country.[115] But the treatment of the native government towards the Christian missions disproves the claim. It is argued that the substantial presence of Christian population in Travancore was not because of the tolerant religious policy but of the annexation policy of Travancore kings. They annexed the territories ruled by the independent Rajas in the eighteenth century, and Christian subjects of those small kingdoms became part of Travancore.[116]

The native government was not in favour of the establishment of Protestant missions in Travancore. In 1806 Ringeltaube, the first LMS missionary to South Travancore, got a passport after the intervention of Col. Macaulay, the then British Resident. Col. Munro, another British Resident, received grants from government for the educational work of the missionaries. The Syrian Christians also faced oppression from the government. They were excluded from public employment and forced to do unpaid work connected with

Hindu temples. The Christians irrespective of tradition and creed experienced harassment and discrimination in different forms. During the years between 1827-30 and 1858-9 Christians were persecuted in South Travancore. The Christians were not treated as equal citizens of the nation. They had to fight with the government for each and every stage of their growth. They always had to depend on missionaries to get favorable treatment from the government. It is interesting to note that till 1838, LMS could not get permission to start a mission station in the capital due to the strong caste and religious prejudices of the government. Missionaries were not even allowed to stay in the capital. Finally they got a plot of waste land at Kannamoola because of the intervention of General Fraser. The CMS missionaries in North Travancore also faced opposition.[117]

Some of the socio-religious disabilities of Christians in Travancore were resolved by Col. Munro. He influenced the native government to rectify those disabilities through royal proclamations. He was instrumental for the law of inheritance for the Christian converts, exemption from all *ūḻiaṁ* services (gratis services) related to temples and free inns for the Brahmins, exemption from supplying provisions for pagodas and shrines, freedom from *ūṛiyam* services to the government, exemption from public works on Sundays. He appointed Christian judges in every district court to ensure justice to Christians.[118] There were also instances in which the British Resident put hurdles to the mission work and the welfare of the Christians.[119]

The Christians, men and women, had to pay various taxes, and were forced to do the works for the temples. They were compelled to carry lights in the Hindu religious processions. They were whipped if they disobeyed. False charges were imposed upon them, and were thrown into prison without proper judicial process. In several occasions Sunday services were disturbed with the support of government officials. During the time of persecution in south Travancore, women were physically assaulted and publicly molested. Churches, schools and houses were burned down. The government officers systematically obstructed the construction of Churches by negating the required permission. In 1827, a royal proclamation was issued to control the erection of worship places. Christian access to government offices, schools, streets and public wells was restricted. Christians were fined for walking nearby the temple premises. The conversion of high caste people were unkindly dealt by the respective caste people and government.[120] When Velu Thampi, the Dewan of Travancore and Paliathu Atchen, the Cochin Dewan fought the British, Christians were tortured, killed and thrown into the backwaters. Men, women, and children were maimed and butchered.[121]

The original but somewhat hidden feeling of the ruling class towards Christianity in Travancore can be read in the letter written by Dewan Velu Thampi to Zamorin Raja in Malabar, in which he expressed his chief concern against the British: 'great apprehension of the extension of the Christian faith in Travancore'.[122] In short, in the context of persecution and discrimination, the Christian community, both Syrian Christians and native converts, survived under the political flag and the moral support of British administration and European missionaries. It is not the tolerant policy of the ruling class that protected Christianity, but the hopeful endurance and faith persuasion of Christians and the dedicated work of missionaries. The ruling class was afraid of the possible conversion of subalterns whose social progress was blocked by the caste system. They might have assumed that the conversion of subalterns, majority of the population, would challenge the hegemony of upper castes and strengthen the power of British rule.

The Status of Women

The life of women in Travancore was defined by the ideal womanhood in Hinduism. The lives of Sita, Savitri and Shakuntala had been evoked to describe the position and responsibility of women in general in the society. Women's destiny was in the hands of men. Husband was her visible god, and final word in her life. She was always under the authority of man from her birth to death. She had to be submissive to her father, husband and son in different stages of her life. Obedience was considered as the greatest virtue of women. It was even believed that a woman could enter heaven only by the merits of her husband.[123] Hindu patriarchal perception of women prevailed in all communities: both upper castes and lower castes.

Women were considered inferior and held in low esteem. They were not given respect but treated with contempt. In fact, they were objects in the hands of men. Women had to uncover their bosoms or upper part of the body before men of superior castes. Because of the low estimation and treatment, women used to exclaim, 'Better to be a clod than to have been born a woman.' The birth of a girl child was not celebrated. Sayings such as 'Why do you sit as if a girl had been born at home?' and 'Through the incapacity of the midwife, the infant is a female!' were common in the society. They had been taught to be submissive in conduct and speech. They were not allowed to speak directly to a male in the absence of a responsible man in the family. Women of some castes were not permitted to speak to even male relatives. The society generally expected women to cook rice and work at home or in the fields.[124]

Though women in general were treated as inferior, the women of high castes, especially the Brahmin women, enjoyed certain privileges and respect within and outside the family. They could wear fine clothing and cover themselves. They wore an upper cloth made of fine cloth.[125] But still they were not fully free from certain community restrictions. They could not be seen by other men. They could not go out without a female servant. Violation of chastity was not tolerated: adulteresses were excommunicated.[126] Women of higher-caste origin, including royal family members, rarely appeared in public.[127]

One of the social evils that enslaved the women was the practice of child marriage. The girl children were given for this wicked system. Though the low caste people were not completely subjected to this evil practice, they were also influenced by its stigma. They also gave their girls for early marriage. The Brahmins performed child marriages according to the *Shankara Smriti*. They married off their girls between eight and ten years of age.[128] Child marriage produced many widows and led several women into misery. It cast doubt on the value and dignity of females.[129] Child marriage existed among the Syrian Christians also.[130] In fact, child marriage, the product of patriarchy, was practised by all communities.

The life of widows was pitiful and disrespected in society. They were restricted with many religious and social regulations. Their mobility within and outside the family was strictly controlled. They were not supposed to perform puja and cook food offered to the deities. The Brahmin widows had to live a life of *sanyasis.* The newly-married couples should not see or meet widows, who were required to fast on *ekadesi.* They were prohibited to re-marry, and fully debarred from assisting any religious ceremony. They were not allowed to wear ornaments and colored garments, or to keep long hair. They were always considered as misfortune within and outside the family. Ill-treatment and neglect led them to even commit suicide. The pathetic life of widows was one of the reasons for female infanticide.[131] But those socio-religious restrictions were not imposed upon widowers. They were free as other men in the society.

The domestic life of women was burdened with routine and customary practices. Women never ate with men in the family. They had to wait for men to finish the meal first, and then had their meal. Sometimes, they had only what was left over.[132] The rules of purity-pollution were strictly applied to women on special occasions such as menstruation, child-birth, death, etc. A menstruating woman had to keep a distance of 12 feet from others. A newly confined woman was required to limit her approach within 18 feet.[133] Childlessness was considered as a curse and sin. But women were always blamed for barrenness.

Except Brahmins, all women had to remove their upper covering before men of superior castes. Though the Nair women had the right to wearing an upper cloth they had to remove it before the Brahmins as a mark of respect and reverence. In North Travancore, Nair women used to go bare breasted by choice. But in the South they strictly wore upper cloth due to the influence of Tamil culture.[134] But the women of low castes were not allowed to wear the upper cloth, or anything above the waist. Their dress code was regulated by royal proclamations and was strictly monitored. Only in 1812, were Christian women of low caste origin allowed to wear jackets. The uncovering of bosoms by Nair women was not legally stipulated. The lower caste women had to go always bare-breasted before all higher castes.[135] They were actually subalterns among the subalterns in society. Since the practice of uncovering bosoms was the upshot of caste, it is possible that the ancestors of low caste women had no such restriction on covering their bosoms in the ancient casteless society of Kerala.

Chastity of woman was checked and regulated with social laws. She had no freedom over her body, emotions and desires. Everything was controlled by men. In fact she was treated as an object in the hands of men. She was victimized in the inter-caste sexual relations. If a high caste (Nair or any other Shudra caste) women cohabitated with a low caste man, she was excommunicated and was sold as a slave. But if it was with a man of superior caste (Brahmin), it was not considered as polluting.[136] In the inter-caste relations, woman is polluted permanently, but man can be purified by certain rituals.[137] The religious and social laws primarily victimized women, particularly the subaltern women. These laws were made by men to control and keep women within the social and religious boundaries.

The women of low and slave castes had many social disabilities and restrictions. They were not allowed to wear gold ornaments or coloured clothes. Lower caste women were permitted to wear ornaments made of silver, and the poor slave women only necklaces of beads. To wear ornaments, they required permission from the government.[138] Apart from domestic work, women of low and slave castes had to work in the fields for their livelihood. Low caste females were not allowed to carry water pots on the hip. They had to walk long distances where she could draw water without the stigma of pollution. The condition of female slaves was more difficult than male slaves. They had to obey the diktats of their master without slight defiance. They had no proper food and clothing. Often, they were not even able to feed their new-born children. Sometimes they had to work on a hungry stomach. They had to live in unhealthy huts in all seasons.[139] Though later it was abolished women criminals were punished by shaving their heads, and then banishing them from the country.[140]

Women's education was denied out of the patriarchal fear that they would be defiant and arrogant. In Travancore, 'Can she read?' 'Can she do needlework?' 'Can she keep accounts?' were not primary questions regarding women.[141] Negation of education to women basically reflects the anti-women outlook of the society. Until the arrival of London Missionary Society missionaries Mr. Charles

Mead and Mrs. Johanna Coelestina Horyst (wife of Charles Mead) and Mr. Charles Mault and Mrs. Martha Mault, no effort had been taken to educate women in South Travancore.[142] The subjugated life of women, especially of the low and slave castes, in Travancore was unparalleled in any part of India. Religious and social laws controlled their mobility, freedom and natural rights. Being objectified in every aspect of life, women in general served men with their sweat and blood. Their dignity and status were defined by men. All through their lives, they carried the wound inflicted by the caste-oriented patriarchal culture. The women of low and slave caste had to serve the men of upper caste and lower caste with their broken body and wounded psyche. They had to be subservient not only before their men but also their upper caste masters. Lack of education coupled with numerous domestic and social restrictions conditioned the women folk not to question those restrictions but to obey them at their calling. The social context of Travancore shaped them to internalize the patriarchal 'truth' that they are inferior to men.

Conclusion

Though ancient Travancore was a casteless society, its social context in the nineteenth century was characterized by caste system. The caste factor in its varied forms played a significant role in all aspects of social life. The hierarchical and oppressive nature of caste system marginalized and excluded the low castes, the subalterns, from the mainstream of society. Caste factor was legitimized by religious faith, and worked on the basis of purity-pollution norms and unjust regulations. It divided the people and assigned them duties and privileges. Thus, a few people enjoyed all privileges and majority lived in humiliation and deprivation. While high castes were untouched by the burdensome taxes and compulsory works, the low castes and slaves paid the price of being born in their respective castes. Even non-Hindu religious communities were defined within the framework of caste. In fact, whole society was immersed in caste consciousness. It was the low castes and slaves who were most adversely affected due to the stigma of caste consciousness. They had only two options: either obey the caste rules and restrictions or end their life. They could not survive without conforming to the caste practices in society.

The political system was controlled by the upper caste elites even though Travancore was a protective state under British rule. They blocked initiatives of reform for the subalterns in the name of religion and caste. They influenced the king considerably and manipulated the native government. The king ruled under the counsel of Brahmins and other upper castes. Each and every step of administration was followed by the diktats of caste people. Interplay of caste and religion reflected in the administration of Travancore government. Whole administrative machinery functioned to help the high castes and ruling class, but not to the ones lived wounded in the tyranny of caste. The corrupt government supported the corrupt judicial system. For the subalterns, judiciary became a seat of injustice. Poor underprivileged sections of society could not even approach the government and court for their legal rights. They always lived in terror created by the ruling class. No voice against the ruling class was tolerated. They had no leader and protector. They were defenseless and exposed to all kinds of cruelties.

The economy of the country was dedicated to facilitate comfortable life for the Brahmins and ruling class. The natural and revenue resources were used for religious and caste purposes. The higher castes owned the whole land and controlled the economy of the kingdom. The subalterns were exploited to strengthen and amass the wealth of high castes and ruling class. The lavish life of the king and ruling class emptied the exchequer. They earned wealth at the expense of the poor laboring class. The low castes were polluted but their labor was not polluted. Heavy taxes were imposed upon them to fill the treasury emptied by the rituals and festivals. Both men and women of low castes and slave castes had to work like cattle in the fields. No question against the landlord could be raised. No complaint could be lodged against the landlord. They had to grapple the life with two options: work or starve. No education could be allowed and afforded. Their children used to be working with them from morning to evening.

There was no religious freedom for the low castes. They were deprived of temples and priests. In fact, they were not part of the so-called Hindu religion. Their approach was considered as polluting and denied entry to the temples. Even the non-Hindu religions could not come out of the influence of Hindu religious practices and caste life. At the same time, other religions, particularly the mission work of Christianity, was opposed by the dominant castes. Christian mission activities were interpreted and treated as part of British rule. Religious tolerance was a myth because the conversion of low castes to Christianity was checked by all possible political and judicial means.

The women, particularly of low castes and slaves, were more subjugated. They had to face all kinds of restrictions and disabilities imposed by the patriarchal religious and social systems. They had to go through the socio-religio-cultural discrimination within and outside the community. They were controlled by their men and upper caste masters. Their discrimination was based on the experience of caste and gender. They were more vulnerable due to the socio-religious restrictions. The women of low castes had to face social restrictions such as keeping a specific distance with caste people, they had no right to wear upper cloth, or enter a temple, etc. These harsh restrictions were imposed upon them only because of their birth in low caste. As women they were not allowed to dress like high caste women, even covering their bosoms. Ornaments were not permitted for them like other women. They were not allowed to carry water pots on the hips which is more convenient. They lived like an object and were treated with contempt. They were physically exploited and mentally tortured. She lived in the shadow of a man and served him with reverence. She was a subaltern among subalterns.

The social disabilities of low caste men and women were introduced by Brahmins. Therefore, it can be inferred that social disabilities such as restrictions on clothing were not there before the arrival of Brahmins in Travancore. The ancestors of low caste women were once free human beings who were not subjected to humiliation. In the social context of valuing people, particularly subaltern women, in terms of caste and gender, a strong new voice had been raised to restore the lost human freedom. The caste tyranny was not left completely unquestioned. While submissive to the caste rules for survival, the subalterns resisted the forces of oppression. Subaltern resistance began to develop in southern Travancore where caste and patriarchal restrictions were strictly applied. It gradually led to a revolt popularly known as the Upper Cloth Revolt.

NOTES

1. P. Shungoonny Menon, *A History of Travancore from the Earliest Times* (Madras: Higginbotham and Co., 1878), p. vii; Samuel Mateer, *Land of Charity* (London: John Snow & Co, 1871), p. 2.
2. Mateer, *Land of Charity*, pp. 3-10.
3. *Keralolpatti* (Mangalore: Stolz & Reuther, Basal Mission Press, 1898), pp. 3-17; Samuel, *Land of Charity*, pp. 13-14; Menon, *A History of Travancore from the Earliest Times*, pp. 16ff.
4. *Keralolpatti*, p. 13; Robin Jeffrey, *The Decline of Nair Dominance* (New Delhi: Manohar, 1994), p. 11.
5. Menon, *A History of Travancore from the Earliest Times*, p. 24.
6. M.N. Srinivas, *Social Change in Modern India* (Berkeley and Los Angeles: University of California Press, 1968), p. 3. Membership to a caste is not by selection but by birth. The inequality of caste is defended by the Hindu theological notions of *dharma* and *Karma-Samsara. Dharma* basically denotes the path in which each caste must pursue. It includes rules and regulations, responsibilities and way of life which members of each caste should follow. There is specific *dharma* for each caste. Therefore, degraded jobs of low castes are considered as his/her *dharma,* and there is no negation of rights or privileges as such but only the upholding of the *dharma* of the caste. The present condition of a particular caste is justified by the theory of *karma* and re-birth. Therefore, in the mechanism of caste there is neither oppressor nor victim (G.S. Ghurye, *Caste and Race in India* (London: Routledge and Kegan Paul, 1932; Reprint of Fifth Edition, Bombay: Popular Prakashan, 1994), p. 2; Marc Galanter, *Competing Equalities, Law and The Backward Classes in India* (New Delhi: Oxford University Press, 1984), p. 11; K. Wilson, *Dialectics of Consciousness* (Madras: Oneworld Educational Trust, 1993), p. iv.
7. V. Nagam Aiya, *Travancore Census Report 1891*, vol. I, p. 624.
8. Ibid., pp. 624-5.
9. Letter from Rev. F. Baylis to the Resident, 10-01-1859, Bundle no. 29, Cover File no. 2115 of 1858, *Shanar Disturbances in South Travancore,*

Archives Directorate, Trivandrum; *The Edict of 1851* referred in R.N. Yesudas, *A People's Revolt in Travancore* (Trivandrum: Kerala Historical Society, 1975), pp. 163-4.

10. A. Sreedhara Menon, *Social and Cultural History of Kerala* (New Delhi: Sterling Publishers, 1979), p. 65. Travancore, the part of South India was actually outside *Aryavarta*, the geographical area specified by Manu, where caste *(Varna)* rules and regulations were to be applied. *Aryavarta*, the country of Aryans, was located between the Himalayas and the Vindhyas and between the eastern and western seas. In this sense, Travancore was a casteless society, and people had not experienced caste regulations in the ancient period. It means the low castes and slaves once enjoyed natural human freedom which they lost after the implementation of caste system (K.A. Nilakanta Sastri, *A History of South India,* Fourth Edition (Madras: Oxford University Press (1955), 1992), pp. 68f; James Massey, *Caste-Class Victims and Their Assertion for* Justice (New Delhi: Centre for Dalit/Subaltern Studies, 2013), pp. 103f.
11. Elamkulam P. N. Kunjan Pillai, *Studies in Kerala History* (Trivandrum: Valsa Printers, 1970), pp. 309-13.
12. A. Sreedhara Menon, *Social and Cultural History of Kerala*, pp. 66-70.
13. J.W. Gladstone, *Protestant Christianity and People's Movements in Kerala* (Trivandrum: Seminary Publications, 1984), p. 15.
14. *Dr. Babasaheb Ambedkar: Writings and Speeches*, vols. 3 and 5, Compiled by Vasant Moon (Bombay: Education Department, Government of Maharashtra, 1987), pp. 101, 107.
15. The rank of Shudras in South India was next to the Brahmins. But they were considered polluted in the caste order in North India. The Aryans or Brahmins conferred the title Shudra to the middle and higher classes of the Dravidians because in South India there were other classes which were equal to the servile Shudras of North India. (Robert Caldwell, *A Comparative Grammar of the Dravidian Family of Languages* (London: Harrison, 1856; revd. edn., Madras: University of Madras, 1961), pp. 112-13.
16. They were placed between the Shudras and the slaves. Today they belong to the category of Other Backward Classes.
17. The slave castes were the outcastes. Presently, they call themselves as 'Dalits.' Constitutionally and legally they are known as Scheduled Castes.
18. Samuel Mateer, *Land of Charity*, pp. 29-32; I.H. Hacker, *A Hundred*

Years in Travancore (1806-1906) (London: H.R. Allenson Limited, 1908), p. 14.

19. Hacker, *A Hundred Years in Travancore (1806-1906)*, p. 14; Mateer, *Land of Charity*, pp. 34-8.
20. Formerly they were called Shanars. Detailed description of Nadars is given in the next chapter.
21. Mateer, *Land of Charity*, p. 41; Hacker, *A Hundred Years in Travancore (1806-1906)*, p. 14.
22. Hacker, *A Hundred Years in Travancore (1806-1906)*, p. 16; Mateer, *Land of Charity*, pp. 42-6; Samuel Mateer, *Native Life in Travancore* (London: W.H. Allen & Co., 1883), pp. 41-2. The condition of slaves in Travancore is explained more in the section on 'Slavery'.
23. Samuel Mateer, *Land of Charity*, pp. 48-9; Hacker, *A Hundred Years in Travancore (1806-1906)*, pp. 11-12.
24. P.G. Jogdand, 'Caste System in India: Dr. Ambedkar's Perspective', in *Dalit Assertion in Society, Literature and History,* ed. Imtiaz Ahmad and Shashi Bhushan Upadhyay (New Delhi: Orient BlackSwan, 2010), p. 102.
25. The low and slave castes of Travancore are not 'caste' people in the strict sense. They do not belong to any of the four orders of the caste hierarchy. They are actually outside the caste system. They can be better called 'outcastes'.
26. M.N. Srinivas, *India: Social Structure* (Delhi: Hindustan Publishing Corporation, 1986), p. 11.
27. William Logan, *Malabar*, vol. I (Madras: Government Press, 1887; rpt., Trivandrum: Charithram Publications, 1981), pp. 144-5.
28 G.S. Ghurye, *Caste and Race in India*, 9-10; A.H. Day, *Dawn in Travancore: A Brief Account of the Manners and Customs of the People and the Efforts that are being Made for their Improvement* (Kottayam: C.M.S Press, 1860), pp. 8-9; Mateer, *Land of Charity*, pp. 28 and 31.
29. Mateer, *Land of Charity*, pp. 32 and 64.
30. Mateer, *Native Life in Travancore*, p. 332.
31. P. Shungoonny Menon, *A History of Travancore from the Earliest Times*, pp. 380-2.
32. Mateer, *Native Life in Travancore*, pp. 333-4.
33. A. Sreedhara Menon, *Social and Cultural History of Kerala*, p. 68; Mateer, *Native Life in Travancore*, pp. 332-3; Mateer, *Land of Charity*, p. 64.
34. Menon, *Social and Cultural History of Kerala*, p. 67; K.P. Padmanabha

Menon, *History of Kerala,* vol. II (Ernakulam: Cochin Govt. Press, 1929), 273-4.

35. *Dr. Babasaheb Ambedkar: Writings and Speeches*, vol. 5, p. 101; vol. 3, p. 107.
36. J. Bhattacharya, *Hindu Castes and Sects* (1896), p. 259, cited by G.S. Ghurye, *Caste and Race in India*, pp. 12-13.
37. *Selected Proclamations by the Sovereign from 1811-1939 AD* (Trivandrum: Government Press, 1937), Archives Directorate, Trivandrum, pp. 18-20, 64-5, 136-7 & 227.
38. John Wilson, *Indian Castes* vol. II (1877), p. 79, cited by Ghurye, *Caste and Race in India*, p. 13.
39. 'Bare-breasted' implies different things. Nair women were allowed to cover themselves with an upper cloth. For them, being bare-breasted meant removing the upper cloth in front of Brahmins as a mark of respect. Since the women of low caste origin were not allowed to wear the upper cloth in any case and were not legally permitted to wear anything above the waist, they used to cover their torso with a scanty cloth or a jacket after the order of Col. J. Munro, the Resident Dewan, in 1812 that legally allowed the Christian women of low caste origin to wear jackets. The condition of slave women was more pathetic as they could not cover their upper body at all.
40. Mateer, *Native Life in Travancore*, p. 291.
41. C.M. Agur, *Church History of Travancore* (Madras: S.P.S. Press, 1903; New Delhi: Asian Educational Service, 1990), pp. 74 & xlviii; *Selected Proclamations by the Sovereign*, pp. 5-7; Mateer, *Native Life in Travancore*, pp. 292-3.
42. Robin Jeffrey, *The Decline of Nair Dominance*, p. 52; Mateer, *Native Life in Travancore*, pp. 293-4.
43. Mateer, *Land of Charity*, p. 42.
44. Petition of British missionaries to the Raja of Travancore on 19 March 1847, cited by R. N. Yesudas, *A People's Revolt in Travancore*, pp. 161-2; Mateer, *Land of Charity*, pp. 43-4; Mateer, *Native Life in Travancore*, p. 58.
45. The Petition of British Missionaries to the Raja of Travancore on 19 March 1847, cited by R.N. Yesudas, *A People's Revolt in Travancore*, 161; Hacker, *A Hundred Years in Travancore (1806-1906)*, pp. 42-3; C.M. Agur, *Church History of Travancore*, pp. 74-5.
46. Mateer, *Native Life in Travancore*, pp. 305 ff; P. Shungoonny Menon, *A History of Travancore from the Earliest Times*, p. 477; Mateer, *Land of Charity*, p. 44.

47. Mateer, *Land of Charity*, pp. 28, 46.
48. Though William Logan narrates the situation in Malabar, it was more or less applicable to Travancore also.
49. *Cheri* and *chāla* where the outcastes lived were located outside the village where high castes lived.
50. William Logan, *Malabar*, vol. I, p. 85.
51. Mateer, *Native Life in Travancore*, p. 130.
52. P. Shungoonny Menon, *A History of Travancore from the Earliest Times*, 371; *Selected Proclamations by the Sovereign*, pp. 1-2; Mateer, *Native Life in Travancore*, p. 301.
53. Mateer, *Native Life in Travancore*, p. 295.
54. C.M. Agur, *Church History of Travancore*, pp. 568-71.
55. Ralph T.H. Griffith (tr. & cr.), *The Hymns of the Rigveda*, new rev. edn., rpt. (Delhi: Motilal Banarsidass, 1986), pp. 602-3. *Purushasukta* is alleged to be a later addition, and only three classes—Brahma, Kshatra and Visha—are repeatedly mentioned in the *Rigveda*. They represent the poet-priest, the warrior-chief and common people respectively. G.S. Ghurye, *Caste and Race in India*, p. 44.
56. Quoted from *Travancore Census Report*, 1875, p. 191 in Robin Jeffrey, *The Decline of Nair Dominance*, p. 11.
57. Robin Jeffrey, *The Decline of Nair Dominance*, p. 11. All non-Nambudiri Malayali Brahmins were called 'Pottis' (Nagam Aiya, *The Travancore State Manual*, vol. II, p. 286, cited by Koji Kawashima, *Missionaries and a Hindu State: Travancore 1858-1936* (New Delhi: Oxford University Press, 1998), p. 23 (fn).
58. *Madras Census 1891*, p. 299, cited by G.S. Ghurye, *Caste and Race in India*, 14; Mateer, *Land of Charity*, p. 27; Mateer, *Native Life in Travancore*, p. 333.
59. Mateer, *Native Life in Travancore*, 91; R.N. Yesudas, *A People's Revolt in Travancore*, pp. 26-7; Kochu Krishnan Nadar, *Nadar Charitram* (Travancore: S.B. Press, 1956), pp. 9ff.
60. Mateer, 'The Pariah Caste in Travancore', *The Journal of the Royal Asiatic Society of Great Britain and Ireland*, vol. XVI (1884), 184f, cited by J.W. Gladstone, *Protestant Christianity and People's Movements in Kerala*, p. 38.
61. Menon, *A History of Travancore from the Earliest Times*, pp. 252-5 & 341; Agur, *Church History of Travancore*, p. 898; *Minutes of Evidence taken from the Select Committee on the Affairs of the East India Company*, vol. VI (Political), p. 226, cited by R.N. Yesudas, *British Policy*

in *Travancore 1805-59* (Trivandrum: Kerala Historical Society, 1977), p. 17 (fn.).

62. *Minutes of Evidence taken from the Select Committee on the Affairs of the East India Company*, vol. VI (Political), pp. 227 and 275 & Secretary to the Governor General to Chief Secretary to Government, Fort St. George, 12 October 1855, Political Consultations, no. 276, FF. 285-90, cited by R.N. Yesudas, *British Policy in Travancore 1805-1859*, pp. 18-19 & 39-40.
63. Yesudas, *British Policy in Travancore 1805-1859*, pp. 19 & 20.
64. Menon, *A History of Travancore from the Earliest Times*, p. 37.
65. Louise Ouwerkerk, *No Elephants for the Maharaja*, pp. 33-4.
66. Menon, *A History of Travancore from the Earliest Times*, pp. 39-40.
67. Mateer, *Land of Charity*, pp. 15-16.
68. Ibid., p. 18.
69. Menon, *A History of Travancore from the Earliest Times*, pp. 278 and 284-6; G. Buhler (tr.), *Sacred Books of the East Edited by F. Max Muller*, vol. 25, *The Laws of Manu* (Delhi: Motilal Banarsidass, 1988), pp. 216ff.
70. Elamkulam Kunjan Pillai, *Studies in Kerala History* (Kottayam: 1970), pp. 116 and 265, cited by J.W. Gladstone, *Protestant Christianity and People's Movements in Kerala*, pp. 21-2.
71. Koji Kawashima, *Missionaries and a Hindu State: Travancore 1858-1936*, p. 17.
72. Letter from Acting Dewan to the Resident, 8 March 1858, Bundle no. 29, Cover File no. 2115 of 1858, *Shanar Disturbances in South Travancore*, Archives Directorate, Trivandrum; Samuel Mateer, *Land of Charity*, p. 24.
73. John Abbs, *Twenty-Two Years' Missionary Experience in Travancore* (London: John Snow & Co, 1870), pp. 30-1.
74. Letter from Rev. F. Baylis to the Resident, 1 January 1859, Bundle no. 29, Cover File No. 2115 of 1858, *Shanar Disturbances in South Travancore*, Archives Directorate, Trivandrum.
75. Mateer, *Land of Charity*, pp. 24 and 296-7.
76. Letter from Rev. E. Lewis to the Resident, 21 January 1859, Bundle no. 29, Cover File no. 2115 of 1858, *Shanar Disturbances in South Travancore*, Archives Directorate, Trivandrum.
77. Mateer, *Land of Charity*, p. 297.
78. C.M. Agur, *Church History of Travancore*, p. 18; Mateer, *Native Life in Travancore*, p. 345.

79. Mateer, *Native Life in Travancore*, pp. 346-51.
80. Mateer, *The Land of Charity*, pp. 31-2.
81. Menon, *A History of Travancore from the Earliest Times*, p. 366.
82. Abbs, *Twenty-Two Years' Missionary Experience in Travancore*, p. 34.
83. Menon, *A History of Travancore from the Earliest Times*, pp. 372-3. No woman was appointed as judge.
84. Mateer, *Native Life in Travancore*, pp. 341-2.
85. A. Sreedhara Menon, *A Survey of Kerala History,* rev. edn. (Madras: S. Viswnathan 1996, rpt. 1998), p. 391; Mateer, *Native Life in Travancore*, pp. 290-1; Menon, *A History of Travancore from the Earliest Times*, pp. 372-4 & 441.
86. Menon, *A History of Travancore from the Earliest Times*, p. 441; K.P. Padmanabha Menon, *History of Kerala*, vol. II (Ernakulam: Cochin Govt. Press, 1929; New Delhi: Asian Educational Services, 1983), pp. 266-7; A. Sreedhara Menon, *Social and Cultural History of Kerala*, p. 69.
87. Elamkulam P. N. Kunjan Pillai, *Studies in Kerala History*, pp. 324-5.
88. A. Sreedhara Menon, *Social and Cultural History of Kerala*, p. 76.
89. Pillai, *Studies in Kerala History*, p. 313; M.N. Srinivas, *India: Social Structure* (Delhi: Hindustan Publishing Corporation, 1986), p. 15.
90. Nagam Aiya, *Travancore State Manual*, vol. III, pp. 311-14, cited by Robin Jeffrey, *The Decline of Nair Dominance*, p. 25.
91. Gladstone, *Protestant Christianity and People's Movements in Kerala*, 45.
92. *Janmi* means 'Landlord'.
93. A. Sreedhara Menon, *Social and Cultural History of Kerala*, pp. 77-8.
94. 'Travancore and Its Land Tenure', *Calcutta Review,* vol. cxii (January, 1901): pp. 130-1, cited by Robin Jeffrey, *The Decline of Nair Dominance*, p. 25.
95. Jeffrey, *The Decline of Nair Dominance*, p. 25.
96. Ibid., pp. 26-8.
97. Kawashima, *Missionaries and a Hindu State: Travancore 1858-1936*, pp. 20-3 & 52.
98. Mateer, *Land of Charity*, pp. 167-8.
99. Ibid., 169-70.
100. Menon, *A History of Travancore from the Earliest Times*, p. 63.
101. Mateer, *Native Life in Travancore*, pp. 116-17.
102. Menon, *A History of Travancore from the Earliest Times*, p. 72.
103. Mateer, *Land of Charity*, pp. 176-81.
104. Ibid., pp. 159-60.

105. Kawashima, *Missionaries and a Hindu State: Travancore 1858-1936*, pp. 23-4 & 52; Mateer, *Land of Charity*, pp. 181-2.
106. Menon, *A History of Travancore from the Earliest Times*, pp. 430-5.
107. Duncan B. Forrester, *Caste and Christianity* (London and Dublin: Curzon Press Ltd & NJ: Humanities Press Inc, 1979), p. 97; L.W. Brown, *The Indian Christians of St. Thomas* (Cambridge, 1956), p. 173 & C.J. Fuller, 'Kerala Christians and the Caste System', *Man* II (N.S), pp. 53-70 at 64-64, cited by Duncan B. Forrester, *Caste and Christianity*, p. 99; F.E. Keay (1938), *A History of the Syrian Church in India* (Madras: SPCK, 1951), pp. 22-4; Shalva Weil, 'Symmetry between Christian and Jews in India: the Cnanite Christians and the Cochin Jews of Kerala', *Contributions to Indian Sociology,* vol. 16, no. 2 (1982), pp. 175-96 at 185; Samuel Mateer, *Native Life in Travancore*, pp. 158-68, 296; James Massey, *Dalits in India* (New Delhi: Manohar, 1995), p. 46.
108. Agur, *Church History of Travancore*, pp. 18, 53, 60 & li-lii; Susan Bayly, *Saints, Goddesses and Kings: Muslims and Christians in South Indian Society, 1700-1900* (Cambridge, 1989), p. 293, cited by V.V. Thomas, *Dalit Pentecostalism* (Bangalore: ATC, 2008), p. 111; Mateer, *Native Life in Travancore*, p. 346.
109. Mateer, *Land of Charity*, p. 231.
110. Robin Jeffrey, *The Decline of Nair Dominance*, p. 18; John Abbs, *Twenty-Two Years' Missionary Experience in Travancore*, pp. 35-9; Samuel Mateer, *Land of Charity*, pp. 227-8 & Mateer, *Native Life in Travancore*, pp. 146-57.
111. V. Nagam Aiya, *The Travancore State Manual*, vol. II (Trivandrum: Government Press, 1906), p. 224.
112. John A. Jacob, *A History of the London Missionary Society in South Travancore 1806-1959* (Nagarcoil: The Diocesan Press, 1990), pp. 6f.
113. I.H. Hacker, *A Hundred Years in Travancore (1806-1906)*, pp. 16-17.
114. Agur, *Church History of Travancore*, pp. 3-4 & 7.
115. Menon, *A History of Travancore from the Earliest Times*, p. 396.
116. Agur, *Church History of Travancore*, pp. 15-17.
117. Samuel Mateer, *Native Life in Travancore*, pp. 393-5.
118. Agur, *Church History of Travancore*, pp. 42-4.
119. Ibid., p. 47.
120. Ibid., pp. 52-6.
121. Ibid., pp. 58-9.
122. Ibid., p. 57.
123. Hacker, *A Hundred Years in Travancore (1806-1906)*, p. 83.

124. Mateer, *Native Life in Travancore*, pp. 208-9.
125. Mateer, *Land of Charity*, p. 62.
126. Menon, *A History of Travancore from the Earliest Times*, pp. 76-8.
127. Ibid., pp. 380-2.
128. K.P. Padmanabha Menon, *History of Kerala*, vol. III (Ernakulam: Cochin Govt. Press, 1937; New Delhi: Asian Educational Services, 2001), pp. 65-7.
129. Leela Dube, 'Caste and Women', in *Caste: Its Twentieth Century Avatar*, ed. M.N. Srinivas (New Delhi: Penguin Books, 1996), p. 14; Mateer, *Native Life in Travancore*, p. 209.
130. Child marriage was practiced among the Christians; there was a common notion that if there is a girl under or about the age of 14, she is eligible for marriage. Among Jacobites, boys were married at age of 10 or 12 and the girls between 6 and 7. In child marriages, the girl had to live with the groom and had to work hard in the house. One survey shows that in the year 1891 in South Travancore there were child wives: 26 at the age between 0 and 4, 1129 at 5-9, and 559 at 10-14. (A.H. Day, *Dawn in Travancore* (Kottayam: C.M.S Press, 1860), p. 58.)
131. Mateer, *Native Life in Travancore*, pp. 209-11.
132. Mateer, *Land of Charity*, p. 65; Mateer, *Native Life in Travancore*, p. 204.
133. William Logan, *Malabar*, vol. I, pp. 144-5.
134. Robin Jeffrey, *The Decline of Nair Dominance*, p. 11; *Travancore Census Report 1875*, p. 228, cited by Robin Jeffrey, *The Decline of Nair Dominance*, p. 53.
135. Agur, *Church History of Travancore*, xlvii, 1, liii & lvii; *Selected Proclamations by the Sovereign*, pp. 301-2, 319-20; Menon, *A Survey of Kerala History*, p. 393.
136. Menon, *Social and Cultural History of Kerala*, pp. 67 and 95.
137. Leela Dube, 'Caste and Women', p. 10.
138. *Selected Proclamations by the Sovereign*, pp. 82-3; Mateer, *Land of Charity*, p. 60; Mateer, *Native Life in Travancore*, pp. 206 & 340-1.
139. Mateer, *Native Life in Travancore*, pp. 201-7.
140. Menon, *A History of Travancore from the Earliest Times*, p. 441.
141. Mateer, *Native Life in Travancore*, pp. 208-9.
142. Hacker, *A Hundred Years in Travancore (1806-1906)*, pp. 84-7 & Joy Gnanadason, *A Forgotten History* (Madras: GLTC, 1994), pp. 69-70.

CHAPTER 2

The Upper Cloth Revolt: A Subaltern Movement

In Chapter 1, the historical background of Travancore in the nineteenth century was analyzed from a subaltern perspective. In this chapter, the movement is described in detail. No community is without history. The histories of some communities are documented in written form while others are in oral form. The history tells us what the past of a particular community was. If we study the history of any people group who were oppressed in the past we come across a few historical events which contain stories of their pain and assertion. Such historical events have defined the future course of certain communities. They have even shaped the faith of respective peoples, giving them dignity, identity and subjecthood. In the context of a dehumanizing social setup, some painful historical events have encouraged and helped people to search for a new space in society; be it social, religious, cultural, economic or political. The Upper Cloth Revolt in South Travancore was a decisive historical movement in the life of the Nadars, the subalterns in Travancore. It was a movement particularly fought for the cause of its women. It contains liberative experiences and moments of resistance against the forces of hegemony in society.

Subaltern: Defined and Located

The idea of subaltern has its roots in the British military system. 'Subaltern', a military term, basically stands for a junior officer below the rank of Captain in the British Army. Its literal meaning is 'subordinate'. In adjective form, it means 'of lower status'.[1] It was Antonio Gramsci, an Italian Marxist leader, who first popularized the expression 'subaltern' in the area of ideological discourses. As an academic and ideological term it appeared first in his prison notes when he was imprisoned between 1929 and 1935. Antonio Gramsci was born in 1891 in the small town of Ales in Sardinia. He was the General Secretary of the Communist Party in Italy. He was put behind the bars by Benito Mussolini in 1929. While in jail, he wrote 2,848 pages of notes on various subjects such as Italian history, education, politics, state, civil society, the philosophy of praxis, etc. He used the expression 'subaltern' in section two of his notes on 'Italian History' and 'The Philosophy of Praxis'. Selected portions of the prison notes of Antonio Gramsci in Italian language were translated and published in different languages. *Selections from the Prison Notebooks of Antonio Gramsci* is the edited version of his prison notes in English.[2]

Since the publication of the prison notes of Antonio Gramsci, the expression 'subaltern' has been used as a tool/concept in academic discourses. It was Ranajit Guha and a group of thinkers who first initiated an extensive study on subalterns in Indian academia. Within the framework of their definition of the expression 'subaltern', they have published a number of volumes which deal with South Asian History and Society under the research scheme of *Subaltern Studies*[3] from a subaltern perspective.[4] The 'subaltern' expression is conspicuous by its presence in the theological discourses in India also. James Massey, Sathianathan Clarke, V.V. Thomas, etc.[5] have employed it in their respective areas of study and reflection. Since Antonio Gramsci, the expression 'subaltern' has been defined and understood, and widened its scope and space by many scholars in different contexts.

Antonio Gramsci's Understanding of 'Subaltern'

Selections from the Prison Notebooks of Antonio Gramsci gives the basic understanding of the expression 'subaltern' by Antonio Gramsci. 'Subaltern' is a construct in the interrelated socio-economic-political context of Europe in the first part of twentieth century. Before locating the subalterns in respective contexts, we need to be aware of the limitations or complications involved in the prison notes of

Gramsci. It is very much clear in the words of the editors of *Selections from the Prison Notebooks of Antonio Gramsci*, 'The problem of making a selection from Gramsci's *Prison Notebooks* is complicated by two factors: the fragmentary character of the writings and the uncertain status of the Notebooks in Gramsci's intentions.'[6] Though the prison notes have its own inadequacies to explain the expression 'subaltern' unambiguously, it is not much difficult to understand to whom he applied it.

Antonio Gramsci understood subaltern in relation with the term 'hegemonic'. For him, '"hegemonic" is . . . to designate an historical phase in which a given group moves beyond a position of corporate existence and defence of its economic position and aspires to a position of leadership in the political and social arena.'[7] Gramsci called non-hegemonic groups as 'subordinate,' 'subaltern' or sometimes 'instrumental' though it is difficult to distinguish any systematic difference between subaltern and subordinate in his discourse.[8] It can be interpreted that non-hegemonic groups are those who are not only dominated by other group/s but also unable to create space in the socio-political arena of life. They are the ones who cannot move beyond their present existence, be it social, political, economic or religious, and advance in life. It means the subalterns are non-hegemonic people in a particular social context. They may be politically powerless, socially voiceless and disempowered and economically exploited because of the supremacy of hegemonic forces/groups in society. In Gramsci's context, working class/proletariat was the subalterns. Since the subalterns are contextual in nature, the contextual factors help to identify and name who are subalterns.

Subaltern Studies in India

The Subaltern Studies Group, who articulated on the expression 'subaltern' in Indian academic circles, has taken the meaning 'of inferior rank' given in the Concise Oxford Dictionary to categorize who are subalterns. Accordingly, they framed the subaltern groups in Indian society: those who are of inferior status. For them, the expression, 'subaltern' stands for the general attribute of subordination in South Asian society. It means subalternity can be in terms of class, caste, age, gender, office or in any other way. Any category/group which has the status 'of inferior rank' in a particular location or field can be considered as subaltern. They also argue that subordination can be understood only in a binary relationship: subordination and dominance, for 'subaltern groups are always subject to the activity of ruling groups, even when they rebel and rise up'.[9]

In their attempt to study South Asian history and society from the subaltern perspective, Subaltern Study Group clarifies the usage of the expression 'subaltern' and its binary categories. For them, the term 'elite' refers to the dominant groups which consist of both foreign and indigenous. All non-Indians, mainly the British officials, foreign industrialists, merchants, financiers, planters, landlords and missionaries belong to the category of foreign elite. The dominant indigenous groups are operating at two levels: all-India and regional and local. The biggest feudal magnates and native bureaucrats constitute the class of dominant indigenous groups at the national level. The members of the dominant class in all-India level and the groups who are inferior to the dominant all-India groups in the social hierarchy belong to the category of elites in the regional and local level. The last category of the elite is heterogeneous in its existence due to the nature of regional and social developments. While dominant in one region the same group/class may be the dominated in another location.

The Subaltern Study Group also explains groups who may come in the category of subaltern class: the lowest strata of the rural gentry, impoverished landlords, rich peasants, and upper-middle peasants. These groups are identified not only as 'subaltern' but also as 'people'. Moreover, they also caution that though the aforementioned groups are 'naturally' subalterns some of these classes may act for the elites or as the elites in some local or regional settings.[10]

Identifying the subalterns within the framework of the meaning 'of inferior rank/status' does not bring out the real subaltern if it contradicts the social reality of Indian society. Although the Subaltern Study Group tried to understand the subaltern in terms of class, caste, age, gender, and office, they kept the door of the category open by giving option for interpreting 'of inferior rank' 'in any other way'. Those who experience 'inferior status' in terms of social standing, economic condition, religious identity and status, political power, administrative hierarchy, etc., can be named as subalterns. This approach brings more groups under the umbrella of subaltern category without considering the social context of India, which is characterized by caste system. Throughout the centuries, socially poor have been economically, politically, religiously non-hegemonic groups. The synonymous use of 'people' and 'subaltern' gives more ambiguity than clarity in identifying the real subaltern groups. 'People' can be referred to any community who may or may not be poor or non-hegemonic in status and power. The subaltern categorization by Subaltern Study Group is more or less economic than social cataloguing. In fact, they homogenized the subaltern groups though they are heterogeneous by caste. In their profiling, a group of people can be defined as subalterns because they are of inferior status/category in a particular region/field even though they belong to different castes. This leads to define and identify specific groups who qualify to be called as subalterns in the Indian social setting.

Dalits as Subalterns

Sathianathan Clarke in his book *Dalits and Christianity: Subaltern Religion and Liberation Theology in India* attempts to situate Dalits in the subaltern space. He gives a critique of the attempt of the homogenization of subalterns by putting together all categories of differentiation in terms of caste, class, age, gender, offices and any other way. He takes a departure; from the generalization of the subaltern class to the identification of subalternity in a particular community. He argues that many groups may share equal disabilities at one level in the society. Nevertheless all may not face the same degree of handicap and oppression in all facets of societal life. Any attempt to put different groups with different struggles and aspirations under one category may lead to unjustifiable generalization. Therefore, he tried to concentrate on the caste dimension. This is not to deny any other class or group as subaltern, but the ideology of caste plays a big role in determining the contextual manifestation of subalternity in the caste-ridden Indian context. Since caste has religious sanction, its role cannot be overlooked in defining subalternity.[11] Clarke quotes Partha Chatterjee: 'No matter how we choose to characterize it, subaltern consciousness in the specific cultural context of India cannot but contain caste as a central element in its constitution.'[12] As caste is the determining factor, for Clarke it is Dalits who are the subalterns. Indeed they are subalterns in all senses. He says, 'The subaltern, thus, are the communities (Dalits) that are cumulatively and comprehensively disadvantaged and subordinated through the caste system, which operates to benefit the dominant groups.'[13] He also attempted to examine in his work how Dalits, particularly Dalit Christians, resist the inequalities and discriminations caused by caste system through their religiosity, which helps them express their collective experience.[14] The point to be upheld in line with the arguments of Sathianathan Clarke is that Dalits are subalterns because they have been considered and treated as inferior people in a caste-ridden society. They have been disadvantaged, subordinated by the ruling-class and caste-people for centuries. If caste is the criterion for being a subaltern group, one cannot avoid the possibility of including other marginalized communities in the subaltern category.

Dalit-Bahujan as Indian Subalterns

For his part, James Massey proposes that Dalit-Bahujans[15] are subalterns. Though he accepts the possibility of using the expression, 'subaltern' in constructing new theoretical and theological formulations, he does not admit it without caution, 'subaltern' being a European construct. Therefore, he cautions that since each context is different in its nature and function, it is important that one should know whether this expression can be applied in our context. According to Massey, Gramsci used this expression in a very general sense to make a distinction between ruling classes and non-ruling classes.[16] For Gramsci subalterns are the politically dominated/powerful group, the ruling class of his time. Hence, the expression 'subaltern' cannot be used without taking the contextual realties into consideration.

James Massey is also critical of the Subaltern Study Group led by Ranajit Guha. For him, their views which categorize and interpret the subaltern are very much generalized. Their understanding of the subaltern include all categories of people, both 'caste people' and 'non-caste people' as they are based on 'class, caste, age, gender, and office'. Therefore, the views of Ranajit Guha and his colleagues are more suitable and applicable to the European context. However, the Indian context is rooted and shaped in caste structures. No attempt of generalization of subalterns without applying caste will work well. The caste factor makes the Indian context different.[17] Massey tends to agree with Sathianathan Clarke on the caste dimension of subalternity, 'This is not to deny that collectives held together by commonalities of age, gender, class and office do share in the state of subalternity. The institution and ideology of caste engenders contextual manifestation of subalternity, which is intrinsically tied up to religion in India.'[18]

In his attempt to understand 'subaltern' in terms of caste, James Massey goes beyond Clarke and includes more communities in the frame of subalternity. He affirms that caste gives birth to subalternity. Caste is the main factor in the formation of subaltern consciousness. More than 80 per cent of the Indian population has a history of discriminations and disabilities inflicted by caste.[19] The report of the Mandal Commission substantiates that the majority of the population falls in the category of backward communities.[20] There is no sign of any reducing influence even today.

The expression 'Dalit' has been understood as subaltern, and 'Bahujan' (Other Backward Classes, Religious Minorities of lower caste origin) can be added. Subalterns may be called Dalit-Bahujan. For Massey Dalit-Bahujan (Dalits-Tribals-OBCs-Religious Minorities of OBC/Dalit origin) constitute the majority of the population. They have been historically victimized by the caste system.[21]

The caste factor of subalternity is understood not only in social aspect but also in economic dimension. It is observed that 'Caste must replace class as the fundamental explanatory framework. . . . "Caste" is the form in which "classes" appear in Indian society.'[22] Gail Omvedt argues that caste has played a historical role in the social relations of production in Indian society. According to her, 'Caste is "a material reality with a material base", it is "not only form but also concrete material content", and it has 'historically shaped the very basis of Indian economy and society and continues to have crucial economic implications today'.[23] It implies that subalternity (being in inferior rank/position/condition/status) in any form (social, political, religious, economic) has direct or indirect influence of caste in Indian context. One's caste decides where s/he falls: in subalternity or outside the frame of subalternity.

The subalternity of subaltern women is not decided by caste alone. Caste, patriarchy, and economic structure, which perpetuate dependence, operate as interrelated mechanisms and crush a subaltern woman's life.[24] Therefore, their experience is different from high caste women and subaltern men. In explaining the relationship between caste and gender, Uma Chakravarti views that 'The patriarchy/ies in India is/are shaped by caste: gendering the caste system.'[25] She further argues that women's subordination to caste and gender oppression has also been continued through the support of women. Though high caste women also face patriarchal oppression, they are privileged by their caste identity and its advantages. They have access to resources and power centres through their men. The subaltern women are deprived of such advantages. The upper caste women are contented with their caste privileges compared to the subaltern women who are victims of caste in society. They consider subaltern women as inferior to them because of their caste identity. They support their men than women in the context of subaltern victimization. It is caste which becomes successful in creating divisions among women.[26] Sharmila Rege observes that even violence against women has caste distinctions. 'While upper caste women are subjected to controls and violence within the family, it is the absence of such controls that makes lower caste women vulnerable to rape, sexual harassment and the threat of public violence.'[27] However, the subaltern women are subalterns within a subaltern community. They are controlled and silenced by men of their community. The caste, gender and economic dependency make subaltern women subservient not only to their own men but also to the upper caste men and their societal restrictions. This experience even shapes their perspective different from the upper caste women.

Indian society is basically characterized by caste. People are primarily categorized on the basis of caste. It is caste which decides the status of a community/person in society. Therefore, Antonio Gramsci's class-based definition of subaltern cannot be employed to identify Indian subalterns. The caste identity surpasses all other identities including class identity in the Indian context. The subaltern study group has also not defined the subalterns in terms of caste alone. They defined subaltern mostly in relation to tribal/adivasis and anti-colonial struggles. For them, caste is one of the decisive factors for naming subalterns. Since caste is the primary norm to define the position of a community, inferior or superior, the historical victims of caste are the real subalterns in India. Though they are heterogeneous they can be collectively named as 'Dalit-Bahujan', which consists of the Dalits, the Other Backward Classes (OBC), the Tribals and the Religious Minorities of OBC/Dalit origin. This category includes both men and women as historical victims of caste. Their historical victimhood of caste still continues in different forms. The painful experiences of caste by the subalterns shape their outlook and contribute to the emergence of their resistance against the forces of subjugation. At the same time, the subaltern experiences of Dalit-Bahujan women inform them of how caste rules and gender prejudices equally contribute to their subalternity.

The Nadars

Stories of Origin and Settlement of Nadars

Nadar is one of the prominent castes in Tamil Nadu and in Thiruvananthapuram District of Kerala. Earlier they were known as 'Shanan' or 'Shanar', which is believed to have derived from the Tamil word, 'Sanrar' or 'Sanror' which means the 'learned' or the 'noble'. 'Nadar' is derived from the Tamil word 'Nadan' which means 'ruler of a country or village' or 'one who lives in the country'. They were also called 'Gramini'.[28]

One myth says that Nadars are the children of God Indra.[29] According to another version of this myth, 'the ancestors of the Nadar were the sons of seven maids, *kannis,* created by the vision of God Narayana. The God brought up seven boys on the milk of the cow of Indra and then left them under the protection of Bhadrakali.'[30]

The Cauvery region of the Chola kingdom, Madurai and South Travancore are considered as the possible places of the origin of Nadar caste.[31] Robert Caldwell argues that the Nadars might have emigrated from Jaffna, the northern coast of Sri Lanka. He informs that he could find there a community having the name 'Shandror' from which 'Shanar', previous caste title of the Nadars, might have been derived. One group called Nadans (a group within Shandror) entered Tirunelveli (previously known as Tinnevelly) in the present Tamil Nadu, by way of Ramnad, during the period of the Pandyas. They brought with them the seeds of palmyra. After a period of time, another group called Shanars, who were considered as a lower division of the Shandror caste, came to the south of Travancore state. They were invited by Nadans (later known as Nadars) who migrated earlier, to serve as climbers of palmyra trees in Tirunelveli. Gradually, there was a blending of Shanars and Nadans/Nadars in the region.[32]

V. Nagam Aiya considers Shanars as one of the Hindu castes having a Dravidian lineage. A few hints in the Tamil literature and their traditions show that the Shanars are a warlike group who migrated to south from north India. Earlier, they might have lived in the areas between the Krishna and the Godavari rivers. They even might have settled down as rulers.[33] Their peculiar customs and the expressions such as *Nadar* and *Nadalvar* within the Shanar race, point to the fact that formerly they were a ruling race. They were overthrown later by the Dravidians.[34] It is also argued that the Nadars share ancestral roots with Jain Saint Mahavira, King Chanta Asoka and dynasties like Chahamanaas, Rashtrakutas and Mauryas and communities like Rajputs.[35]

In the caste hierarchy, some Nadars identify themselves as Shudras, but others claim Kshatriya status. It is claimed that they are the descendants of the Pandya kings. However, some claim Kshatriya status by arguing that their ancestors were once hereditary tax collectors, and exercised civil authority under the Pandyas and the Nayaks. They functioned as landlords or petty rulers.[36] The inferior position of later Nadars is attributed to their association with toddy tapping. Many of them were involved in tapping toddy from palmyra trees. Therefore, they were considered as 'a half polluting caste'.[37] In the beginning of nineteenth century, according to Robert L. Hardgrave, 'The Nadars occupied a socio-limbo somewhere between the Shudras and the outcaste untouchables.'[38] For Robert Caldwell, 'They may in general be described as belonging to the highest division of the lower classes, or the lowest of the middle classes; poor, but not paupers; rude and unlettered, but many degrees removed from a savage state.'[39] Raja Rama Rao describes the in-between position of Nadars in this way, 'They are inferior to Shudras and superior to Parayas.'[40]

The Nadars, originally consisted of five groups in Tinnevelly. They are *Karukku-pattayar* (believed to be superior), *Kalla*, also called *Pulukka Sanan* (servants of the other four groups mainly Karukku-pattayar and also involved in climbing), *Nattati* (settled at the village near Sawyerpuram in Tinnevelly district, traditionally engaged in cultivation, trade and money lending), *Kodikkal* (standard bearers of the fighting men. They were betel cultivators and climbers also) and *Mel-nattar* (those who lived in the western part of Tinnevelly and in Travancore). Also there was another group called Nadar barbers. The present Nadars have a very vague knowledge of these sub-castes, and there is no agreement on the number and names. These divisions were occupational or territorial. Apart from toddy-tapping, many Nadars involved in other occupational activities such as agriculture, trade, etc.[41]

The Nadars of Travancore

It is opined that the Nadars migrated to the southern part of Travancore from Tinnevelly (Tirunelveli) District in the present Tamil Nadu. It is also likely that they came to Travancore through Tirunelveli from their earlier settlement/s. In Travancore they identified with the title 'Nadar'. But others called them 'Shanar'. The traditions of some Nadar families claim that their ancestors had been called by the ancient kings of Travancore. Moreover, the numerical strength of Nadars in southern Travancore points to the inference that they were supported by the ancient kings. The term 'Nadar' was used as caste name and title. The ancient kings of Travancore had granted titles such as *Tiruppapur Nadar, Udaya Martanda Nadar, Nagamani Martanda Nadar*, to some families of Shanars.[42] 'In appearance they are a dark-skinned race with low foreheads, sunken eyes and prominent cheek bones. There is nothing peculiar about the dress or ornament of Shanar men or women to distinguish them from the other Hindu castes of the same social position except that they are back-tufted.'[43] They were courageous and excellent warriors. They were also enlisted in the army of King Marthanda Varma.[44]

Polygamy, polyandry and widow marriage were not permitted in the community. Even a woman divorced for adultery was not allowed to remarry. Nadars stayed away from liquor and beef. They followed the *makkathayam* system of succession. Among the Nadars there were Saivites and Vaishnavites. They also worshipped *Pallliyar* (Ganapati) and *Subrahmanya. Bhadra Kali* was their chief deity. A so-called demon worship with animal sacrifice existed among them. The Nadars used to bury the dead, but in some localities the dead were burned. Honoured individuals were buried in a seated posture, facing east. They had their own family burial grounds. They had hereditary families of priests known as *Aiyar* or *Aiyar Pandaram.*

Apart from their traditional occupation of cultivating and climbing the palmyra tree and of manufacturing jaggery out of palmyra sap, many Nadars were involved in agriculture and trade. Though Tamil was their mother tongue, they used to speak Malayalam also. The literacy rate was low. With the arrival of Christian missionaries they began to get educated and consequently became aware of their social conditions. Many Christian converts were placed in government jobs. The number of Hindus among Nadars decreased due to the large-scale conversions to Christianity.[45] Nadars were on the whole palmyra climbers and landless agricultural workers in Travancore.[46]

The Nadars as an Oppressed Community

Whatever may be their claim of origin and position in the caste hierarchy, the Nadars of nineteenth century in Travancore had to face a lot of socio-economic-religious restrictions. They were categorized as people of low caste origin in the social hierarchy, not permitted to go near the so-called high caste people. They had to keep a distance of 36 feet from a Brahmin and 12 feet from a Nair. The violators of the caste rules were punished, and even killed. It is doubtful whether they could ever have attempted to break the distance of pollution in the strict caste society.[47] They lived in a society where the distance of pollution was one of the yardsticks of social status. They were deprived of the liberty of free-movement in the localities where the upper castes lived.

The Nadars had no entry into temples managed by the high castes, and were restricted to remain outside those temples. Though they had their own temples they were not allowed to worship gods like Siva, Brahma, and Vishnu whom the higher castes worshipped. The Nadars worshipped Veerabadran, Sudalai Madan, Irulan, Mutharamman, and Bhadrakali whom the low castes venerated. They could offer only toddy and arrack to their gods, but not ghee or milk.[48] The division of gods in terms of caste leads to the question – whether caste divided the existing gods or when new gods were introduced the lower castes were given the 'old' gods? Whatever may be the answer, the Nadars had no freedom to worship any deity whom they wished to worship because they were subalterns.

The Nadars had to pay the price of their being called lower caste in many ways. Their income was extracted in the form of fines, taxes and gifts. *Prāyaśchitam* (penitence), one kind of fine, was most cruel on the Nadars. Officers could fix any amount as a fine for any violation. Often it was collected without a reason. The Nadars had to pay a tax on inherited ancestral property. They had to pay poll tax, even for the dead. They were taxed on their job, house, land, trees, job equipment (ladder and belt used to climb the trees), *tali* (marriage symbol of women), some kind of dress, ornaments, conducting marriage, etc. The tax collectors used to collect more than what was prescribed and remitted less amount to the Government. Tax defaulters were harshly punished; their ears were pierced with red hot iron. Sometimes, a weighty stone would be loaded on their back and they were made to stand in the hot sun. The Nadars had to provide *ūḻiaṁ* (service without payment) and *viruti* (supplying things free of cost) services to the government. They also had to give gifts to the royal families, officers, and landlords (*janmi*) during festivals. They were forbidden to carry umbrellas or wear *chappals*. They were not allowed to live in tiled houses or to own cows. Decoration of marriage pandals was not permitted.[49] In fact, the life of Nadars was one of constant struggle, painful and humiliating. They had been deprived of basic human rights in every sense. Their life was unjustly taxed and exploited. They had to break their bodies for the luxury of the high castes. As subalterns they had no other option but to bear the pain of subjugation for the survival. But they never submitted to oppression without resistance. The Upper Cloth Revolt was one of the manifestations of their resistance.

Nadar Women

The life of Nadar women was more agonizing than their men in Travancore society. As women of low caste origin, they endured all common disabilities imposed upon them by the high caste. At the same time, they also had to undergo several restrictions and prohibitions of the nexus of caste and patriarchy. They were restricted within and outside the family/caste. Nadar women were not allowed to wear gold ornaments or to dress like Nair women. Coloured clothes were prohibited. They were forbidden to use the upper cloth. The Nadar women had to carry water pots on their head keeping both hands on the pots. Women tax defaulters had to face public molestation and sexual harassment.[50] Caste restriction did not allow them to get education also.[51] The life of Nadar women was crushed by the restrictions of caste and patriarchy. They were subjected to male domination inside and outside the community. Though Nadar men supported and participated in the struggles of Nadar women, it cannot be assumed that Nadar women had equal status with their men in the community. Nadar women had to bear the burden of domestic work, caste restrictions and patriarchal rules. They were the subalterns among the Nadars. However, their long struggle, pain and humiliation led them to break the caste-cum-man rules by wearing the upper cloth, the privilege of high caste women. It proves that subaltern women can also resist the forces of subjugation and break the restrictions.

Situating the Nadars in Subaltern Location

Nadars were subordinated in all aspects of life: social restriction on mobility, no religious freedom, no economic advancement. They were deprived of a dignified life and had to be subservient to the ruling upper caste people. They were subalterns not only because of their subordinated condition but also because of their defiant nature. While being submissive they resisted the caste restrictions. As J.W. Gladstone commented, 'They were subalterns because they had no temple, no leader, no land, no home, and were in inferior status and oppressive condition.'[52] The Nadar women were subalterns within a subaltern community because of their inferior status in terms of caste and gender.

At present, Nadars have been classified as Other Backward Class (OBC) by Government of India, especially in the states such as Kerala, Tamil Nadu, Karnataka, Maharashtra and the Union Territory of Puducherry. The OBC[53] are basically the historical victims of caste. The Nadars, categorized as OBC, are subalterns too. Though the Nadars have come out of the old restrictions imposed by the caste system, they are attributed the so-called 'inferior status' by caste people and their structures.

The Nadars Today: Caste, Patriarchy and Customs

The Nadar community had a long journey of struggle and hard work throughout the centuries. Their upward mobility has helped them achieve position and power in contemporary Tamil Nadu.[54] There are Christians of various denominations and Hindus in the community. They maintain their ethnic identity, observing some of their community customs and practices. Many are agriculturists, educationists, and business people. They have created their space in socio-economic-political-religious realms of the society. What they are today is because of their hard work and determination. The past memories give them motivation and confidence to explore new ventures in life. The Upper Cloth Revolt is an important part of their history, especially of the Nadars of former Travancore.

The Nadars fought against dehumanizing caste practices. The caste system placed them in low status and deprived them of their dignity and freedom. Today, however, the community, which had resisted the tyranny of upper castes, perpetuates caste hierarchy. They consider themselves superior to certain communities. Irrespective of religion, the Nadars continue to keep their caste identity. They discourage inter-caste marriage, which B.R. Ambedkar considered as the real remedy for annihilating caste,[55] but promote inter-religious marriage between community members. Christian Nadars prefer to take membership in the Church/denomination where they are the majority or where the pastor belongs to their own community. There are even caste organizations among the Nadars: Nadar Mahajana Sangam, Kerala Nadar Mahajana Sangam, Vaikunda Swami Dharma Pracharanasabha, the All India Nadar Association, etc. Though they claim that they stand for the welfare of Nadars, in essence they aim for the caste consolidation of Nadars. In the Upper Cloth Revolt, they revolted against caste, but caste is being perpetuated among them. As long as they maintain a rigid caste identity and solidarity, the real intention of Nadars in Upper Cloth Revolt is questioned. It can even be suggested that in the Upper Cloth Revolt, they were trying to climb up the caste hierarchy.

It is true that Nadar men supported and were actively involved in the struggles of their women against the caste-based patriarchal restriction on the dress code of lower caste women. They had suffered physically and mentally. Many Nadar men were arrested and jailed during the Upper Cloth Revolt. They fought for the right of their women but this does not mean that Nadar women have equal status with their men in the community today. Nadar women do not have the freedom that their men enjoy in the family and community circles. Men are the decision makers. Though many Nadar women have received higher education and achieved positions in government and in society, their mobility and freedom are restricted by patriarchal norms within the community. They are expected to be submissive and obedient to men in the family. With a few exceptions, a girl's opinion is not sought for fixing her marriage. Male members of the family/community decide everything related to the marriage of a girl. In fact, the space, freedom, voice, opinion, etc., of Nadar women is controlled by her brother, father, husband, father-in-law, and brothers-in-law. She is watched in the family. Her dress code is also defined by her men. The community which fought for the equality of women in dress code restricts the space of women.

The life of Nadars in the post-Upper Cloth Revolt is characterized by socio-economic-political advancement. While they have improved their lives, Nadars have been gripped by certain customs and practices. One of such practice is dowry. The dowry system is rampant among them. Previously, Nadar women were not allowed to wear gold ornaments. Nowadays dowry is given mostly in gold. The dowry is a huge burden for parents who are economically not sound. The community which stood for the dignity of women encourages a practice that values women in terms of gold/dowry. There is also a gap between rich and poor among the Nadars. The rich may not fix a marriage alliance with a poor family because of dowry, and women are the victims. Once victimized by caste and patriarchy, now they are victimized by practices within the community. The community has to evaluate its current attitude towards caste, the subjugation of women, and dehumanizing practices like dowry and to become a community of egalitarian values. They have to stand for a society where women are treated equally and oppressive caste practices and customs are shunned. A subaltern community must always strive for non-hegemonic relations and liberating experiences in society.

Dress Code of Women in Travancore

The dress code was one of the means to convey the social status and power of a particular caste in Travancore. There were different patterns of dress, identifying women of respective castes. Three kinds of jackets were used by the women of different social backgrounds to cover the upper parts of their bodies. High caste women used to wear a jacket called *muditchiravakkay*. Its body and sleeves were short, and was fastened in front with a knot. Coloured jackets were permitted to Brahmin women only. The Muslim women used to wear a type of jacket called the *kuppāyam*. Its body and sleeves were long, and was tied in front with a thread. Another form of jacket, *ravakkay* was used by Christian women: its body was long and sleeves were short. It was bound in front with a string. This type of jacket was allowed to the Christian women of lower caste origin, particularly the Nadar women. But before 1812, they were forbidden any covering above the waist.[56]

Women of high castes used to wear jackets with upper cloth. Upper cloth is a small piece of cloth worn across the breasts and over the left shoulder. It was the privilege of high caste women. Though

Nair women were permitted to wear the upper cloth, they had to take it off in the presence of Brahmins and royal family members, and before the temple deities. They were even completely stripped off by the servants of the Raja if they had violated the custom. There was no such restriction for Brahmin women. While Nadar Christian women were allowed to wear jackets, they were forbidden to wear upper cloth. Hindu women of low caste origin were not legally permitted to wear anything above the waist. Therefore, the question of the upper cloth was not raised among them. But they used to make use of the benefits of the orders issued by the Resident or Dewan regarding the dress code of the Christians of low caste origin such as legal permission to cover the upper body with jackets.[57] The dress code of women in Travancore shows that it was not the dignity of women, but the size and colour of the jacket that was prioritized and protected. The value of women was measured by the mode and colour of the dress. The upper cloth was an important element of dress which conveyed the status of women.

Symbolism of Upper Cloth

Kings and regional chieftains used to honour their loyal followers by either allowing them to wear fine clothes or by bestowing on them a special costume.[58] Joanne Punzo Waghorne argues that 'these objects (garments, dress) helped to build up a new "body", a new substantial identity for the recipient, transforming him from what he was into new, honored and honorable companion of the king'.[59] With the Upper Cloth, the Nadar women attempted to build up a new body and identity to experience human dignity and freedom.

The upper cloth was symbolized and interpreted differently among various interested groups. For the Nadar men and women it was a symbol of their social aspirations to shake off their social disabilities. The missionaries understood it as a sign of modesty and being civilized. The Nairs interpreted bare breasts/chests as a symbol of humility and difference in status and power because they had different understanding behind the symbol. As Brahmins used to appear before the deity bare chested in the temple, Nairs were expected to bare breast/chest before the Brahmins, the gods on earth. Those below the Nairs were also required to be bare breasted/chested before their superiors in the caste hierarchy. In this sense, the Nairs believed that Nadar women were unworthy for the upper cloth, a symbol of privilege.[60] But the Nadars believed that their women were indeed worthy of it. For them, it was not only a symbol of privilege but also a symbol of dignity, respect, and selfhood. When Nadar women claimed the privilege with the support of their men, Nairs responded violently. Moreover, the Nadars understood the dress of their women as one of humiliation and contempt in the eyes of high caste. Therefore, they encouraged their women to appropriate the dress symbolism of high caste people who enjoyed power and status in society, a bold and risky step in Travancore society.

The Nadars, Christianity and Upper Cloth Revolt

The Protestant Christian mission work in South Travancore began with the London Missionary Society (LMS) in 1806. William Tobias Ringeltaube (1770-1816) was the first missionary of LMS in Travancore. Though he was given the freedom to select his place for mission work,[61] Ringeltaube came to Travancore on the invitation of Maharasan Vedamanikam, a convert from Mylaudy, north-east of Kanyakumari. Maharasan became a Christian on his return journey of pilgrimage from Chidambaram in Tamil Nadu. He was a convert of Rev. John Casper Kohlhoff, a Lutheran German missionary stationed in Thanjavur. He was considered the first Protestant convert in Travancore. By caste he was a Pariah. When Ringeltaube left Travancore, Vedamanikam was in-charge of the LMS mission work for two years (1816-17). His family members contributed in different capacities to the development of the Travancore mission.[62] The LMS missionaries primarily worked among the people of lower caste origin. The Nadars were the principal people group who largely responded to the missionary activities of LMS. Thus the Nadars constituted majority of the early converts under LMS missionaries in South Travancore. The facts and figures of mission work show that large-scale conversion of Nadars and the subsequent growth of LMS mission played a significant role in the emergence of Upper Cloth Revolt.

The LMS Mission Work

The LMS mission had a steady growth in South Travancore. It is noticeable that from the beginning of its work in 1806 to 1860, the missionaries made efforts to diffuse the knowledge: religious and secular. They communicated the Gospel and baptized those who accepted the Christian faith. They established schools to enlighten the people through education: religious and non-religious, and built churches and worship places for the new converts in their respective places.

The LMS mission began in an adverse social context in Travancore. Ringeltaube and his associates had to face many challenges from the government and the native high castes. At the same time, he did not encourage those who came apparently with material motives. Therefore, there was less numerical growth visible in the very early stage of the mission. But he baptized 900 individuals and prepared many candidates for baptism within 10 years (1806-16) of his ministry. Six or seven major mission stations and five or six schools were also established.[63]

The substantial development of the mission can be observed before the first episode of the Upper Cloth Revolt in 1822. From 1817 onwards, more people began to accept the Gospel. For instance, there was one congregation of 400-500 members in Tamarakulam in 1818. In the same location, around 1,000 people were also enrolled as members during this period. It was estimated that 1,600 people joined the mission in 1818. A few schools were also opened along with the places of worship in different locations in this period. Charles Mead, who came as an LMS missionary after Ringeltaube, established five new schools in 1818 and baptized about 500 individuals in 1819. By 1820, about 3,000 people came to the Christian faith and native schools were increased to 15. They renounced idolatry and destroyed their old places of worship. Since its inception in Travancore in 1806, it was calculated in 1822 that more than 5,000 natives embraced the Christian faith through the work of LMS mission. There were 22 regular congregations, 17 native teachers, and 20 village schools.[64] The growth of LMS mission informs that a sizable number of natives, particularly Nadars, placed themselves under the Christian faith which taught them the fullness of life and induced them to question the social restrictions on clothing in 1822. The Christian faith considerably influenced them to raise their voice against social disabilities. Christianity gave a new space for people who had been reduced to a dehumanized life condition.

The second episode of Upper Cloth Revolt in 1828-9 was also preceded by considerable conversions of natives in various places. In 1824, there were 48 congregations, 27 native teachers and 47 schools attended by 1,300 students.[65] A Central school or Seminary was also established to prepare the future leaders. The students were also taught English in this school.[66] The growth of missions can be observed from the division of mission fields for better management. For example, in 1827, Nagarcoil area of the mission was divided into two: eastern and western. In the eastern division there were 14 chapels, 1,410 Christians, 36 schools with 1,304 boys and 106 girls. In the western division, there were 12 chapels, 1,441 Christians, and 21 schools attended by 541 children. There were 95 school masters and 34 native readers in both divisions.[67] The data of education and mission activities of LMS demonstrates what made the native Christians courageous to fight against social disabilities. The new faith and education contributed to the critical consciousness of native Christians, particularly the Nadars.

The progress of mission work in South Travancore could not be checked by the persecutions or royal proclamations. After the Upper Cloth Revolt in 1829, more people were added to the mission. For example, in Neyoor Mission District there were 3,667 Christians in 1833.[68] In 1840 it became 6,867 in number.[69] It is worth mentioning that native Christians began to construct and repair the places of worship and schools. In Neyyor Mission District, 'a society for assisting in the erection and repairs of places of worship' was formed in 1833.[70] The native Christians contributed money, material and even land to construct places of worship and schools in many places.[71] It shows their commitment to the faith which emboldened and enlivened their lives to fight against the forces of oppression in society. The subalterns are loyal to the faith and ideology which make them 'subjects' and 'masters' of their destiny.

In 1853, there were seven main stations and 250 outstations supervised by eight missionaries and 105 catechists. There were 17,600 native professing Christians though all were not in full communion with the Church. While 104 boys and 230 girls were taught in boarding schools, 6,000 boys and 1,000 girls studied in day-schools.[72] The Christians of South Travancore were generous in giving for mission work. Though majority of them were poor, they contributed liberally to the auxiliary bodies of the mission such as the Bible Society, Tract Society, Book Society and Dorcas or Poor Fund.[73]

The Upper Cloth Revolt in 1858-9 did not stop conversions. In fact, it motivated more people to embrace the Christian faith. For example, after the final episode of the Upper Cloth Revolt, there were about 3,000 people in Neyyor and Pareychaley mission districts who became Christians. In some villages, people as a whole embraced the Christian faith. It was estimated that in 1861-2 there were about 4,000 people who came under Christian instruction. It was Nadars who mainly responded to the Christian faith in the first half century of the LMS mission work in Travancore.[74] In sum, the success of LMS mission in South Travancore was because of two reasons: the commitment of missionaries to the dissemination of the Gospel and the contextual response of natives, particularly Nadars, to the Gospel in the light of societal realities. The contributions of subalterns are often ignored in the dominant narratives. The growth of Protestant Christianity in Travancore is due to dissent against the dominant religion, and not exclusively the mission work of a numerically few missionaries.

Education and Empowerment of Women

Education and empowerment of women was one of the priorities of LMS. They gave equal importance to the education of male and female individuals. In Travancore, women were not given education till the missionaries initiated the process in the nineteenth century. They understood that women's empowerment in Travancore was possible only through education. The wives of missionaries played a vital role in the education and empowerment of women.[75] In 1823 the first school for girls was established. In the beginning, parents were reluctant to send their children to schools. Girls were mainly taught reading, writing, sewing, lace making, etc.[76] but the enrollment of girls in schools increased year by year. In 1827, 106 girls were studying in different schools in one of the divisions of a mission district.[77] In 1838, there were 120 girls in the boarding school run by Mrs. Martha Mault.[78] In this boarding school, girls were taught to make lace and prepared to be school teachers. In 1853, there were 230 girls in boarding schools and 1,000 girls in day-schools.[79] Many local women qualified as school mistresses or deaconesses. In 1856-7, twenty devoted women were employed in different vocations such as school mistresses, deaconesses or instructors of women in one of the mission districts.[80] Education initiated by missionaries indeed facilitated the empowerment of women in South Travancore and prompted Nadar women to question the social restriction on the mode of dress. Education is the social capital of subalterns.

The Nadar Christians: Nature and Spirituality

There were two main reasons behind the large-scale conversion of Nadars in South Travancore. First, they experienced a kind of freedom in the new faith, particularly freedom from the fear of demons or evil spirits. Second, they desired emancipation from the societal oppression of caste. In fact, in the new religion they could find horizons of spiritual and social emancipation.[81] The conversion of Nadars was not simply an emotional expression but an experiential encounter with the Gospel. For example, many of them renounced their primitive worship after experiencing its futility in their lives.[82] The oppressive social conditions may have led some Nadars to become Christians for temporal advantages, but all conversions cannot be placed in this category.[83] Many took a conscious decision to follow the Christian faith. There were three classes of Christians among them: unbaptized converts or candidates for baptism, the baptized but not yet fully confirmed for communion, and the communicants or Church members, a comparatively small number in the congregations.[84] Though not exclusively, the early converts were spiritually promising in nature. They had biblical knowledge, and conviction. Children had a basic knowledge of scriptures. As people of low caste origin, their spirituality was shaped in the furnace of persecutions and in struggles against social disabilities.[85] The Nadars, who were comparatively wealthy, expressed their commitment to the new faith by contributing liberally to the building of worship places and to the establishment of new schools.[86] The new faith not only met their spiritual and material needs but also taught them to resist injustice and oppression. The Upper Cloth Revolt was an outcome of the internalization of this new faith.

The Role of Native Catechists and Teachers

Native catechists and teachers played a significant role in building the Christian community. They were the main link between the people and the missionaries. This continued throughout the eventful years of mission work in the nineteenth century. In order to prepare the native agency, a seminary was established in Nagercoil.[87]

A native catechist was primarily responsible for a village congregation. He would read and preach the Word of God in the congregation. The native teachers, mostly catechists, gave general knowledge and knowledge of the Bible to children in the schools. They made regular house visits and catechized men and women. They never ignored any chance to diffuse knowledge and enlighten the people. Visiting the sick and irregular church members, distributing Christian lietrature, and performing other religious duties were part of their daily work. Indeed, the success of mission work was credited to them.[88] They also conducted Bible classes attended by young men and women. Local preachers worked under the English missionaries. Every missionary was pastor of a particular mission station. Under him were local persons who had to report to him regarding the conditions of the congregations and schools. Reporting used to happen once a week or month. The missionaries used to give instruction to local preachers and help them to prepare sermons.[89] It was their own people who helped the locals to internalize the faith and prepared them to renounce the evil practices and to respond against the social evils, one of these being the clothing taboo. They might have taught them why women of certain communities were privileged to wear fine dress while others were deprived of it. So subalterns were taught and conscientized by subalterns of the same flock.

The Mass Conversion of Nadars

It is observed that the conversion of Nadars was a mass movement in nature. In many villages, they had left their old religion *en bloc* and embraced the new faith to start a new life. Schools and places of worship were opened. The missionaries called this phenomenon a 'movement'.[90] This mass movement of Nadars into Christianity, after destroying their old temples and idols, was not just an attempt to escape from the cruelties of caste. According to J.W. Gladstone, 'Destroying of their old temples and idols . . . was a forsaking of a religion that did not offer spiritual satisfaction, and accepting a new religion in which they found a new life, new meaning and satisfaction.'[91] Even if it is for social advancement, as C.F. Andrews noted about material motive behind mass movements, 'yet this desire had a good and noble side, and was not without spiritual value'.[92] John W. Grant observes that conversion for social advancement is undoubtedly Christian because the New Testament categorically endorses the empowerment of the poor and downtrodden in society.[93] Above all, this mass conversion ultimately helped the Nadars to question social restrictions. Through conversion, the Nadars could experience spiritual satisfaction and improve their condition in the caste-ridden society. It was a spiritual exercise which opened new paths of empowerment. It gave them spiritual and moral strength to fight social disabilities. This was proved in the Upper Cloth Revolt.

The Upper Cloth Revolt

The Upper Cloth Revolt was an outcry of the Nadars against a caste system which was supported by the native government in Travancore and the religion of the land. The revolt was an outcome of the bold move by Nadar women to cover themselves as they thought fit. The Nadar women with the support of their men appeared wearing the upper cloth, and claimed this privilege. According R.N. Yesudas, 'This was the first organized revolt against custom and caste in India.' He also called it a 'People's Revolt'.[94]

Factors which Led to the Upper Cloth Revolt

There are some basic factors which influenced the Nadar Christian women to break the caste and patriarchal ban on upper cloth. When they violated the social customs by wearing the upper cloth, high caste men, particularly the Nairs, unleashed violence against Nadar men and women. This violent revolt is later known as Upper Cloth Revolt in South Travancore.

The Influence of Nadar Women in Tinnevelly (Tirunelveli)

The life of Nadar women in Tinnevelly inspired their counterparts to question the restriction on upper cloth in South Travancore. The Nadar women were not forbidden to cover their bosoms and wear upper cloth in Tinnevelly. Many Nadar women of wealthy families in South Travancore had the habit of wearing upper cloth before the arrival of missionaries. Opposition might have developed when more Nadar women appeared with upper cloth. Since their migration, the Nadars in South Travancore used to spend half of the year in Tinnevelly and other half of the year in Travancore due to their seasonal occupations, particularly palmyra cultivation. During their stay in Tinnevelly, the Nadar women were free to dress with the upper cloth.[95] Apart from their continuous contact, the Nadars of Travancore used to take wives from Tinnevelly and vice-versa.[96] The women from Tinnevelly continued the dress code in Travancore. Moreover, long before the issue of upper cloth surfaced in the form of violent revolt, the Nadar Christian women in Neyoor used to appear with jacket and upper cloth.[97] It also encouraged their sisters in other regions to follow it. It is also argued that before their migration from the Pandya kingdom, the Nadar women were not forbidden to use upper cloth and cover their bosoms.[98] It means they lived an unrestricted life in Tamil country. Thus, the unrestricted use of upper cloth by the Nadar women in Tinnevelly influenced their sisters to break the ban on wearing upper cloth in Travancore. In the Upper Cloth Revolt, they were also attempting to reclaim the freedom of their ancestors in the Tamil nation.

The Christian Faith

The Christian faith had been influencing the Nadars in south Travancore from the very beginning of its larger dissemination among them in the nineteenth century. The reluctance to perform free services to upper castes and offer donations to the deities, which they had done earlier, is a best case in point regarding the impact of Christian faith in their lives.[99] Many Nadars who came under the instruction of Christian faith also began to question the social evils and restrictions. It was culminated in the emergence of Upper Cloth Revolt. It was Nadar Christian women who first appeared with upper cloth and questioned the restriction.[100] Mrs. Eshakee, wife of Puthathan Cutty, was one among them.[101] The Christian faith taught the Nadars their rights as human beings and as citizens. Gradually, a spirit of defiance was developed among them. They demanded more freedom and asserted the dignity of life in the repressive social context.[102] Their Christian life was shaped in the congregations where the Scripture was expounded with contemporary significance. The believers were advised to live in the spirit of Gospel which upholds equality.[103] J.W. Gladstone opines that, 'When they accepted the Gospel values a new change happened in their socio-religious lives.'[104] They internalized the faith and began to live as free human beings in the caste society. They even questioned their old masters and began to share the Gospel with them also.[105] In the words of R.N. Yesudas, 'Faith gave them unity and brought them under one umbrella'[106] to challenge the unjust social restrictions imposed upon them. It can be inferred that the Gospel which affirms the fullness of life have given them consciousness of freedom, justice and dignity. The fullness of life in their specific context meant a life with dignity. For Nadar women, it was a life without any restriction on wearing the upper cloth. In short, the

Christian faith of Nadar men and women ultimately led them to question social injustice and inequality.

The Missionaries

The Protestant missionaries sided with the people of low caste origin who were underprivileged in Travancore in the nineteenth century. They stood for the values of justice, liberty and equality. They also sowed the seeds of revolution in the minds of the oppressed people against the unjust social order based on caste.[107] They believed that deprivation of basic rights to the low castes was a crime against human beings and God. In their work, they emphasized temporal and spiritual aspects of salvation.[108] It is viewed that the pathetic condition of the low castes provoked the missionaries to stand with them.[109] In the context of the negation of rights and privileges, for the Nadar Christians, the missionaries were their new social leaders.[110]

The Nadar Christians had the support of Christian missionaries in all their struggles for social emancipation, particularly the Upper Cloth Revolt.[111] As R.N. Yesudas notes, 'Missionaries were the real agents. They were steering the event (Upper Cloth Revolt). Action was carried out by the native leadership who were connected to the Missionaries.'[112] The missionaries encouraged the Nadars to be defiant to the dehumanizing customs and practices of the land and to break the restriction on wearing upper cloth. The missionaries were even criticized for supporting the converts without considering the time, the country and the nature of government, etc.[113] It is quite natural that the dominant takes refuge in time and context if new initiative is taken against the status quo. They will behave as if they are not against the reform; but in reality they are not in favour of it.

J.W. Gladstone observes that 'Missionaries preached and acted. They preached the Gospel values and encouraged the converts to live on those values. They taught them the God who loves them in the oppressed situation.'[114] The role of missionaries can be seen in the government report also. It says that '. . . they (Nadars) probably desired a total abolition of all restrictions as to dress, and calculated upon the sympathies and support of the European missionaries residing among them.'[115] The sympathies and support can be interpreted as spiritual and moral support given by the missionaries. As religious leaders and pastors, it is obvious that the missionaries must have encouraged the Nadars in their sermons and deliberations. They might have even promised the support of British administration. It was the missionaries who approached the court and petitioned on behalf of the Nadars. The missionaries supported the cause of the Nadars based on their faith and its values. The missionaries inculcated the faith which combats against life-negating systems and structures. On the one hand, missionaries taught them the values of Christian Gospel; on the other hand, Nadars internalized those values to fight against discrimination. It culminated in the assertive action of Nadar women to start wearing the upper cloth.

Johanna Coelestina Horyst and Martha Mault: Woman Missionaries

Women missionaries played an important role in empowering the Nadar women, particularly in asserting their dignity in a male dominated caste society. They educated the women in social matters. It was Mrs. Johanna Coelestina Horyst and Mrs. Martha Mault who were instrumental in starting schools, particularly boarding schools, for girls in South Travancore. Apart from regular schooling, the girls were also taught lace-making, embroidery, crotchet, spinning, etc. Gradually, schools for girls were established throughout the mission stations.[116] In the context of the strict restriction on the dress code of lower caste women, they also encouraged the Nadar women to improve their attire. They not only taught them how to wear jackets but also stitched the jackets for them.[117] By catering knowledge and motivating to modify the dress code of Nadar women, the woman missionaries actually facilitated the assertion of Nadar women against socio-patriarchal regulation on dress. While woman missionaries supported the Nadar women to modify their dress code, they were also subjected to patriarchal culture. The activities of these woman missionaries show the compartmentalization of mission activities within the framework of patriarchy. Their work was limited to women's education, teaching embroidery, etc. They were not equal to the men in the mission fields. It means missionaries also had patriarchal mindset.

Education and Social Advancement

Education equipped the Nadars to fight against social oppression and deprivation of rights. The Nadars, both men and women, who were educated in schools aspired for freedom from all social disabilities. It was the Nadars who embraced Christianity mainly benefited from education. Education gave them space to improve, and made them more intelligent and industrious. According to J.W. Gladstone, 'education awakened critical consciousness in them'.[118] The improvement of the Nadars, particularly in the case of dress, disturbed the Nairs who had suppressed them for many years.[119] In fact, education enabled the Nadars to think of their situation critically and led the Nadar women to modify their dress with upper cloth. This modification in dress was challenged by the Nairs in all possible ways such as court cases, physical violence etc. Critical consciousness is the first step towards the liberation of subalterns. Education is the tool to achieve it.

The Teachings and Work of Vaikunta Swami

The teachings and work of Vaikunta Swami (1809-51) was another influential factor behind the revolt. Vaikunta Swami, also known as Muthukutti Swami, a Nadar by caste, was born at Thoppil in the present Kanyakumari district. He claimed to be an incarnation of Vishnu and apparently possessed miraculous powers. He had followers who were attracted to his social and religious teachings. He was one of the social revolutionaries in Travancore in the nineteenth century. He raised his voice against the evils of caste system and the administration of the native government. In 1836 he founded 'Samatva Samajam', an organization to fight the social disabilities of the low castes in society. His activities annoyed the ruling class, and he was arrested in 1837 and put in jail in Trivandrum. Though he died before the major episode of Upper Cloth Revolt in 1858-9, it would be unreasonable to say that his teachings and work for social equality did not influence the Nadars to fight against caste restrictions.[120] The involvement of Nadar Hindus in the later stage of the Upper Cloth Revolt can be considered as an outcome of the influence of Vaikunta Swami. He is another example of subaltern resistance and agency for liberation.

The Abolition of Slavery

The abolition of slavery in 1855 was one of the factors which intensified the Upper Cloth Revolt. While it encouraged the Nadars to question the social restrictions, the Nairs were more irritated against the ongoing reforms by Nadars. It finally resulted in the violent response of the Nairs in the last stage of the Upper Cloth Revolt in 1858-9. The Nadars utilized the opportunity of the abolition of slavery for challenging their disabilities, and consequently more Nadar women appeared wearing upper cloth. The emancipation of slaves frustrated the Nairs mainly because of two reasons. As the main owners of the slaves, the Nairs were the losers. They were also afraid of losing their social status in future if the missionaries, whose intervention caused the abolition of slavery, continued their support to the demands of the low castes.[121] In this context, the Nairs perceived the appearance of Nadar women wearing the upper cloth as a threat to their social position.

Proclamation of 1858 by Queen Victoria

After the first war of Indian Independence in 1857, the administration of India was directly taken over by the British government from East India Company. Queen Victoria issued a proclamation which was declared officially in India by Lord Canning on 1 November 1858. This proclamation basically outlined the policy of British government in the management of Indian affairs in future. It declared,

Firmly relying ourselves on the truth of Christianity and acknowledging with gratitude the solace of religion, we disclaim alike the right and the desire to impose our convictions on any of our subjects. We declare it to be our royal will and pleasure that none be any wise favored, none molested or disqualified, by reason of their religious faith or observances, but that all shall alike enjoy the equal and impartial protection of the law; and we do strictly charge and enjoin all those who may be in authority under us that they abstain from all interference with the religious belief or worship of any of our subjects, on pain of our highest displeasure.

And it is our further will that, so far as may be, our subjects, of whatever race or creed, be freely and impartially admitted to offices in our service, the duties of which they may be qualified, by their education, ability, and integrity, duly to discharge.[122]

During his official visit Lord Harris, the Governor of Madras, read out the proclamation in Travancore.

The proclamation of 1858 by Queen Victoria was understood and interpreted by the Nairs and the Nadars differently. It added fuel to the fire in the context of existing animosity between the two communities over the use of the upper cloth. While it gave encouragement to the Nadars for their attempts of social advancement, the Nairs were equally happy with the promise of the non-interference of administration in the religious matters. But the Nairs misinterpreted the proclamation that the British government had withdrawn its protection of missionaries and native Christians. They even propagated that missionary activities were prohibited in Travancore.[123] The proclamation was given wide publicity. Government officials pasted the proclamation in market places, main roads and streets to inform people about the new development in the political situation of the nation and to convey the idea that the appearance of Nadar women with upper cloth was not supported by the British government. It encouraged them to take law and order in their own hands and unleash violence against the Nadars.[124] Thus the Queen's Proclamation became one of the causes for the Upper Cloth Revolt. The misinterpretation of the proclamation by Nairs shows the hegemonic behaviour of the dominant. They exploit the ignorance and powerlessness of subalterns and misuse the resources and government machinery to retain their domination.

The First Episode of the Upper Cloth Revolt (1822-3)

In the beginning of nineteenth century, the lower caste women were not allowed to cover their bosoms. Their dress was a single cloth which hardly covered the body above the waist and below the knee. In 1812, Col. John Munro, Dewan of Travancore, issued a proclamation permitting women of low caste origin converted to Christianity, to cover their upper body.[125] So Nadars modified their dress. It irritated the Nairs, and a complaint was submitted to Col. Munro against the modification of dress. In response to the complaint, Col. John Munro issued an order regulating the dress of the Christian women of low caste origin in 1814. According to the order, they were allowed to wear only a jacket, like Christian or Muslim women. They were forbidden to imitate the Nair dress.[126] In 1815, another proclamation was issued to state that as their religion demanded, the Christian women who belonged to low castes such as the Nadars were permitted to cover themselves.[127] These orders/ proclamations are silent about the Hindu Nadar women. It implies that they were legally not permitted to cover their bosoms. Perhaps they had modified their dress after their Christian sisters. This can be understood from the proclamations of 1829 and 1859.

In spite of the legal restrictions on dress, the Nadar Christian women began to wear not only jackets but also upper cloths. They appeared in public with the costume of high caste Hindu women. In May 1822, the Nadar Christian women were ill-treated for appearing properly dressed with upper cloth in the Kalkulam mission district. The appearance of Nadar women displeased the Shudras, particularly the Nairs. They mocked and abused the poor women in markets and streets.[128] This was the beginning of the Upper Cloth Revolt which continued in different periods till 1859.

The Padmanabhapuram Court Order and the Nadar Christians

When the Nadar women were attacked in Kalkulam and Eraniel districts, Mr. Charles Mead approached the Padmanabhapuram (Palpanabapuram) court to get justice for them. But his complaints were withheld. Then he approached the Resident and pleaded him to protect the Nadar men and women from the outrage of the Nairs. The Resident immediately acted and asked the Christian judges of Nagarcoil and Padmanabhapuram to submit a report on the issue. The reports were favourable to the Christians. Finally, the Court reinvestigated the complaints of both parties, and one case which was filed against the Nadars was adjudicated in favour of them. The decree of this case was an encouragement to the Nadar women to appear in public with upper cloth. A complaint was filed against some Nadars who failed to pay the toddy-rent and encouraged their women to wear the upper cloth. When it was argued that they had to be fined, the Court asked Mr. Charles Mead to verify the religion of the accused and to inform if the Christian religion required the women to wear the upper cloth. He replied that the Christian women ought to wear the upper cloth when they had to go to church or appeared in public. Thus the court decreed (Vakil No. 177, dated 7th Vykasi, 998 ME (1823) that Shanoo Neelenkutty and others who were accused of allowing their women to wear the upper cloth were not to be fined.[129]

The Nadar Christian women considered the Padmanabhapuram court order an official sanction to change their attire.[130] The ruling class and high castes could not tolerate the Nadar women wearing jackets and the upper cloth. Though Mr. Charles Mead advised the Nadar women not to offend the Nairs unnecessarily, they always appeared with an upper cloth.[131] It was not that easy to question the restriction on dress in Travancore society which was notorious for its caste-rigidity. But Nadar men and women raised their voice and risked their lives to challenge the protectors of life-negating practices in society. They also paid the price for the freedom of future generations. History shows that subaltern protest is risky and painful in nature.

The Second Episode (1828-9)

The animosity between the Nadar Christians and the upper castes, particularly the Nairs, continued even after the Padmanabhapuram court order in 1823. The Nadar Christians were accused of breaking the laws of the land and of creating disorder. The Nadar Christian women had not discontinued to wear the upper cloth. Occasional quarrels were common between the two groups.[132] But an organized attack against the Nadars was started in 1828. The main reason behind the fresh violence was the innovation of dress by the Nadar Christian women. The Nairs were actually disturbed by the improvement of Christians of low caste origin, particularly the Nadars, in education and religion.[133]

Suppression

The Nadar Christians both men and women had to face severe persecution, which began in the late 1828. It started with threatening language by the Nairs. Gradually, threat was replaced by personal assault and public outrage. They threatened to kill missionaries and burn the chapels and schools. They systematically planned attacks and carried them out with the support of government officials. They burned down chapels, schools, and books. Raman Thampi who sold his land to construct a mission house at Neyoor was imprisoned for seven years. The Nairs obstructed worship services and compelled the Nadars to work on Sundays though they were legally exempt.[134]

The outrages of Nairs mostly affected the Nadar Christians who lived in Autoor, Arumanai, Tripparapoo, Cannanoor, Pulipanam, Oodayavelly and other villages in the Neyoor region. The Nairs had the support of Pidagacars, the district officials, for their mischievous activities. They burned schools and chapels and seized many men as captives in Autoor.[135] In order to escape from the assailants many Nadars retired to the mountains. Christian converts were threatened and their homes were destroyed. A school master, a new convert who was also the principal man of the village was captured and tortured. His house was looted and set fire. Plundering and burning down the homes were common during those days of violence. Some men were even falsely charged with murder,[136] imprisoned for many months without any judicial intervention. It is also reported that all-high castes, Muslims and Catholics were against the Nadar Christians who attempted to improve their status.

The Nair goons under the leadership of Pidagacars used to march towards the villages and threatened the Nadar Christians. They were fully armed to carry out their plan. They were even supplied guns. In one incident, one school master and some Christians were seized as captives. They were tied with ropes and the ends of the ropes were attached to the trunks of the elephants which marched back and forth. The hands and feet of captives were fettered with irons. Vedamanickam of Pambadikonam in Autoor was beaten to death.[137]

It was not only the dress code that gave offence. The Nadar Christians in Cannanoor were attacked for their unwillingness to perform *ūḻiaṁ* services or wage-free labour on Sundays. They were already exempted from this. But on Sunday, 21 December 1828, some ex-government officials forced a Christian to carry a bundle of leaves for elephants at the Padmanabhapuram Fort. Seeing this unjust action, a group of Christians questioned the Nairs and released their brother, placing the bundle upon the head of one of the Nairs. He was made to carry the bundle back to their place. The Nairs considered this as an insult. They never expected such humiliation from the Nadars who were inferior to them in social hierarchy. The Nairs became infuriated and planned to teach the Nadars a lesson. On 23 December 1828, they assembled near the Cannanoor Church, armed with guns, swords, cleavers, rice-beaters, clubs, etc. Having received the news of possible attack, the Nadars left their homes and escaped. But a few Nadar women and children, who remained in homes, had to face the fury of the Nairs. It was surprising that the Tahsildar, the main responsible person of the government in the violence affected region, had not 'known' of the incident in time.[138] It shows the vulnerability of Nadar Christians and the protection of Nairs. The administrative support enabled the Nairs to express their caste fury against the Nadar Christians. For the Nairs, violence was the answer and the method to suppress the innovation of Nadars in future. But it proved wrong in the future course of the revolt.

Eswara Pillai and his associates secretly produced gunpowder and firearms. During the assault, the Nadar Christians reacted according to their capacity. On 29 December 1828, some of them encouraged by the visit of Charles Mead, seized a few Nairs of Autoor who came to the Eraneel market and brought them to his bungalow. But after a while they were released.

As they threatened to assassinate the missionaries earlier, on 3 January 1829 the Nairs conspired to kill Charles Mead, staying in Mandacad. He perceived the impending danger and assembled his Christians and asked any one of them to take a letter to Fort Oodagherry. One Christian took the letter to the Commander. Under the leadership of Captain Sibbald, the 15th Regiment Madras Infantry reached Mead's house at night and gave him protection for a fortnight. When the army came the Nairs were at *pooja*. Hearing the arrival of the British army they ran away in different directions. Thus the missionary's life was saved. Although he was advised to be away from his people for some time, Mead remained with them throughout their struggle. Though the arrival of army controlled the violent actions of the Nairs they set fire to another chapel during this time.[139] This shows the intensity of Nair rage against the Nadar Christians. They were ready to go to any extent to stop the social advancement of Nadar Christians in Travancore. Moreover, the fear of losing social status always haunted the Nairs. It led them to react more violently. Throughout the revolt they used other subalterns against the Nadars. The subalterns had no other option except to carry out the orders of their masters. This continues even today in religious and caste conflicts. The dominant either divides the subalterns in religious and caste lines or co-opts them to implement their agenda.

Violence against Nadar Women

The Nadar Christian women suffered violence, humiliation, and molestation throughout the revolt. They were harassed in markets, streets and other public places for wearing the upper cloth. They were beaten and abused publicly.[140] The Nairs did not even spare old women. In Autoor, they cut off the ear of a woman who was above ninety years old. In many places, the Nadar women were forced to remove their upper cloths[141] or they were also torn off. When they had to appear before the Dewan, who was investigating the unrest, they were not allowed to wear the upper cloth when they entered the Padmanabhapuram Fort.[142] Yesudial, a Nadar Christian woman of Kallikkavilai, was beaten to remove her upper cloth when she was going to the local market. Neethiyudial, another Nadar Christian woman, was also physically assaulted and forced to take off her upper cloth in Kunattur.[143] When the Nadars left homes at the point of impending violence, their women and children who stayed behind were cruelly assaulted by the Nairs. The dress of one woman was completely stripped and others were forcibly bare-breasted.[144] The body of Nadar women had become vulnerable location for violence: violence of caste and patriarchy. They were socially and personally dishonored. Their bodies were stripped to prevent the advancement of a community. Their nakedness had not exposed the bodies of poor women but the primitiveness of so-called civilized bodies, the Nairs. When the Nadar women showed their boldness by covering their bodies with upper cloths, the Nairs showed their cowardice by removing them from the bodies. The women endure double humiliation among the subalterns during communal conflicts. The dominant intentionally target them to subjugate their communities.

Mrs. Yesuvadial: Martyr of the Upper Cloth Revolt

Different forms of violence had been unleashed by the upper caste men. The Nadar women were assertive and courageous throughout the struggle for restoring their dignity and freedom in the casteist and patriarchal society. They had to face physical, mental and sexual violence and even death. During the second Upper Cloth Revolt, a group of women under the leadership of Mrs. Yesuvadial appeared with an upper cloth in public and challenged the restriction on dress in Kannanoor. They were beaten by the caste men and Mrs. Yesuvadial was injured by gunshot. Although they attempted to shoot her by gunfire, she did not die. The enraged upper caste men tied and dragged her for nearly five kilometers and brought her to a place called Maruthoorkurichy. Then, she was stripped off and tied to a jack fruit tree upside down. After some time she died.[145] She became a martyr for the cause of the dignity of lower caste women. She risked her life by raising voice against the caste and male hegemony of upper castes. She personifies not only the courage of Nadar women but also the resistive power of subaltern women.

Enquiry, Trial and Punishment

Apart from the arrest of a few Nair leaders by Captain Sibbald, the Resident directed the Dewan Vencatta Row to visit and take necessary steps to maintain peace in those districts where conflict happened. The Dewan conducted his court at Padmanabhapuram and held regular investigations. The Appeal Court of Travancore was also sent to assist the Dewan in the enquiries. The Nair Brigade under Captain H.W. Daly was assigned to watch the native officers and their proceedings. In the beginning of the public enquiries at Palpanabapuram Fort, Charles Mead was permitted to appeal on behalf of the Nadar Christians. Then this permission was withdrawn and the Nadars had to plead for themselves. They did not get any legal protection, and the enquiry was not impartial. None of the Nairs were taken into custody in prison. The Nadar Christians were confined to prison without granting bail. Many were falsely charged with murder cases. Witnesses were supplied and bribed by the Tahsildar and the police officials. The Nadar Christian prisoners were chained two by two and produced before the court. Since they were chained with irons their legs were swollen. In prison they were deprived of the legal rights of prisoners. One prisoner was badly beaten for his request to read his affidavit once more. The prisoners who were falsely charged with murder cases were not allowed to have advocates. In fact, the Nadar Christians were ill-treated not only in court but also in prison. The Nairs were given all facilities to plead their cases through advocates. After all enquiries, the Nairs who instigated violence were punished with the imprisonment of short periods, and some of them nominal punishments, even though they had committed grave crimes. But the Nadar Christians were sentenced with longer imprisonment. But Mead who decided to remain with his people had not stopped his attempts to get the prisoners released. He appealed to the Native government and the British government. Finally, he personally met the new Resident and pleaded for the release of his people. The intervention of this Resident led to the release of prisoners.[146] What is interesting is that enquiry, trial and judgment were carried out by the high caste officials and judges. Therefore, it is not reasonable to think that they were above the influence of caste in a society which was irredeemably influenced by caste consciousness. The legal ignorance of the Nadar Christians was also exploited throughout the legal procedure. It may be the story of subalterns all over the world. They have limited access to judiciary because of their scarce economic resources and social capital.

The Proclamation of 1829

The second episode of the Upper Cloth Revolt was followed by a proclamation on 3 February 1829 prohibiting the Nadar Christian women to wear upper cloth. It was issued by Her Highness the Ranee (Queen) Parvathi Bai. This proclamation had seven sections dealing with different subjects such as wearing the upper cloth, performing *ūḻiaṁ* services, erecting places of worship, etc. But the main intention of the proclamation was to prohibit the Nadar Christian women from wearing the upper cloth. The first clause of the proclamation goes like this:

> Whereas some disturbances have taken place in the Kalcolam, Yeraniel, and Velavancode districts between the Shanars and Nairs originating in a pretension of the women of the Shanars to wear upper cloth contrary to orders and ancient customs, and in a refusal of that caste to perform the Sirkar Ooliam work required of them in common with other inhabitants, I deem it proper to publish the following Proclamation:
>
> *First,* As it is not reasonable on the part of the Shanar women to wear cloths over their breasts, such custom being prohibited, they are required to abstain in future from covering the upper part of their body. An order (circular) had been issued on the 7th Edavam 989 to all places prohibiting the Shanar women of the families of such Shanars as may have embraced Christianity from wearing cloths over their breasts, and requiring them to substitute for these the kupayam (a kind of short-bodice used by other Christians and by Mohomedan Native females), but with regard to their (the Shanar's) allegation as an authority for wearing cloths over their breasts that decree had been passed subsequently by a Law Court permitting the Shanar women on the contrary the use of cloths on the upper part of their body, such a decision since if it be admitted as establishing as a rule, it would be in direct contravention of the order alluded to, cannot but be considered as invalid. Therefore the order referred to is hereby re-published to be held as a document (or authority) in this respect.[147]

This proclamation not only prohibited the Nadar Christian women to wear upper cloth but also invalidated the Padmanabhapuram Court order of 1823 allowing them to wear the same. It was a proclamation which endorsed the violence of Nairs and put down the dignity of subaltern women. It is surprising that the proclamation was issued by a woman against her gender. It implies that it was not gender but caste which mattered. It also shows that the priority and perspective of upper caste women are entirely different from subaltern women. The proclamation became a tool in the hands of Nairs to continue their violent tirade. While the Nairs considered this proclamation as success it could not stop the Nadar Christian women to wear the upper cloth. The third episode was the result of the failure of the proclamation to understand the determination and pain of poor women who had only the support of their men and missionaries in their journey of struggle for dignified life.

The Third Episode of the Upper Cloth Revolt (1858-9)

Nadar Christian women had not stopped wearing upper cloth in spite of the strong proclamation of 1829. They continued in their attempts to adopt the costume of high caste women. Mrs. Eshakee, wife of Puthathan Cutty, a catechist, dressed like a Nair woman and appeared before her former landlord and his wife.[148] Now, the Nadar Hindu women also modified their dress after Christian women. It aggravated the upper castes and culminated in an aggressive resistance against the innovation of dress in 1858.[149] When the conflict developed, a public warning was given on 27 December 1858.

> It has been brought to the notice of the Sirkar that some Shanar women have begun to wear upper-clothes in a fashion different from that hitherto customary and that this gives occasion to quarrels between Shanars and Shudras and other high caste people. If any modifications be desired of long established usages, the proper course would be to represent the matter to the Sirkar and abide by its decision. But conduct in violation of old usages is not proper, and is punishable. This, the Shanars should bear in mind, and shape their conduct accordingly.[150]

Apart from this warning, the proclamation of 1829 was also republished.[151] By these actions the government conveyed that the Nadar women should not challenge the tradition and custom of the land. The warning and the re-publication of the proclamation failed to stop the impending revolt. The governments of the day also followed the practice of warning the subalterns by invoking the laws related to public order if they raise their voice to protect their rights.

The Missionaries and the Use of Upper Cloth

The government and the upper castes accused the missionaries of encouraging the Nadar women, particularly the Christians, to wear upper cloth. But the missionaries argued that they never promoted the costume of upper caste women. Though they supported the advancement of Nadars, they advised the Nadar women to be content with jackets. They also advised them to petition the government regarding the modification of dress. They even discouraged the use of upper cloth in their sermons.[152] As one missionary stated, 'we (the missionaries) have never recommended the practice to anyone. The Christian converts at this place have never asked my permission to wear it nor have I tendered my advice to them on the subject'.[153] The missionaries in their petition to the King of Travancore also underlined this argument.[154] If the missionaries had not advised, then it was the self-initiative of Nadar women to wear the upper cloth and challenge the caste people. In the context of the conflict, the missionaries might have advised the Nadar women to abstain from wearing upper cloth. But it cannot be assumed that they had not supported them at all. Their effort to bring the intervention of Madras government is proof of their sympathy and support.

The Participation of the Nadar Hindus

The Nadar Hindu women were not legally allowed to wear the upper cloth or the *kuppāyam*, the dress permitted to their Christian sisters, till 1859. However, they followed their Christian counterparts in wearing *kuppāyam* and upper cloth. If they had not imitated the dress code of their Christian counterparts, the Proclamation of 1829 would not have asked them to restrain from modifying the dress. The participation of Nadar Hindus was minimal in the first two stages of the revolt. After the proclamation of 1829, however, they began to join hands with their brothers and sisters who were fighting for the liberty of wearing the upper cloth since 1814. Beyond religious lines, the Nadar Hindus and Christians joined in a common cause, to assert the right of their women to wear upper cloth, the symbol of privilege and status.[155] Nadar women irrespective of religion appeared with upper cloths in public.[156] Nadar Christians supported and even helped their Hindu brothers and sisters to prepare petitions against the restriction. Nadar Christian women also taught their Hindu sisters how to modify the dress.[157] The Nadars fought together against their common enemy, the Shudras, mainly the Nairs.[158] In the conflict, the Nadars as a whole were attacked, their houses plundered and burned.[159] Though the Nadar Hindus participated in the revolt, the Christians were the chief target. Beyond religious boundaries they could unite and challenge their oppressors in the caste-driven society. However, the dominant succeed in dividing the subalterns on the basis of religion in contemporary Indian society.

Opposition against Social Advancement

The violent action against the Nadar Christians began in October 1858. They were manhandled in the market places and streets. Mud was thrown on them.[160] On 25 December 1858 the Nadar Christians were attacked in Cullengully, and after two days a mission chapel was burned in the same village.[161] In Pareychaley, within three weeks, many houses, chapels and schools were set on fire.[162] In Neyoor many were ill-treated and houses were plundered. On 25 December 1858 one catechist with his wife and son were imprisoned for complaining against the government officials who cut his trees without permission. A chapel was destroyed at Maycode on 27 December 1858.[163] The Nairs even attempted to beat up Nadar Christians in the presence of the Dewan.[164]

The Nadars also reacted against the mischief of the Nairs. On 30 December 1858, a group of 350 Nadars under the leadership of Cinna Nadar (Shinanadyan) attempted to destroy shops in Kottar

Bazaar. They looted the shops and made the merchants panic and immediately close their shops in the bazaar.[165] The Christians in Nagercoil also put up a defence. They assembled and guarded against the miscreants. Women and children joined the group to protect their main place of worship in Nagarcoil.[166]

A group of 200 Vellalas attacked the Nadar Christians at Talagoody on 4 January 1859. They searched the Christians day and night and threatened to burn down their houses and the chapel. The chapel was closed, and the Christians fled. On 7 January 1859, the Shudras of about 500 fully armed came to Comarapooram and broke and plundered the houses. Next day another group assaulted the poor Christians in Sempenvilly and destroyed the houses of catechists and Christians. They burned books and beat up the schoolmaster. The same group obstructed the worship service at Kodoopoothoor and dispersed the congregation, locking the chapel.[167]

Some Nairs also attacked the British Residency in Nagarcoil on 10 January 1859.[168] On that day another mission chapel was burned down in Vadacuncarey. Again on the same day, a number of Nadar Christians were seized from the Monday Market in Eraneel and taken to the police station without any charge against them. Later they were charged with theft.[169] On 10 January 1859 the Nairs and the Vellalas took law in their hands and looted the Nadars who were doing their regular jobs in the market in Neyoor. Afterward they were seized and taken to the police station. The main reason for this incident was the appearance of Nadar Hindu women with upper cloths in the market. Then assailants came to the Christian village and threw stones at the houses.[170] On 13 January 1859 a number of schools and chapels were destroyed in different places, and on the next day a Nadar village in Tovala was set on fire.[171] A school used as a chapel in Gunamkadu was burned down on 14 January 1859.[172] The same day also witnessed arson, loot and physical assault in Titoovillay and Anditope.[173] On 27 January 1859 another chapel was set on fire in Kalooventidal.[174] The mission chapel at Cullengully in Maycode was burned down on 4 February 1859.[175] In James Town schools were broken, and many catechists fled from the station.[176]

As a result of continuous violence, many Nadar Christians left their villages. The congregations were left without catechists.

Several schools were closed, Sunday services stopped. The roads used by Christians to go to the market and other places were blocked. Nadar Christians were even forced to leave their faith and apply 'Holy Ash' on their foreheads.[177] The situation was such that many of them had already migrated to Tinnevelly or planned to do so.[178] The missionaries also faced the outrage of the Shudras, mainly the Nairs. They lived in fear and anxiety. They had been always threatened by Nair criminals. They could not visit congregations and schools. They were looked with contempt by the government officials in police stations and other offices.[179] They were even assaulted while visiting the Christian prisoners in jail.[180] The attempt of Nadar Christians to get rid of social oppression in the form of restrictions was countered by the Nairs through violent methods. By destroying the schools, the Nairs tried to destroy the education opportunity of Nadars. By burning the chapels, they aimed to destroy the faith of Nadar Christians. Making them homeless was the final nail.

The Suffering of Nadar Women

The Nadar women, particularly the Christians, suffered untold miseries during the revolt. They had gone through physical assault, molestation and public harassment. They were mercilessly ill-treated by the miscreants. Though they were harassed, hither and thither calculated attempts began in October 1858. Consequently, the first case of violence was reported on 8 October 1858 when the Nairs assaulted a Nadar Christian woman and tore her jacket in the market place in Trivandrum mission district. They even spread the rumor that the government had issued order to strip the jackets of Nadar women.[181] Even though the Proclamation of 1829 allowed the Nadar Christian women to wear jackets, the Shudras forcibly tore their jackets also.[182]

A group of two hundred Shudras, mainly Nairs, attacked the Nadar Christians in Thalakudi, stripped off the jackets of the women, and tore their upper cloths on 4 January 1859. In another incident on 7 January 1859, a mob of five hundred Shudras came to attack the Christians in Comarapooram. The Nadar Christian women were dragged out of their houses and stripped. They were subjected to indescribable deeds and sexually molested. In Arambooly, on 9 January 1859, women were ordered to take off their jackets. When they refused to obey the diktat of the Nairs, they were beaten up brutally and stripped. Tearing off the jackets happened again on 10 January 1859 in Neyyor.[183]

On 11 January 1859, a big crowd accompanied by government officials attacked the Nadar Christian women in the market place at Neyyatinkkara and threatened to continue the assault if jackets were worn by them. As it was threatened the previous day, a government peon stopped some women in front of the police station and tore up their jackets and hung them on a tree. Though the peon was caught guilty and ordered to give back the jackets, the dignity of women was not restored.[184]

The upper-caste rioters planned to attack Nadar Christians in Neyyoor in the beginning of 1859. They decided to execute their plan on the day when Baylis, the missionary at Neyyoor, was away at Muttam. When the Nadar Christians came to know about the preparations of the rioters, they were helpless to convey the news to the missionary. Then a Nadar woman came forward. She disguised herself as a mad woman and walked upto Muttam; she communicated the message to F. Baylis. He arrived the next morning. He and other missionaries approached the Resident and the Maharaja and requested them to diffuse the hostile situation. Though Nadar women were attacked in Neyyoor, the courage of this woman avoided a large scale attack on Nadars.[185] In fact, she risked her life to protect the community.

At Mandkad, Muslims also joined with the Shudras and disturbed the Nadar women. While going to the market, poor women were insulted and their jackets were torn off.[186] In Pareychaley, severe conflict continued for twenty days. Though the Nadar Christian women wore only jackets, they were beaten up cruelly and their jackets were taken off in the presence of government officials. In one incident the Muslims and the Nairs physically attacked them and took off the jackets of forty women who were going to the church.[187] In Aramanoor, a barber of the Ezhava caste assaulted a Nadar Christian woman and tore her jacket. The wife of a reader was also assaulted by this barber and a Muslim, and her jacket was torn off and hung upon a tree. The public streets, markets and thoroughfares in Balaramapuram and Neyyatinkkara became unsafe for the Nadar women. Whenever they appeared they were always threatened and assaulted.[188] Though cases were instituted about the burning of houses, schools, and chapels, no case was made against the molestation of women.[189] By taking off and tearing the jackets, the Nairs not only molested the Nadar women sexually but also inflicted pain in their psyche. The mischievous deeds of Nairs tore the dignity of Nadar women. But the combined assault and harassment of Nairs, Muslims and even of the Ezhavas, could not distract the determination of Nadar women. This also shows how the subalterns are used to subjugate other subalterns. Critically unconscious subalterns join hands with the dominant to persecute the co-subalterns.

Unjust Judicial Procedure and Government Machinery

The Nairs enjoyed the support of government officers in their atrocities against Nadar Christians. High-caste officials extended their support to their brothers who were protecting caste practices through violent means. The caste feeling was evident in the actions of government officers from the Dewan to the peon. Thus an impartial discharge of official duty from them was beyond imagination. Complaints of the Nadar Christians were not entertained by casteist officers.[190] Moreover, in many cases, violence was perpetrated by the lower level government officials. Instead of controlling the mobs that attacked the people and destroyed the properties, local officials functioned as instigators.[191] The vulnerability of Nadar Christians can be observed in the decision of sending a Nair Brigade to bring the situation under control, under a European officer.[192] Otherwise, it is obvious that the Nair Brigade would act in favour of Nairs who already had the support of the administration. The prejudiced behaviour can be sensed from the name of the force itself. It shows the helplessness of Nadars who were in peril and the senselessness of the government machinery which was passionate to support the Nairs.

There was also an unjust judicial treatment against the Nadar Christians. Even though the Nairs were caught guilty in many cases, they were not punished for one or the other judicial reasons. But the Nadars were always unduly punished. No impartial treatment was shown to Nadars at any stage of legal process. On one occasion, Nadars, both Hindus and Christians, who threatened rebellion, and Nairs who burned a Nadar village were brought to the Nagarcoil jail. While the Nadars were chained and hand-cuffed and manhandled by the peons and Maravars who were armed with sticks and swords, the Nairs were given gentle treatment. Moreover, the case of Nairs was settled within a short period, and a few of them were given short-term imprisonment and rest were acquitted. The case of Nadars was prolonged and none of them was acquitted even though there was no evidence for the allegations made against them. They were fettered and imprisoned without bail or communication with relatives.[193] Many of the Nadar Christians were falsely charged and arrested and kept in fetters for months in the jail without trial or bail.[194] The law of the land, the government and the judiciary worked against the Nadars who refused to yield to the practices which negated the freedom and dignity of low caste people in Travancore. Though they were imprisoned for many months, the caste elites could not paralyse the liberative passion of the Nadars.

British Intervention

In order to suppress the revolt, the Dewan sent Shungoony Menon, the Deputy Peishcar, to restore peace in the region. The situation became uncontrollable and the Dewan himself had to visit those places. Later the Nair Brigade under Captain Daly proceeded south and tried to apprehend the leaders of the rioting groups. It took long to reinstate peace among the people. Meanwhile, the missionaries had submitted a petition to the Raja about violence against Christians.[195]

During the dreadful time of the revolt, the Nadars planned to put up collective resistance to the violence. They raised money and men to counter the Nairs. They even sought the help of Tinnevelly Nadars to prevent the atrocities of Shudra oppressors.[196] It was reported in the letter of Resident to the Dewan and the Chief Secretary to the Madras Government.[197] It attracted the urgent intervention of authorities to check the on-going conflict.

In the meantime, there were also attempts to break the movement, apart from the intervention of the Nair brigade. The Dewan reported to the Resident that the missionaries should be kept away from the Nadars. He discouraged the move to consider the missionaries as intermediaries between the government and the Nadars. He also planned to use some influential Nadars to create dissension and break the movement.[198] The Resident too was not fully sympathetic to the missionaries and the Nadars even though he was suspicious of the actions and reports of the Dewan and the native government.[199]

The appeal of missionaries to British authorities led to the intervention of the Madras Government. The position of the Governor in the Council of the Madras Government was expressed as follows.

> The Resident will be careful to give no countenance to the idea that the British government of which he is the representative, recognizes any exclusive distinctions, or the right of any set of men to prevent others from following in all matters of social or domestic life, such course as they may see fit – provided it be not repugnant to public decency and morals. It will be his duty to impress these views on His Highness the Raja, and to point out to him that such prohibitions and those contained in the Circular Order of May 1814 or in the Proclamation of the 3rd February 1829, are unsuited to the present age and unworthy of an enlightened Prince and that he is not to look for the support of British Government in any attempts to maintain them, as respects any class of his subjects.[200]

This order was actually an endorsement of the new mode of dress for the Nadar women and the humiliation to the Travancore government whose caste prejudice and inaction led to a violent revolt against the defenceless group of people. It also made the Resident accountable.

The intervention of the Madras Government prompted the Travancore government to consider modifications in the Proclamation of 1829.[201] The pressure mounted on the Resident to convince the Raja of the views of the British Government and settle the issue without delay.[202]

Sir Charles Trevelyan, the Governor of Madras, again wrote to the Resident General Cullen,

> I have seldom met with a case in which not only truth and justice but every feeling of our common humanity are so entirely on one side. The whole civilized world would cry shame upon us if we did not make firm stand on such occasion. If anything could make this line of conduct more incumbent on us it would be the extraordinary fact that persecution of a singularly personal and indelicate kind is attempted to be justified by a Royal Proclamation the special object of which was to assure to Her Majesty's Indian subjects the liberty of thought and action, so long as they did not interfere with the just rights of others. I should fail in respect to Her Majesty if I attempted to describe the feelings with which she must regard the use made against Her own sex of the promises of protection so graciously accorded by her.[203]

The high castes criticized the missionaries responsible for the British Government's views.[204] But they could not see the ground realties perpetuated by their fellow brothers against the low castes.

The Resident reported to the Governor that His Highness, the Raja of Travancore, had no objection to modify the Proclamation of 1829.[205] After considerable discussion the Dewan communicated the position of the Raja. He wrote to the Resident that,

> His Highness certainly feels that the provisions of the Proclamation of 1004 M.E. (1829 AD), on the subject of the dress of the inferior castes require to be greatly modified. His Highness now proposes to abolish all rules prohibiting the covering of the upper parts of the persons of Shanar women, and to grant them perfect liberty to meet the requirements of decency any way they may deem proper, with simple restriction that they do not imitate the same mode of dress that appertains to the higher castes. . . . His Highness would not have made even this simple reservation, were it not for the fear that the sudden and total abolition of all distinctions of dress, which have from time immemorial distinguished one caste from another may produce most undesirable impressions on the minds of the larger portion of his subjects, and cause their serious discontent; still I am to observe that, by the present concession, the demands of decency have been fully answered without needlessly offending the feelings peculiar to the other castes. It is of course, needless to remind you of those many circumstances which would make the introduction of decisive reforms,

especially in matters of caste and religion, much more difficult in Travancore than in Her Majesty's territories. While, therefore, the progress of education among the people in general may be expected to have the way for much greater changes, His Highness hopes that the arrangement now proposed, the only one which seems calculated to answer the object in view; without the probability of disturbing the peace of the country, would meet with your approval and that of the Madras Government. A corresponding proclamation will be issued by His Highness on hearing from you.[206]

The views of the Raja were a total surrender to the caste prejudices even though he was willing to accept the modification of the previous proclamation which totally prohibited the Nadar women to cover themselves modestly.

Sir C.E. Trevelyan accepted the proposal of the Raja and hoped to see the effective implementation of the new proclamation.[207] Accordingly a new proclamation was issued on 26 July 1859. Thus ended four decades of a fight against a modest dress for women with considerable success.

The Proclamation of 1859

Ultimately, in 1859, the British government forced the Raja of Travancore to declare the old dress-code obsolete, having earlier voiced its abhorence for it. As promised to the British government, Shri Padmanabhadasa Uthradam Thirunal Marthanda Varma, the Raja of Travancore issued the proclamation on 26 July 1859. It was proclaimed that,

In as much as we have been informed of the grievance occasioned by the Proclamation of the 23rd of Magaram, 1004, on the subject of the upper cloth of Shanar women, and it is our will and pleasure to treat all people, as far as we can, in such a manner as none shall feel aggrieved; we hereby proclaim that there is no objection to Shanar women either putting on a jacket, like the Christian Shanar women, or to Shanar women of all creeds dressing in coarse cloth, and tying themselves round with it as the Mukkavattigal (low-caste fisher women) do or to their covering their bosoms in any manner whatever; but not like women of high castes. [208]

The proclamation stipulated that Nadar women should not emulate the attire of high-caste women. High-caste women had upper cloths made of fine or coloured cloth. It was implied that the Nadar women for their part could wear upper cloths made of coarse or simple cloth.

Nadar women appeared in markets and public places with jackets and upper cloths.[209] This demonstrates their courage. The Upper Cloth Revolt was the first incident, in which a community fought against their social disabilities, particularly of their women, imposed by the upper castes, in Travancore.

The Upper Cloth Revolt: A Subaltern Movement

The Upper Cloth Revolt, the protest movement of a community, was fought against the social restriction of casteist and feudalistic systems in Travancore. It was an 'inevitable reaction'[210] of the Nadars, the subalterns against the ruling class and the high castes. It was also a social reform movement because it had an 'element of deliberate action on the part of a few in the society'[211] against the callous customs and practices in society. Moreover, it was a conscious attempt of Nadars to 'mitigate their deprivation and secure justice'.[212]

According to T.K. Oommen, 'Who was involved and what was involved and ideology define the movement and perspective.'[213] In the Upper Cloth Revolt, the Nadars were involved to assert the right of Nadar women to cover their bosoms with the upper cloth. It was the Nadar women who took the bold initiative of wearing upper cloth in the caste-ridden patriarchal society. The issue involved in the Upper Cloth Revolt was a customary restriction on the dress code of low-caste women. The Nadar men and women fought for the self-respect of the community and its women. In fact, it was a revolt of a community who had been subalternized by the ruling class and caste people in various ways. The people who initiated the movement were of 'inferior status', the mark of subalternity in the caste society. The Nadar women who were subalternized in the name of caste and gender were the main agents of this movement. Thus, the Upper Cloth Revolt was a subaltern movement. It was fought against the factors that contributed to the subaltenization of low caste people. It was a voice against the subjugation and the objectification of the people, particularly the women of low caste origin. In the Upper Cloth Revolt, the Nadars revolted against the domination built on the denial and silence of the subalterns. It had an ideology in the form of Christian faith which promoted human dignity, justice and equality. Therefore, it is potentially resourceful to develop a subaltern theological expression.

Conclusion

The Upper Cloth Revolt was a protest of Nadars against a humiliating custom in Travancore. It was a revolt against the rules laid by a dominant class who decided a dress code for the low-caste women. This movement not only gave new direction in the social and religious life of Nadars but also created a platform for initiating other social movements against social inequalities in Travancore. The Nadars, particularly the Christians among them, had gone through a painful experience. They lost their homes, schools, and worship places in the caste violence. Though they suffered for their attempts at social advancement and of reclaiming the rights of their women, they challenged the caste elites and ruling class in a society where low castes were subjected to numerous life-negating practices and customs. The Nadars as a subaltern community expressed their anger against the oppressive practices by being defiant in various ways. Their subalternity became subversive in the Upper Cloth Revolt. The perpetual subalternity was questioned in this movement and the subalterns emerged as the leaders of change. In the Upper Cloth Revolt the subalterns emerged from the periphery to the centre. They came up and asserted their right to have a dignified life. Their assertion itself was a revolutionary act in the caste society. It was initiated at the risk of their life. The social hegemony of dominant castes was challenged in the bold action of Nadar women.

Christianity gave the Nadars protection, encouragement and space to live a life of dignity and freedom. Though they were subalterns, they identified the oppressive practices protected by the old religion. While the old religion kept them subjugated, the new faith gave them energy to challenge the dehumanizing institution. It gave them resources to re-orient their lives. The Upper Cloth Revolt was the result of the internalization of new religious resources. Therefore, it can be considered as a faith movement. The Nadars, particularly the

Christians, were encouraged by the new faith to fight against the evil forces throughout the movement. The Biblical faith taught them the fact that every human being is created in the image and likeness of God with equal rights. The missionaries as their religious and social leaders helped them to understand their faith contextually.

In the Upper Cloth Revolt, women were not only the subject of narration but also the agent of a historical event. It was Nadar women who wrote the narrative of the Upper Cloth Revolt. They were 'writing' a history of a community. It was not a political history of an individual but a history of an oppressed community, especially its women. Though they were supported by their men, the Nadar women were courageous to take bold steps to break the chain of oppression by the upper caste men. They were aware of the risk they had taken in the society which functioned within the framework of religiously sanctioned and socially recognized caste system and patriarchy. Even though they were physically assaulted and sexually molested, they were persistent in their struggle. Their painful journey of struggle created a new history of women's liberation. In the Upper Cloth Revolt, women mediated the process of liberation. Perhaps it is the first women's rights struggle for justice by women in India.

The Upper Cloth Revolt is a model historical episode in the journey of subaltern women's liberation. It was a joint venture of Nadar men and women. When Nadar women raised their voice for a dignified life, Nadar men supported them. They were not discouraged by their men to avoid conflicts and disturb the existing social equations. It is quite common among the subalterns because of their fear of survival. Here, the dissenting voice for change was made possible by the equal participation of both subaltern men and women. The Upper Cloth Revolt has also opened up a new horizon for theological engagement which is not yet explored-interpreting historical event theologically. The contextual liberation theologies give guidelines for the attempt of theologizing subaltern historical events like the Upper Cloth Revolt. A survey of libration theologies is given in the next chapter.

NOTES

1. Catherine Soanes and Angus Stevenson, eds., *Concise Oxford English Dictionary, Indian Edition* (New Delhi: Oxford University Press, 2007), p. 1434.
2. Antonio Gramsci, *Selections from the Prison Notebooks of Antonio Gramsci*, edited and translated by Quintin Hoare and Geoffrey Nowell Smith (Chennai: Orient Longman, 1996), xvii ff.
3. *Subaltern Studies* is a collection of edited works which attempted to understand South Asian history and society from a subaltern perspective. A group of scholars such as Ranajit Guha, Partha Chatterjee, Gyanendra Pandey, David Arnold, David Hardiman, Dipesh Chakrabarthy, Gautam Bhadra, etc., edited the multi-volume work.
4. James Massey, 'Subaltern People and the Rise of their Movements,' in *A Vision of Mission in the New Millennium*, ed. Thomas Malipurathu and L. Stanislaus (Mumbai: St. Paul's, 2001), 24-5; James Massey, *Caste-Class Victims and Their Assertion for Justice* (New Delhi: Centre for Dalit/Subaltern Studies, 2013), 12-13.
5. Massey, ibid., idem, *Caste-Class Victims and Their Assertion for Justice* (New Delhi: Centre for Dalit/Subaltern Studies, 2013); Sathianathan Clarke, *Dalits and Christianity: Subaltern Religion and Liberation Theology in India* (New Delhi: Oxford University Press, 1998); V.V. Thomas, *Dalit Pentecostalism* (Bangalore: ATC, 2008).
6. Antonio Gramsci, *Selections from the Prison Notebooks of Antonio Gramsci*, x.
7. Ibid., xiv.
8. Ibid.
9. Ranajit Guha, 'Preface,' in *Subaltern Studies*, vol. I, ed. Ranajit Guha (New Delhi: Oxford University Press, 1994), vii.
10. Ranajit Guha, 'On Some Aspects of the Historiography of Colonial India,' in *Subaltern Studies,* vol. I, ed. Ranajit Guha (New Delhi: Oxford University Press, 1994), p. 8.
11. Sathianathan Clarke, *Dalits and Christianity: Subaltern Religion and Liberation Theology in India*, p. 7.
12. Quoted from Partha Chatterjee, 'Caste and Subaltern Consciousness,' in *Subaltern Studies*, vol. VI, ed. Ranajit Guha (New Delhi: Oxford University Press, 1989), p. 169 in Clarke, *Dalits and Christianity: Subaltern Religion and Liberation Theology in India* (New Delhi: Oxford University Press, 2002), p. 7.

13. Clarke, *Dalits and Christianity: Subaltern Religion and Liberation Theology in India,* p. 7.
14. Ibid., pp. 4-7, cited by Goldie Osuri, *Religious Freedom in India* (London & New York: Routledge, 2013), pp. 11-12.
15. Here, Dalit-Bahujan is understood as a social category than a political entity, as interpreted by some political parties for vote-bank strategy.
16. James Massey, 'Subaltern People and the Rise of their Movements', pp. 24-5; Massey, *Caste-Class Victims and their Assertion for Justice,* pp. 12-13.
17. Massey, 'Subaltern People and the Rise of their Movements', pp. 25-6.
18. Quoted from Sathianathan Clarke, *Dalits and Christianity: Subaltern Religion and Liberation Theology in India,* in James Massey, 'Subaltern People and the Rise of their Movements', p. 26.
19. Massey, *Caste-Class Victims and their Assertion for Justice,* pp. 14-15.
20. B.P. Mandal, *Reservations for Backward Classes, Mandal Commission Report of the Backward Classes Commission, 1980* (along with Introduction) (New Delhi: Akalank Publications, 1990), p. 61.
21. Massey, *Caste-Class Victims and their Assertion for Justice,* p. 15; *Reservations for Backward Class Mandal Commission Report of the Backward Commission,* p. 19.
22. Partha Chatterjee, 'Caste and Subaltern Consciousness', pp. 174-5.
23. Quoted from Gail Omvedt, 'An Introductory Essay', in Gail Omvedt, ed., *Land, Caste and Politics in Indian States* (Delhi, 1982), pp. 9-50; in Partha Chatterjee, 'Caste and Subaltern Consciousness', p. 176.
24. Guy Poitevin, *The Voice and the Will, Subaltern Agency: Forms and Motives* (New Delhi: Manohar, 2002), p. 181. They also act as complementary to each other. One system will strengthen the other and vice-versa
25. Uma Chakravarti, *Gendering Caste: Through a Feminist Lens* (Calcutta: STREE, 2006), p. 175.
26. Ibid., pp. xii-xiii (Foreword) and p. 144.
27. Sharmila Rege, 'Caste and Gender: The Violence Against Women in India', in *Dalit Women in India: Issues and Perspectives,* ed. P.G. Jogdand (New Delhi: Gyan Publishing House & Pune: University of Pune, 1995), p. 19.
28. Edgar Thurston, *Castes and Tribes of South India,* vol. V, p. 134 and vol. VI, p. 368 (Madras: Government Press, 1909).
29. Robert L. Hardgrave Jr., *The Nadars of Tamilnadu* (Berkeley and Los Angeles: University of California Press, 1969), pp. 19-20. The

myth goes like this. 'Seven celestial virgins, while bathing in a stream, caught the eyes of the God Indra. He hid their saris, which were on the bank, and when the virgins emerged from the water, he caught and consorted with each. The seven virgins each gave birth to a male child, but on returning to their celestial world, they abandoned their sons. The Goddess Bhadrakali took pity upon them and brought them up as her own sons. One day, the River Vaigai, near Madurai, breached and as the city was threatened with a flood, the Pandya king ordered all men to carry earth in baskets to rebuild the bund. The seven sons refused to obey the king. "We are meant to carry crowns upon our heads, not baskets", the young men cried. The king was furious and ordered that one of the boys be buried in sand up to his neck and his head be trampled by an elephant. The order was carried out, but the crushed head continued to cry out, "I will not touch the basket". The furious king ordered that the second brother too be treated likewise. This time the head cried, "Shall this head prove false to the others?" The king was greatly frightened by these strange happenings and freed the remaining five sons from whom the Nadar race was sprung.'

30. H.R. Pate, *Madras District Gazetteers, Tinnevelly*, vol. I (Madras: Government Press, 1917), cited by K.S. Singh, ed., *People of India, Tamilnadu*, vol. XL Part Two (Madras: Anthropological Survey of India, 1997), p. 1052.
31. Hardgrave Jr., *The Nadars of Tamilnadu*, p. 20.
32. Robert A. Caldwell, *The Tinnevelly Shanars*, First Edition (Madras, 1849), 4-5, cited by Robert L. Hardgrave Jr., *The Nadars of Tamilnadu*, 20-1. It is viewed that first migration happened during the time of Imperial Cholas (K.S. Ramaswami Sastri, ed., *The Tamils,* vol. III, New Delhi: Cosmo Publications, 2002), p. 44. It is also observed that Shanars might have migrated to South Travancore 'either from or through the Tinnevelly district (T.K. Velu Pillai, *The Travancore State Manual*, vol. I, Trivandrum: Government of Travancore, 1940), p. 856.
33. V. Nagam Aiya, *The Travancore State Manual,* vol. II, Trivandrum: Government Press, 1906, p. 392. 'The Shanars are called Kali Puthirar (the sons of Kali or Bhadrakali, the great Bellona of India), and this goddess is considered as their tutelary deity. Enathi-Natha-Nayanar, one of the sixty-three disciples of Siva, is described as having belonged to the Shandrar caste in the Tamil work, *Periyapuranam* and as Sakshi-kulotbhava in the Sanskrit work. One strong argument in favor of this conjecture is that in the southern part of Tinnevelly the highest class of Shanars called Nadars are the acknowledged proprietors of the soil

and even when a Nadar has sold a piece of land, he retains the right to a sort of quit-rent. Indeed, this system is very like that of our lords of Manor' (*The South Indian Sketches* by Miss S. Tucker) (footnote in the same page).

34. V. Nagam Aiya, *The Travancore State Manual,* vol. II, p. 393. The expression 'Nadalvar' occurs in some ancient stone inscriptions of Travancore (footnote in the same page); T.K. Velu Pillai, *The Travancore State Manual,* vol. I, 856.
35. M. Immanuel, *The Dravidian Languages: The Nadars Through the Ages* (Nagarcoil: HRPT, 2002).
36. K.S. Singh, ed., *People of India, Tamilnadu,* vol. XL Part Two, p. 1053; Edgar Thurston, *Castes and Tribes of South India,* vol. VI, pp. 365-6; K.S. Ramaswami Sastri, ed., *The Tamils,* vol. III, p. 44.
37. K.S. Singh, ed., *People of India, Tamilnadu,* vol. XL, Part Two, p. 1053; K.S. Ramaswami Sastri, ed., *The Tamils,* vol. III, p. 44.
38. Hardgrave Jr., *The Nadars of Tamilnadu,* p. 21.
39. Quoted from Robert A. Caldwell, *The Tinnevelly Shanars* (London, 1850), p. 5 in J.W. Gladstone, *Protestant Christianity and People's Movements in Kerala* (Trivandrum: Seminary Publications, 1984), p. 28.
40. Quoted from Raja Rama Rao, *Ramnad Manual* (Madras, 1889), p. 36 in Hardgrave Jr., *The Nadars of Tamilnadu,* p. 21 (fn.).
41. Edgar Thurston, *Castes and Tribes of Southern India,* vol. VI, pp. 376-77; Robert L. Hardgrave Jr., *The Nadars of Tamilnadu,* pp. 32-5; Dennis Templeman, *The Northern Nadars of Tamilnadu: An Indian Caste in the Process of Change* (New Delhi: Oxford University Press, 1996), pp. 26-7 and K.S. Singh, ed., *People of India, Tamilnadu,* vol. XL, Part Two, p. 1053.
42. V. Nagam Aiya, *The Travancore State Manual,* vol. II, p. 393; Joy Gnanadason, *A Forgotten History* (Madras: GLTC, 1994), p. 24.
43. V. Nagam Aiya, *The Travancore State Manual,* vol. II, pp. 393-4.
44. T.K. Velu Pillai, *The Travancore State Manual,* vol. II (Trivandrum: Government of Travancore, 1940), p. 343.
45. V. Nagam Aiya, *The Travancore State Manual,* vol. II, pp. 394-5 and 398; T.K. Velu Pillai, *The Travancore State Manual,* vol. I, p. 856.
46. There is no substantial evidence to prove that five-fold sub-castes existed or strictly observed among Nadars in south Travancore as existed in Tamil Nadu. The possible divisions were the palmyra climbers/toddy tappers and those involved in trade or non-toddy tapping

jobs. It does not mean that those involved in non-toddy tapping jobs were not subject to social disabilities.

47. G.S. Ghurye, *Caste and Race in India* (London: Routledge and Kegan Paul, 1932; Reprint of Fifth Edition, Bombay: Popular Prakashan, 1994), pp. 9-10; Samuel Mateer, *Land of Charity* (London: John Snow & Co., 1871), pp. 28-31.
48. *Madras Census* 1891, 299, cited by G.S. Ghurye, *Caste and Race in India*, 14; Mateer, *Land of Charity*, p. 27; Mateer, *Native Life in Travancore* (London: W.H. Allen & Co, 1883), pp. 91 & 333; R.N. Yesudas, *A People's Revolt in Travancore* (Trivandrum: Kerala Historical Society, 1975), pp. 26-7; Kochu Krishnan Nadar, *Nadar Charitram* (Travancore: S.B. Press, 1956), pp. 9ff.
49. R.N. Yesudas, *The History of the London Missionary Society in Travancore* 1806-1908 (Trivandrum: Kerala Historical Society, 1980), pp. 16-18; Mateer, *Native Life in Travancore*, pp. 292-4; Mateer, *Land of Charity*, p. 41; C.M. Agur, *Church History of Travancore* (Madras: S.P.S. Press, 1903; New Delhi: Asian Educational Service, 1990), p. 74 & xlviii; *Selected Proclamations by the Sovereign from 1811-1939 AD* (Trivandrum: Government Press, 1937), Archives Directorate, Trivandrum, pp. 5-7; Robin Jeffrey, *The Decline of Nair Dominance* (New Delhi: Manohar, 1994), p. 52; D. Peter and Ivy Peter, *Liberation of the Oppressed A Continuous Struggle* (Nagarcoil: Kanyakumari Institute of Development Studies, 2009), pp. 31-3.
50. Mateer, *Land of Charity*, pp. 41 & 60; I.H. Hacker, *A Hundred Years in Travancore (1806-1906)* (London: H.R. Allenson, 1908), p. 14; J. Bhattacharya, *Hindu Castes and Sects* (1896), 259, cited by G.S. Ghurye, *Caste and Race in India*, pp. 12-13; D. Peter and Ivy Peter, *Liberation of the Oppressed: A Continuous Struggle*, p. 33. *Selected Proclamations by the Sovereign*, pp. 82-3; Mateer, *Native Life in Travancore*, pp. 206 & 340-1.
51. Hacker, *A Hundred Years in Travancore (1806-1906)*, pp. 84-7.
52. Interview with J.W. Gladstone, Former Moderator of Church of South India and Professor of Church History and Former Principal of Kerala United Theological Seminary, Trivandrum, 15 April 2013.
53. Jotirao Govindrao Phule talks about Shudras and Ati-Shudras. Today, they represent the Other Backward Classes (OBC) and the Dalits/Scheduled Castes (SC) respectively. For him, the ancestors of both were 'blood brothers'. They came from same family stock. When they fought against the injustices of Brahmins, they were divided into dif-

ferent categories by using the '*pernicious fiction of the caste system*'. Cf. Jotirao Govindrao Phule, *Slavery,* translated by P.G. Patil (Bombay: Education Department, Government of Maharashtra, 1991), xlix-li. B.R. Ambedkar argues that there was a time the forebears of 'Shudras' (OBCs) and the 'Untouchables' (SC) were not the 'Shudras' and the 'Untouchables' as defined today. They were made 'Shudras' and 'Untouchables' by the Brahmins. Cf. *Dr. Babasaheb Ambedkar: Writings and Speeches*, vol. 7, Compiled by Vasant Moon (Bombay: Education Department, Government of Maharashtra, 1990), pp. 9-16 & 274-80.

54. Leonard Fernando and G. Gispert-Sauch, *Christianity in India* (New Delhi: Penguin/Viking, 2004), p. 242.
55. *Dr. Babasaheb Ambedkar Writings and Speeches*, vol. 1, compiled by Vasant Moon (Bombay: Education Department, Government of Maharashtra, 1989), p. 67.
56. Letter from Rev. E. Lewis to the Resident, 21 January 1859, Bundle no. 29, Cover File no. 2115 of 1858, *Shanar Disturbances in South Travancore*, Archives Directorate, Trivandrum; Samuel Mateer, *Land of Charity*, pp. 41, 61-2 & 305. Though they appeared with jackets, Nadar Hindu women were given the privilege of wearing jacket legally only in 1859.
57. C.M. Agur, *Church History of Travancore*, xlvii, l, liii & lvii; Samuel Mateer, *Land of Charity*, pp. 58 & 61-2; *Travancore Census Report 1875*, p. 228, cited by Robin Jeffrey, *The Decline of Nair Dominance*, 53; Krishna Kurup, *Kerala Charitram Parasuramaniloode* (Kottayam, 1962), p. 200 ff., cited by J.W. Gladstone, *Protestant Christianity and People's Movements in Kerala*, p. 82; K.P. Padmanabha Menon, *History of Kerala*, vol. III (Ernakulam, 1936), p. 192 and Tiruvangad C. Krishna Kurup, *Kerala Charitram Parasuramaniloode* (Kottayam, 1962), pp. 201-2, cited by R.N. Yesudas, *A People's Revolt in Travancore*, pp. 18-19.
58. Eliza F. Kent, *Converting Women* (New York: Oxford University Press, 2004), p. 201.
59. Ibid., p. 203.
60. Ibid., p. 205.
61. R.N. Yesudas, *The History of the London Missionary Society in Travancore 1806-1908*, p. 26.
62. Mateer, *Land of Charity*, p. 260; Joy Gnanadason, *A Forgotten History*, pp. 40-4, 50-3; C.M. Agur, *Church History of Travancore*, pp. 35 & 92-3. It is also argued that the SPCK Mission, based in Tinnevelly,

introduced Protestant faith in Travancore. There were Christians under SPCK in South Travancore before the arrival of L.M.S. Mission (John A. Jacob, *A History of the London Missionary Society in South Travancore 1806-1959*, Nagercoil: Diocesan Press, 1990, pp. 16-18); 'Catholic faith was introduced in South Travancore in 16th century' (C.M. Agur, *Church History of Travancore*, 22f; Gnanadason, *A Forgotten History*, pp. 46-7).

63. Mateer, *Land of Charity*, pp. 264-5.
64. Joseph Mullens, *Missions in South India* (London: W.H. Dalton, 1854), p. 104; Mateer, *Land of Charity*, pp. 269-71; *London Missionary Society Report*, May 1819, UTCA, pp. 54 & 123-5; *London Missionary Society Report*, May 1820, UTCA, pp. 61-3; *London Missionary Society Report*, May 1821, UTCA, p. 63.
65. Agur, *Church History of Travancore*, p. 789.
66. *London Missionary Society Report*, May 1825, UTCA, p. 96.
67. Agur, *Church History of Travancore*, p. 808.
68. *Report of the Neyyoor Station*, 24 October 1833, CWMA, cited by J.W. Gladstone, *Protestant Christianity and People's Movements in Kerala*, p. 94.
69. *Annual Report of the LMS*, 1840, p. 65, cited by J.W. Gladstone, *Protestant Christianity and People's Movements in Kerala*, p. 94.
70. *Report of the Neyoor Station*, 24 October 1833, TR-IL, Box 2, F2, J B, CWMA, 6, cited by J.W. Gladstone, *Protestant Christianity and People's Movements in Kerala*, p. 94.
71. *Report of the Neyyoor Station*, 24 October 1833, TR-IL, Box 2, F2, J B, CWMA, 6 & Cox to Ellis, Letter, MS, TR-IL, dated Trivandrum, 11 September 1840, Box 3, F 1, J A, CWMA, cited by Gladstone, *Protestant Christianity*, p. 94.
72. Mullens, *Missions in South India*, p. 106.
73. Ibid., pp. 116-17.
74. Agur, *Church History of Travancore*, p. 940, I.H. Hacker, *A Hundred Years in Travancore (1806-1906)*, p. 52.
75. John A. Jacob, *A History of the London Missionary Society in South Travancore 1806-1959*, p. 69.
76. *London Missionary Society Report*, May 1825, UTCA, p. 96.
77. Agur, *Church History of Travancore*, p. 808.
78. Mullens, *Missions in South India*, p. 106.
79. Ibid.
80. John Abbs, *Twenty-Two Years' Missionary Experience in Travancore* (London: John Snow & Co, 1870), p. 209.

81. Gladstone, *Protestant Christianity and People's Movements in Kerala*, p. 95; Mullens, *Missions in South India*, p. 111.
82. Samuel Mateer, *Land of Charity*, p. 223.
83. Hacker, *A Hundred Years in Travancore (1806-1906)*, pp. 35 & 51-2.
84. Mullens, *Missions in South India*, p. 113.
85. Agur, *Church History of Travancore*, pp. 787, 808-9 & 982; John Abbs, *Twenty-Two Years' Missionary Experience in Travancore*, pp. 22 & 96.
86. Agur, *Church History of Travancore*, p. 786; *London Missionary Society Report*, May 1819, UTCA, pp. 124-5.
87. Mullens, *Missions in South India*, p. 116.
88. Agur, *Church History of Travancore*, pp. 808-9; Mateer, *Land of Charity*, pp. 274 & 328.
89. Mullens, *Missions in South India*, pp. 115-16.
90. C. Mault, *Report of the Nagercoil Station*, MS, dated Nagercoil, 10 June 1828, TR-IL, Box 1 F3, CWMA, cited by Gladstone, *Protestant Christianity and People's Movements in Kerala*, p. 93.
91. Gladstone, ibid., p. 97.
92. C.F. Andrews, *Handbook of English Church Expansion North India* (London: A.R. Mowbray & Co., 1908), pp. 38-9.
93. John W. Grant, *God's People in India* (Madras: CLS, 1960), p. 8.
94. Yesudas, *A People's Revolt in Travancore*, pp. 2, 4.
95. The Petition of Missionaries of the LMS to the King of Travancore, 7 February 1859, in *Copies of the Official Papers Sent from India Touching the Recent Disturbances in Travancore*, Box no. 15 (MF), UTCA, 39-41; Samuel Mateer, *Land of Charity*, p. 298.
96. Letter from Rev. E. Lewis to the Resident, 21 January 1859, Bundle no. 29, Cover File no. 2115 of 1858, *Shanar Disturbances in South Travancore*, Archives Directorate, Trivandrum.
97. Letter from Rev. F. Baylis to the Resident, 17 January 1859, Bundle no. 29, Cover File no. 2115 of 1858, *Shanar Disturbances in South Travancore*, Archives Directorate, Trivandrum.
98. Yesudas, *A People's Revolt in Travancore*, p. 3.
99. Abbs, *Twenty-Two Years' Missionary Experience in Travancore*, pp. 55-6.
100. V. Nagam Aiya, *The Travancore State Manual*, vol. I (Trivandrum: Government Press, 1906), p. 528.
101. P. Shungoonny Menon, *A History of Travancore from Earliest Times* (Madras: Higginbotham and Co., 1878), p. 507.

102. *LMS Report of the James Town Mission District for the Year 1859*, UTCA, 3.
103. Abbs, *Twenty-Two Years' Missionary Experience in Travancore*, pp. 161 & 224-5.
104. Interview with J.W. Gladstone.
105. Menon, *A History of Travancore from Earliest Times*, p. 507.
106. Interview with R.N. Yesudas.
107. Yesudas, *A People's Revolt in Travancore*, p. 2.
108. R.N. Yesudas, *British Policy in Travancore 1805-1859* (Trivandrum: Kerala Historical Society, 1977), pp. 24 & 49.
109. Jeffrey, *The Decline of Nair Dominance*, p. 51.
110. Gladstone, *Protestant Christianity and People's Movements in Kerala*, p. 96.
111. Menon, *A Survey of Kerala History* (Madras: S. Viswanathan, 1998), p. 396; Letter from the Acting Dewan to the Resident, 8 March 1858, Bundle no. 29, Cover File no. 2115 of 1858, *Shanar Disturbances in South Travancore*, Archives Directorate, Trivandrum; Letter from the Deputy Peishkar Shungoony Menon in-charge of the Southern Division to the Dewan of Travancore, 3 January 1859, Bundle no. 29, Cover File no. 2115 of 1858, *Shanar Disturbances in South Travancore*, Archives Directorate, Trivandrum.
112. Interview with R.N. Yesudas.
113. Menon, *A History of Travancore from Earliest Times*, pp. 504-5.
114. Interview with J.W. Gladstone.
115. V. Nagam Aiya, *The Travancore State Manual*, vol. I, p. 528.
116. Hacker, *A Hundred Years in Travancore (1806-1906)*, pp. 84-7; Gnanadason, *A Forgotten History*, pp. 69-71.
117. Samuel Mateer, *Land of Charity*, 278; I.H. Hacker, *A Hundred Years in Travancore (1806-1906)*, p. 36; C.M. Agur, *Church History of Travancore*, p. 779.
118. Interview with J.W. Gladstone.
119. Jacob, *A History of the London Missionary Society in South Travancore 1806-1959*, p. 120; Minute by the President, 28 February 1859 in *Copies of the Official Papers Sent from India Touching the Recent Disturbances in Travancore*, Box no. 15 (MF), UTCA, pp. 10-11.
120. A. Sreedhara Menon, *A Survey of Kerala History*, pp. 400-1; Samuel Mateer, *Land of Charity*, p. 223; Yesudas, *A People's Revolt in Travancore*, p. 136.
121. The Petition of Missionaries of the LMS to the King of Travancore, 7 February 1859, in *Copies of the Official Papers Sent from India Touch-*

ing the Recent Disturbances in Travancore, Box no. 15 (MF), UTCA, p. 40; Jacob, *A History of the London Missionary Society in South Travancore 1806-1959*, p. 120; Samuel Mateer, *Land of Charity*, p. 297.

122. V.D. Mahajan, *India Since 1526* (New Delhi: S. Chand and Company, p. 270 (Part B).

123. The Petition of Missionaries of the LMS to the King of Travancore, 7 February 1859, in *Copies of the Official Papers Sent from India Touching the Recent Disturbances in Travancore*, Box no. 15 (MF), UTCA, p. 39; Letter from Rev. F. Baylis to the Resident, 1 January 1859, Bundle no. 29, Cover File no. 2115 of 1858, *Shanar Disturbances in South Travancore*, Archives Directorate, Trivandrum; John Cox, *LMS Report of the Trivandrum and Quilon Mission Districts for the Year 1858,* UTCA, p. 8; Agur, *Church History of Travancore*, p. 932.

124. Letter from the Deputy Peishkar Shungoony Menon in-charge of the Southern Division to the Dewan of Travancore, 3 January 1859, Bundle no. 29, Cover File no. 2115 of 1858, *Shanar Disturbances in South Travancore*, Archives Directorate, Trivandrum; V. Nagam Aiya, *The Travancore State Manual*, vol. 1, p. 528.

125. *Translation of an Order from Colonel J. Munro Resident Dewan to the Sarvadicariacars of Trevandrum and Neiyattangurray Taluq dated Quilon the 19th of Dhanoo 987 (1812)* 'I have heard that the women of Elaver and such like castes who have embraced Christianity have been prevented from covering their bosoms; but as I have granted my permission to the women converted to Christianity to cover their bosoms as obtains among Christians in other countries, you will take steps that there be no obstacles put to the women converted to Christianity wearing clothes over their breasts.' Agur, *Church History of Travancore*, pp. l & 935; Menon, *A Survey of Kerala History*, p. 396.

126. *Translation of circular order from Colonel Munro, Dewan, dated at Baleamporam the 7th Yedavam in the year 989 (1814) regulating the dress of Christian women.* 'It having been complained by the Pidagacars, that the women of Elavers, Shanars and others of this description in this country wear cloths over their bosoms, a practice which never has been in use formerly and that in consequence of the said dress having been assumed, the difference between the one and other caste cannot be known, and everything is allowed to be polluted, you are hereby therefore directed to take measures that no women of Ealavers, Shanars and others of such description are ever allowed to wear clothes on their bosoms as the Nayar women, and that they (the former) are not prevented at the same time from wearing jackets called coopayam

like the women of Christians, Shonagas and Moplas.' Agur, *Church History of Travancore*, liii.

127. Agur, *Church History of Travancore*, p. xlvii.
128. Ibid., p. 779; A. Sreedhara Menon, *A Survey of Kerala History*, p. 396.
129. Agur, *Church History of Travancore*, pp. 780-1 & xlviii.
130. Gladstone, *Protestant Christianity and People's Movements in Kerala*, p. 84.
131. Agur, *Church History of Travancore*, p. 782; R.N. Yesudas, *The History of the London Missionary Society in Travancore 1806-1908*, p. 176.
132. Menon, *A History of Travancore from Earliest Times*, p. 504.
133. Agur, *Church History of Travancore*, p. 826.
134. Mateer, *Land of Charity*, pp. 278-9.
135. Agur, *Church History of Travancore*, p. 829.
136. Ibid., p. 830; Samuel Mateer, *Land of Charity*, p. 279.
137. Agur, *Church History of Travancore*, pp. 832-3.
138. Ibid., pp. 834-5.
139. Ibid., 837-40.
140. Mateer, *Land of Charity*, p. 279; Agur, *Church History of Travancore*, p. 827.
141. Agur, *Church History of Travancore*, pp. 829-30.
142. Mateer, *Land of Charity*, p. 280.
143. Agur, *Church History of Travancore*, p. 835.
144. Ibid., pp. 834-5.
145. G. Issac Arul Dhas, *Kumari Mannil Kristhavam (Tamil) Christianity in Kanyakumari* (Nagarcoil: n.p., 2010), p. 138.
146. Agur, *Church History of Travancore*, pp. 841-51.
147. *Neetu*, vol. 20, pt. 1 (Central Archives, Thiruvananthapuram), pp. 48-50; *Selected Proclamations by the Sovereign*, pp. 224-7; Agur, *Church History of Travancore*, lvii.
148. Menon, *A History of Travancore from Earliest Times*, p. 507.
149. Ibid., p. 504; Agur, *Church History of Travancore*, p. 931; John J. Dennis, *LMS Report of the Nagercoil Home Stations for the Year 1859*, UTCA, p. 1.
150. Proclamation issued by the Dewan of Travancore, 27 December 1858, Bundle no. 29, Cover File no. 2115 of 1858, *Shanar Disturbances in South Travancore*, Archives Directorate, Trivandrum.
151. Letter from the Deputy Peishkar Shungoony Menon, in-charge of the Southern Division to the Dewan of Travancore, 3 January 1859, Bundle no. 29, Cover File no. 2115 of 1858, *Shanar Disturbances in South Travancore*, Archives Directorate, Trivandrum.

152. Letter from Rev. F. Baylis to the Resident, 10 January 1859, Bundle no. 29, Cover File no. 2115 of 1858, *Shanar Disturbances in South Travancore*, Archives Directorate, Trivandrum; Letter from Rev. F. Baylis to the Resident, 17 January 1859, Bundle no. 29, Cover File no. 2115 of 1858, *Shanar Disturbances in South Travancore*, Archives Directorate, Trivandrum.
153. Letter from Rev. E. Lewis to the Resident, 21 January 1859, Bundle no. 29, Cover File no. 2115 of 1858, *Shanar Disturbances in South Travancore*, Archives Directorate, Trivandrum.
154. The Petition of Missionaries of the LMS to the King of Travancore, 7 February 1859, in *Copies of the Official Papers Sent from India Touching the Recent Disturbances in Travancore*, Box no. 15 (MF), UTCA, pp. 40-1.
155. Yesudas, *A People's Revolt in Travancore*, p. 136; Mateer, *Land of Charity*, p. 298.
156. Letter from the Deputy Peishkar Shungoony Menon, in-charge of the Southern Division to the Dewan of Travancore, 3 January 1859, Bundle no. 29, Cover File no. 2115 of 1858, *Shanar Disturbances in South Travancore*, Archives Directorate, Trivandrum.
157. Letter from W. Cullen, the Resident of Travancore and Cochin to T. Pycroft, Chief Secretary to Government, Madras, 13 January 1859, no. 4 in *Copies of the Official Papers Sent from India Touching the Recent Disturbances in Travancore*, Box no. 15 (MF), UTCA, 5; Order of T. Pycroft, Chief Secretary to Government, Madras, 27 January 1859, No. 75 in *Copies of Official Papers Sent from India Touching the Recent Disturbances in Travancore*, Box no. 15 (MF), UTCA, 6; C.M. Agur, *Church History of Travancore*, p. 935.
158. Agur, *Church History of Travancore*, p. 932.
159. Letter from Rev. E. Lewis to the Resident, 21 January 1859, Bundle no. 29, Cover File no. 2115 of 1858, *Shanar Disturbances in South Travancore*, Archives Directorate, Trivandrum.
160. John Cox, *LMS Report of the Trivandrum and Quilon Mission Districts for the Year 1858,* UTCA, p. 8.
161. Letter from Rev. F. Baylis to the Resident, 1 January 1859, Bundle no. 29, Cover File no. 2115 of 1858, *Shanar Disturbances in South Travancore*, Archives Directorate, Trivandrum.
162. Mateer, *LMS Report of the Pareychaley Mission District for the Year 1859,* UTCA, pp. 14-15.
163. Agur, *Church History of Travancore*, p. 932.
164. Letter from Rev. F. Baylis to the Resident, 10 January 1859, Bundle

no. 29, Cover File no. 2115 of 1858, *Shanar Disturbances in South Travancore*, Archives Directorate, Trivandrum.

165. Letter from the Deputy Peishkar Shungoony Menon, in-charge of the Southern Division to the Dewan of Travancore, 4 January 1859, Bundle no. 29, Cover File no. 2115 of 1858, *Shanar Disturbances in South Travancore*, Archives Directorate, Trivandrum.
166. Agur, *Church History of Travancore*, p. 933.
167. Letter from the Resident to the Dewan of Travancore, 25 January 1859 (attached letter of Rev. James Russel to the Resident) Bundle no. 29, Cover File no. 2115 of 1858, *Shanar Disturbances in South Travancore*, Archives Directorate, Trivandrum.
168. John J. Dennis, *LMS Report of the Nagercoil Home Station for the Year* 1859, UTCA, 2.
169. Letter from Rev. F. Baylis to the Resident, 11 January 1859, Bundle no. 29, Cover File no. 2115 of 1858, *Shanar Disturbances in South Travancore*, Archives Directorate, Trivandrum.
170. F. Baylis, *LMS Report of the Neyyoor Mission District for the Year 1859,* UTCA, p. 3.
171. Letter from W. Cullen, the Resident of Travancore and Cochin to T. Pycroft, Chief Secretary to Government, Madras, 18 January 1859, no. 4 in *Copies of the Official Papers Sent from India Touching the Recent Disturbances in Travancore*, Box no. 7 (MF), UTCA, p. 6.
172. Baylis, *LMS Report of the Neyyoor Mission District for the Year 1859,* UTCA, p. 4.
173. Letter from the Resident to the Dewan of Travancore, 25 January 1859 (attached letter of Rev. James Russel to the Resident) Bundle no. 29, Cover File no. 2115 of 1858, *Shanar Disturbances in South Travancore*, Archives Directorate, Trivandrum.
174. Letter from Rev. James Russel to the Resident, 31 January 1859, Bundle no. 29, Cover File no. 2115 of 1858, *Shanar Disturbances in South Travancore*, Archives Directorate, Trivandrum.
175. Letter from Rev. F. Baylis to the Resident, 10 February 1859, Bundle no. 29, Cover File no. 2115 of 1858, *Shanar Disturbances in South Travancore*, Archives Directorate, Trivandrum.
176. *LMS Report of the James Town Mission District for the Year 1859,* UTCA, pp. 1-2.
177. Letter from the Resident to the Dewan of Travancore, 25 January 1859 (attached letter of Rev. James Russel to the Resident) Bundle no. 29, Cover File no. 2115 of 1858, *Shanar Disturbances in South Travancore*, Archives Directorate, Trivandrum.

178. Letter from Rev. E. Lewis to the Resident, 21 January 1859, Bundle no. 29, Cover File no. 2115 of 1858, *Shanar Disturbances in South Travancore*, Archives Directorate, Trivandrum.
179. The Petition of Missionaries of the LMS to the King of Travancore, 7 February 1859, in *Copies of the Official Papers Sent from India Touching the Recent Disturbances in Travancore*, Box no. 15 (MF), UTCA, 39-40.
180. Letter of Rev. James Russel and Rev. J.J. Dennis to the Resident, 14 April 1859, Bundle no. 29, Cover File no. 2115 of 1858, *Shanar Disturbances in South Travancore*, Archives Directorate, Trivandrum.
181. Cox, *LMS Report of the Trivandrum and Quilon Mission Districts for the Year 1858,* UTCA, p. 7.
182. Letter from Rev. F. Baylis to the Resident, 10 January 1859, Bundle no. 29, Cover File no. 2115 of 1858, *Shanar Disturbances in South Travancore*, Archives Directorate, Trivandrum.
183. Agur, *Church History of Travancore*, 933; Letter from the Resident to the Dewan of Travancore, 25 January 1859 (attached letter of Rev. James Russel to the Resident), Bundle no. 29, Cover File no. 2115 of 1858, *Shanar Disturbances in South Travancore*, Archives Directorate, Trivandrum; Letter from the Resident to the Dewan of Travancore, 25 January 1859 (attached letter of Rev. James Russel to the Resident) Bundle no. 29, Cover File no. 2115 of 1858, *Shanar Disturbances in South Travancore*, Archives Directorate, Trivandrum; Baylis, *LMS Report of the Neyyoor Mission District for the Year 1859,* UTCA, 3.
184. Cox, *LMS Report of the Trivandrum and Quilon Mission Districts for the Year 1859,* UTCA, p. 2.
185. Gnanadason, *A Forgotten History*, p. 116.
186. Baylis, *LMS Report of the Neyyoor Mission District for the Year 1859,* UTCA, p. 4.
187. Mateer, *LMS Report of the Pareychaley Mission District for the Year 1859,* UTCA, pp. 14-15.
188. Letter from Rev. John Cox to the Resident, 21 January 1859, Bundle no. 29, Cover File no. 2115 of 1858, *Shanar Disturbances in South Travancore*, Archives Directorate, Trivandrum.
189. Baylis, *LMS Report of the Neyyoor Mission District for the Year 1859,* UTCA, pp. 3-4.
190. Letter from Rev. E. Lewis to the Resident, 21 January 1859, Bundle no. 29, Cover File no. 2115 of 1858, *Shanar Disturbances in South Travancore*, Archives Directorate, Trivandrum; Baylis, *LMS Report of the Neyyoor Mission District for the Year 1859,* UTCA, p. 4.

191. The Petition of Missionaries of the LMS to the King of Travancore, 7 February 1859, in *Copies of the Official Papers Sent from India Touching the Recent Disturbances in Travancore*, Box no. 15 (MF), UTCA, p. 39.
192. Letter from W. Cullen, the Resident of Travancore and Cochin to T. Pycroft, Chief Secretary to Government, Madras, 18 January 1859, no. 4 in *Copies of the Official Papers Sent from India Touching the Recent Disturbances in Travancore*, Box no. 7 (MF), UTCA, 6; Letter from W. Cullen, the Resident of Travancore and Cochin to T. Pycroft, Chief Secretary to Government, Madras, 13 January 1859, no. 4 in *Copies of the Official Papers Sent from India Touching the Recent Disturbances in Travancore*, Box no. 15 (MF), UTCA, p. 5.
193. Dennis, *LMS Report of the Nagercoil Home Station for the Year 1859,* UTCA, pp. 2-3.
194. Baylis, *LMS Report of the Neyyoor Mission District for the Year 1859,* UTCA, p. 5; E. Lewis, *LMS Report of the Santhapuram Mission District for the Year 1859,* UTCA, p. 2; *LMS Report of the James Town Mission District for the Year 1859,* UTCA, pp. 1-2.
195. Agur, *Church History of Travancore*, p. 934; The Petition of Missionaries of the LMS to the King of Travancore, 7 February 1859, in *Copies of the Official Papers Sent from India Touching the Recent Disturbances in Travancore*, Box no. 15 (MF), UTCA, pp. 39-41.
196. V. Nagam Aiya, *The Travancore State Manual*, vol. 1, p. 529.
197. Letter from W. Cullen, the Resident of Travancore and Cochin to T. Pycroft, Chief Secretary to Government, Madras, 18 January 1859, no. 4 in *Copies of the Official Papers Sent from India Touching the Recent Disturbances in Travancore*, Box no. 7 (MF), UTCA, p. 6; Letter from the Resident to the Dewan of Travancore, 10 February 1859, Bundle no. 29, Cover File no. 2115 of 1858, *Shanar Disturbances in South Travancore*, Archives Directorate, Trivandrum.
198. Letter from the Dewan of Travancore to the Resident, 5 January 1859, Bundle no. 29, Cover File no. 2115 of 1858, *Shanar Disturbances in South Travancore*, Archives Directorate, Trivandrum.
199. Agur, *Church History of Travancore*, p. 49; Letter from the Resident to the Dewan of Travancore, 6 January 1859, Bundle no. 29, Cover File no. 2115 of 1858, *Shanar Disturbances in South Travancore*, Archives Directorate, Trivandrum; Letter from the Resident to Rev. F. Baylis, 9 January 1859, Bundle no. 29, Cover File no. 2115 of 1858, *Shanar Disturbances in South Travancore*, Archives Directorate, Trivandrum.
200. Order of T. Pycroft, Chief Secretary to Government, 27 January 1859,

in *Copies of the Official Papers Sent from India Touching the Recent Disturbances in Travancore*, Box no. 15 (MF), UTCA, p. 6.

201. The Dewan's Report to the Resident, 12 Febraury 1859, no. 196 in *Copies of the Official Papers Sent from India Touching the Recent Disturbances in Travancore*, Box no. 15 (MF), UTCA, p. 10.
202. Letter from T. Pycroft to the Secretary to the Government of India, 23 March 1859, no. 37 in *Copies of the Official Papers Sent from India Touching the Recent Disturbances in Travancore*, Box no. 15 (MF), UTCA, p. 38.
203. Minute by the President, 7 May 1859 in *Copies of the Official Papers Sent from India Touching the Recent Disturbances in Travancore*, Box no. 15 (MF), UTCA, p. 43; Agur, *Church History of Travancore*, p. 936.
204. P. Shungoony Menon, *A History of Travancore from Earliest Times* (Madras: Higgin Botham and Co., 1878), p. 511.
205. Letter from Resident to T. Pycroft, 12 May 1859, no. 44, in *Copies of the Official Papers Sent from India Touching the Recent Disturbances in Travancore*, Box no. 15 (MF), UTCA, p. 44.
206. Letter from the Dewan of Travancore to the Resident, 17 May 1859, in *Copies of the Official Papers Sent from India Touching the Recent Disturbances in Travancore*, Box no. 15 (MF), UTCA, p. 45.
207. Minute by the President, 30 May 1859, no. 15 in *Copies of the Official Papers Sent from India Touching the Recent Disturbances in Travancore*, Box no. 15 (MF), UTCA, p. 45.
208. *Selected Proclamations by the Sovereign*, pp. 301-2; Mateer, *Land of Charity*, p. 305; Agur, *Church History of Travancore*, p. 937.
209. Mateer, *Land of Charity*, p. 306; Yesudas, *The History of the London Missionary Society in Travancore 1806-1908*, p. 196.
210. Interview with R.N. Yesudas.
211. V.D. Divekar, 'Introduction', in *Social Reform Movements in India: A Historical Perspective*, ed. V.D. Divekar (Bombay: Popular Prakashan, 1991), p. vii.
212. T.K. Oommen, *Protest and Change* (New Delhi: Sage, 1990), p. 30.
213. Ibid., p. 14.

CHAPTER 3

Interaction of Faith and History: A Survey of Liberation Theologies

This chapter attempts to understand the interaction between faith and history in liberation theology. The histories of people are diverse in content and nature. The experiences of the past are remembered with different sentiments, and are used for various purposes. In the religious sphere, history is one of the important keys to understand the faith of the people meaningfully. At the same time, historical experiences stand as resources which can be interpreted to develop new expressions of religious faith. The new meaning of faith is built upon the interaction of faith with history and vice-versa. The liberation theologies, expressions of Christian faith in various historical contexts, have emerged out of the experiences of people which have influence on their present existence. The historical experiences of people have been interpreted to challenge the present and to make the future hopeful. It means the history of people has an important role in developing new Christian theological expressions. In an attempt to understand this, a few contextual liberation theologies are studied in this chapter. As models, they are surveyed for methological insights to interpret the Upper Cloth Revolt theologically. Some basic understanding in the study of history and a few perspectives of reading history are discussed in this chapter. The contextual and historical nature of the interpretations of Christian faith is also briefly discussed.

History: Meaning, Nature and Perspectives

Unfolding the Past for a New Outlook

'History' is derived from the Greek word, '*istoria*' which means 'learning or collection of information, obtained as a result of enquiry'.[1]

It also denotes enquiry, research, investigation or exploration.[2] The meaning of the term 'history' also rests in the German word, *Geschichte*, which refers to an intelligible unfolding of the past.[3] E.H. Carr says, history is 'a continuous process of interaction between the historian and his facts, an unending dialogue between the present and the past'.[4] G.R. Elton views that history is not simply the study of the past but of the present traces of the past. It includes whatsoever was said, thought, done or suffered in different contexts.[5] For Wood Gray, history gives us an understanding and wisdom for the present.[6] John C.B. Webster takes a step further on Carr's explanation of history as an unending dialogue and says it is 'an unending conversation between the past and the present, carried on through the examination of evidence and focused upon concrete events and changes in the past'.[7] History also helps people know who they are today. James Massey makes the point clear: 'it is only our past or history which can tell us our past identity'[8] in the present context. It means history cannot be treated in the frame of past alone, but in the present dimension too. History may have many things to speak to contemporary humans.

History is interpreted as 'contemporary history'.[9] It implies that history is not simply a record of the past, but it involves in seeing the past through the eyes of the present. This is an important aspect of reading and understanding history. Therefore, the main task of a historian is not ended with recording the past events, but interpreting them contemporarily.[10] It calls for the historian to place the past in the present space. Collingwood rightly observed that 'the past which a historian studies is not a dead past, but a past which in some sense is still living in the present'.[11] He argues for the contemporary significance of history/historical events. Past can live in the present only through new readings of it. E. H. Carr also views that the facts which compose history should be employed as key to comprehend the present.[12]

History has not only the face of the past and present but also the face of the future. We are shaped by the past, and the future is shaped through us. In this sense, the past (history) not only shapes the present but also the future. On the one hand, history helps to know what happened in the lives of people and on the other it facilitates to shape the present and the future. In order to shape the present and the future, we look back to the past. In this process, we are not only historians but also participants in history.[13] The 'present' dimension of history is also inevitably linked with the historian who lives in the present and is influenced by the contemporary ethos, ideologies, etc. [14]

In sum, history is a narration of the experiences of human beings in the past, which is found in the different forms of evidences – written or oral. In historical studies, those evidences are systematically arranged, investigated and interpreted to understand the past to give a better framework for the present and future. It indicates that the study of the past can widen the horizons of the present and future. Thus, history is not a mere presentation of the past but a dynamic source to develop a new outlook in the present and for the future.

Objectivity, Content and Context

There are different opinions among historians about the status of history. Some argue that history is a science. For them, history is a science because it employs scientific methods to bring out the 'truth' in the past. Historians scientifically observe the facts and attempt to interpret them objectively. It does not mean that interpretation is completely unbiased. For the scientists, the truth can be repeatedly verified only through experiments. It is not impossible with historians also.[15] Historians have ways of verifying and establishing facts. According to J.B. Bury, 'History is simply a science, no less and no more.'[16] G.R. Elton views that history is both art and science.[17] But for Durant, 'Obviously historiography cannot be a science. It can only be an industry, an art and a philosophy – an industry by ferreting out the facts, an art by establishing a meaningful order in the chaos of materials, a philosophy by seeking perspective and enlightenment.'[18] The whole question is about objectivity. Scientists argue that history cannot achieve objectivity and accuracy as claimed in the experiments done in laboratories. This argument is not valid in the postmodern context. No branch of study can comprehensively bring out the truth. It demands inter-disciplinary approach which incorporates different disciplines. Every science/branch of knowledge has its own method of enquiry or methodology to systematically employ different tools and methods to bring out the truth in respective fields. In this sense every branch of knowledge, including history, is scientific in nature. Every discipline in its research attempts to furnish new information/data/knowledge in a particular field. If this is the criteria to be called a discipline as science, then history is also a science.

History is the story of human beings and their encounter or interaction with respective environments. E.H. Carr says that 'the cult of individualism is one of the most pervasive of modern historical myths'.[19] He continues that no individual can act out of context but only in the web of relations in society.[20] Simultaneously, an event or story, the content of historical narration, cannot be viewed without analyzing the context because it is the result of the interplay of many contextual factors.

Every historical event has reasons. A historical study attempts to comprehend how events took place and why? All historical events, facts, manuscripts/scripts and movements are contextual in nature. They cannot be intelligible apart from the context. While conscious of the role of context in the content of history, historians also realize that the records or the documents, which are used to narrate an event, may not give sufficient information. Records are always incomplete. The best example in this regard is the nineteenth century missionary documentation of Protestant Christianity in India. The role and contribution of native Christians is ambiguous and not documented properly. It shows the need of evaluating and interpreting the historical sources from different perspectives. [21]

Not 'The' History but Histories

It is observed that 'more than new evidences are shifts in methodology and theory which require the re-evaluation of old evidence and the consideration of a new one'[22] important in historical studies. Shifts in methodology refer to the change in viewing the evidence from new/different perspective, a shift in interpreting the facts or historical events and in considering neglected sources as well. The methodological shift leads to the re-examination of existing historical (dominant) narratives and results in producing new ones. Emphasis on viewing history from a different position can be seen in the words of Goethe, 'History must from time to time be rewritten, not because many new facts have been discovered, but because new aspects come into view, because the participant in the progress of an age is led to standpoints from which the past can be regarded and judged in a novel manner.'[23] The new aspects correspond to new perspectives in reading the historical accounts. Time brings into light new aspects through which things to be viewed. History/historical events cannot be escaped from viewing through new aspects. Thus history is led to be re-written or interpreted from diverse perspectives. Some perspectival readings are given below.

Colonial histories were narrations of British rule in India. They credited all achievements to the British colonial rulers, and disregarded the Indians, the colonized. The British policies, institutions and culture were the substance of colonialist narratives. The colonial historical accounts, written from the perspective of colonialists, ignored the perspective of the colonized and their agency in historical movements.[24] Colonial accounts was projected as 'the history' of India in the colonial period. In order to counter the colonialist narrations, attempts were made to narrate the history of colonial India from a nationalist perspective. It was aimed to bring out the agency of natives which was neglected in the history of colonial India. The nationalist perspective produced historical narrations which placed natives as the subjects of Indian history, particularly the history of freedom struggle. Through nationalist historiography, not only new perspective but also a new historical narration emerged. Thus, 'the history' of India was challenged. But the Indian nationalist historiography was also characterized by the colonial mode of writing-elitist thinking and agency.[25] It was 'caught up, since its inception, in the contradictory pulls of such affinity and opposition. The affinity is historical as well as conceptual. The opposition is in terms of incipient nationalism.'[26] It was written by the dominant, and resources were supplied by elite personalities, traditions, institutions, thoughts and visions. The dominant writers were upper caste men who wrote about upper caste men and women as the subjects of Indian history.

Elitist historical reading and narration is countered by the subaltern perspective which shows that the elitist perspective fails to recognize the role and sacrifice of the common people in history. It also falls short of the articulation of the common people. For instance, the national movement was articulated as the product of elite leaders, and the activities of the common people, independent of the elite, were depicted in a negative sense,[27] according to Ranajit Guha.

The subaltern perspective, however, concentrates on the role and contributions of marginalized peoples in history as subjects and attempts to counter the biased histories of the elite upper-caste historians.[28] Subalterns are authors, interpreters and evaluators of their histories. 'Established' histories cannot be taken at 'face value' because the subjectivity and agency of subalterns were always concealed by the dominant who wrote those histories.[29] The traditions, ideologies of resistance, protests and subversive movements of subalterns are either ignored or misrepresented in the 'established' historical accounts.[30] They are devalued because they are historical protests against the hegemony of caste.

Historical narration from a Dalit perspective attempts to retrieve the history of destroyed and distorted by the dominant expressions of history. Abraham Ayrookuzhiel views that, 'these indigenous inhabitants have become a people without their own history, without their own cultural individuality, though they retain a certain amount of cultural distinctiveness. Dalit perspective is a tool to reconstruct this unknown history from the folk songs, stories, myths and to a certain extent in religious symbols.'[31]

The tribal perspective tries to trace out the tribal histories which have been misrepresented in the dominant historical accounts and reconstruct them from a tribal point of view. Tribal history is the history of suffering from exploitation, discrimination, invasion, and more importantly alienation.[32]

Feminist readings of history too critique and analyse the exclusion, experience and invisibility of women in historical writings. They attempt to unearth the patriarchal silencing of women and their experiences of exclusion and subordination in history. This perspective endeavours to reclaim their space in the historical discourses. Through the reading of feminist eyes, feminist historians hope that subordination and marginalization of women in historical writings can be removed.[33] The feminist reading ventures to make historical experiences of women alive, and translates their silenced voices into heard voices. It argues that the historical narrations are partial if the women are not given adequate space in them. Re-reading, deconstruction, hermeneutics of suspicion, etc., are the methods employed in this enterprise.[34]

Post-colonial reading is yet another perspective employed in historical studies. It attempts to analyse the sources and documents on colonized societies produced by the colonial scholars. It exposes the ideological imperialism of colonizers in historical discourses. In this perspective scholars attempt to decolonize historical discourses and bring forth the voice of the subordinated people. They address various aspects of the colonial hegemony that were imprinted in the minds of the colonized. The post-colonial perspective tries to create space for the colonized in historical documentation.[35]

Post-modern perspective emerged to correct the assumption that historians are capable of writing an impassionate objective history. Post-modernists argue that historians cannot fully come out of the bond of his/her subjectivity. The 'subjectivity' influences him/her in the selection of documents, interpretation of the facts, perspective, etc. Therefore, the post modernists propose 'deconstruction'.[36]

We see that there is no single perspective through which history can be written and viewed. Different perspectives give birth to different histories. They are the histories of women, dalits, tribal people, and so on. No historical narration can claim objectivity and comprehensiveness. There can be no comprehensive account of an event but an expression of it, often subjective, read by the people concerned.

Caste, Body and History

There is interplay of caste and body in historical narrations in India. The histories of subalterns cannot be written or interpreted without acknowledging this interaction. Since the subalterns are historical victims of caste, their histories are histories of subjugation and marginalization. The subaltern bodies bear the marks of historical subjugation implemented through the devise of caste. This is why the body is considered the site of historical forces like caste, so far as untouchability, discrimination in work, worship, mobility, etc. are concerned.[37] Caste separated lower caste person from the person of the upper caste in terms of purity and pollution. Clothing, posture and gesture were also determined by caste,[38] resulting in pain, humiliation, exclusion, and brokenness. Those experiences are the histories that are overlooked in the dominant narratives. While caste hegemony places the high caste bodies as subjects in established histories low-caste persons, men and women, are outside the ambit of such accounts. It is subaltern histories that give voice to the subalterns and help retrieve the neglected stories of 'impure' bodies.

The 'Subject' of Indian Christian Historical Narrations

Indian Christian historical narratives in the nineteenth century were Eurocentric and colonial in nature and content. Most of them were produced by missionaries for a western readership. They contained stories of mission activities, missionary methods, and the life of missionaries.[39] The 'natives' are, however, largely neglected in such writing. In the missionary biographies, too, missionaries were over projected, and local people overlooked.[40]

The missionaries/missions designed the program of writing history and took no notice of the social history of native Christian communities. The missionary work – its progress, problems and challenges – was prioritized in the writings,[41] so that the native Christians became 'objects' and missionaries became 'subjects' in the mission histories.

After independence, two shifts have taken place in writing the history of Christianity in India. They are: (1) a desire to understand the origin and growth of the Indian Church from a nationalist perspective and (2) an emphasis on social history to enhance the self-understanding of Christian communities in India. At the same time, historians whose readership was largely western focused much on the religio-cultural encounter of East and West.[42] With such shifts, the Christian community attempted to establish the fact that they are part of this land, and its history,[43] with the communities as its focus. They are the subjects of history. Their sacrificial life and contributions to the growth of Christianity should be the subject of research.

The history of Christianity in India is primarily a social history.[44] It implies that the focus of study should be shifted from missionaries to Indians, Christian to local communities. One has to bear in mind that 'The primary purpose of studying the history of one's own people is to gain increased self-understanding.'[45] 'One's own people' can be taken here as native Christians of different historical and social backgrounds. Therefore, history of natives must be studied with the purpose of enabling respective communities to look back boldly and to get energy to go forward with their hopes and aspirations in society.

Biblical God: God of History

Biblical God is God of History. The Bible affirms that God is engaged in human history. Indeed, the Bible is the witness of God's action in history. It describes the history of an enslaved people and of God's involvement in their journey toward a promised land. The same God commanded the people of Israel through Moses that their history of slavery should be retold from generation to generation. It is clearly narrated in Deuteronomy 6: 20-5, and echoes in I Corinthians 1: 26-8.[46] The commandment to remember one's past underlines the importance of history in the life of a community.

According to the Bible, creation was the first act of God's historical participation in human history (Genesis 1 & 2). After creation, sin entered the human history (Gen. 3). The surfacing of sin as a historical reality in human community can be perceived in Gen. 4-11. The call of Abraham shows again the direct intervention of God in human history (Gen. 12).[47] The life and message of Prophets also demonstrate how God intentionally engaged in human history. Moreover, Jesus' life is the historical narrative of God's intervention in the history of His people.[48] The incarnational act of God in Jesus Christ was the climax of God's solidarity and participation in human history (John 1: 14).[49]

The Bible not only explicates how God acts in human history but also shows how history is useful to human community. History is a means of community formation. The two Chronicles in the Bible underlines this fact. The chronicler attempts to explain to his post-exilid community the history of glory and disgrace of their ancestors. The main purpose of this narration is to inspire as well as caution them as they are going to build up a new community life. History helped them know their identity and re-construct their community on the footsteps of their forebears. It reminded them the mistakes and sacrifices of their ancestors.[50]

In short, the Biblical understanding of history is based on the affirmation of God's participation in the life of entire creation. God's participation leads to history. It is an ongoing process in which God meets his creation, especially humans, in concrete situations. If Biblical God is God of History, the same God has a part in our history too. God continuously participates in our existence and writes our histories along with us. Histories ultimately help to rebuild the communities, particularly the subalterns.

History is Neither 'Sacred' Nor 'Profane'

In the traditional Christian understanding of history, a distinction is made between sacred history and profane history. Sacred history refers to God's action in history for the salvation of humankind, whereas profane history points to the political history. Sacred history is attributed to God and profane history to human beings. It is also believed that an historical event is irrevocable and unrepeated. It is based on the linear view of history where history is understood not only in terms of progress but also in terms of eschatology. Since Jesus Christ has inaugurated an interminable stage, Christianity is the *eschatos*, the last thing. Through Christ event, the end of history has already taken place. Moreover, Christian eschatological vision of history rejects the fulfilment of history within history itself. Fulfilment is beyond the historical existence.[51]

For St. Augustine, sacred history is a continuous event. God's work still continues in the world, especially in the conversion and sanctification of souls.[52] St. Irenaeus considered universal history as part of divine dispensation.[53] The separation of sacred history from profane history or focus of sacred over profane leads to the question that if we make a distinction who is the author of 'profane history'? If we accept this division, it is contrary to the Biblical understanding of history that God participates in human history of any kind. Since God participates in human history, human beings alone cannot be held responsible for 'profane' history. The sacred and profane separation of history directly or indirectly excludes human beings from the sacred history and God from the profane history. There can be no sacred history without human beings because human beings are indispensable part of God's act of salvation. Therefore, history can be neither sacred nor profane but divine-human. Both God and human beings are equally involved in history. It is true that God works in history. But God works through human beings in their history. Human beings may be an instrument in the historical events. Their role also must be acknowledged when we understand and define history. As history is understood as one entity without separation of sacred and profane, so the history of Christianity must be studied as part of general history. A historian is conditioned not only by his/her religious faith but also by the general historical context of his/her time. It must also be acknowledged that God works not only through the Church but also through other institutions in the world.

Context, History and Theology

Christianity is an historical religion. Its doctrines are either the result of historical events or the historical interpretations of faith.[54] But, James Massey argues that systematic theology (traditional/ classical theology) and its Indian version, Indian Christian Theology have not attempted to touch human history directly. The former was developed in the framework of the understanding of two histories: sacred and profane, but the latter was emerged in the framework which does not give any space for history.[55] The contextual liberation theologies understand human history as the bedrock of theological formulations.[56] According to M.M. Thomas, 'a living theology is the manner in which a church confesses its faith and establishes its historical existence in dialogue with its own environment. If the Indian Church is understood merely as a product of Western missions, the Indian theology will only appear as an appendage to Western theology.'[57] K.C. Abraham sees 'creative moments in theology [that] have risen out of the Church's response to new challenges in a given historical context. They bear the social and cultural imprints of the time. Theologians of every age are committed to interpreting the Gospel of Jesus in a way (that is) relevant and meaningful to the realities around them.'[58] James Massey says, 'Any living theological expression has to be rooted in the actual experiences of believers in a particular historical setting.'[59]

In the contextual faith articulations, the starting point of theology is the understanding of the context of people to whom theologizing is intended. Theology which is not informed by a context cannot be considered relevant. Theology becomes meaningful and engaging if it is done in interaction with the experiences of people in a specific environment. The context denotes not only the contemporary realities but also historical experiences which shaped the life of people in particular locations. The principal shifts in Christian theology are as follows. The early formation of Christian theology was made in the historical context of the early Church. The modernization of Christian theology happened in the seventeenth-eighteenth centuries as a reaction to the rationalism promoted by the Enlightenment. The contextual theologies came into surface after the Second World War.[60] The development of different theologies informs that there is an interaction between context, history, and theology. The words of Gustavo Gutierrez affirm it, 'Theology fulfills a prophetic function insofar as it interprets historical events with the intention of revealing and proclaiming their profound meaning.'[61]

Universality and Particularity: Myth and Reality

According to V. Devasahayam, 'Theology is contextual. All theologies have emerged and reflected in particular contexts in spite of claims to the contrary.'[62] Theology is a contextual reflection on faith in the light of human experiences. The particularity of human experience invalidates the notion of universality in theologizing.[63] K.

Kitamori views that the universal is mediated by the particular. The 'particular' refers to history, culture, faith, customs, etc., of respective communities or places. All theologies are particular in nature and content. They are responses to particular situations or issues. Greek theology is not universal theology but a particular theology.[64] Since context varies from place to place and country to country, there is no 'universal context' as such. Different theological expressions confirm the reality of non-universality.[65] The incarnation of God occurred in a particular person, place and time. But it has universal significance, shaped by the particular historical context.[66]

The particularity of human experience in theologizing affirms that theologizing cannot be monopolized by any person or community or ethnic group. It opens the horizons of expressing the knowledge of God in one's own way, and through his/her historical experience. It is an intrinsic right of human beings. It can be exercised only in concrete historical situations. In order to express the knowledge of God in his/her way, one has to attempt to understand what God has done in the past, and what God is doing at present in the community.[67] It means history of a community is very important to know what God has done. The theological value of history rests in the point that God acts in human history.[68] God does engage with all human beings in their respective situations. It is not universal, but particular in nature. What is real is a particular context and historical experience. Universality is abstract and a myth.

Theology as Subjective Speech in a Historical Context

James H. Cone understands theology as human speech about God. It is a human talk about God in his/her language. Since it is a human speech, it can be made only in definite historical situations. Therefore, it cannot be separated from social existence.[69] The fact of theology as 'human speech' shows the anthropological character of theological constructions. Ludwig Feuerbach gives more clarity in this regard. He questioned Hegelian idealism which propositioned that what is rational is only real and what is real should be rational. Feuerbach argued that what is real can be found in concrete life, not in philosophical abstractions. In theological terms, what is real about God is not with the rational analysis of God but with the examination of the experience of humanity in historical context – how do human beings experience God in concrete situations.[70] That is why he said, 'Theology is anthropology'.[71] He argues that 'Man cannot get beyond his true nature. He may indeed by means of his imagination conceive individuals of a so-called higher kind, but he can never get loose from his species, his nature. . . .'[72] It implies that a human being cannot speak anything authentically beyond his/her existence in society. His/her speech about God cannot be removed from his/her space and time in a specific history. It may be possible to place God beyond time and space, but not human beings. Humanity cannot transcend history. Even if human beings articulate the divine, who is beyond history, they can do it only in a language of time and place. The words which they use to describe God are the product of a particular historical context. This limitation makes the God – talk subjective speech – a speech by a person of a historical setting.[73] The subjective speech ultimately owes to the historical changes/forces in respective time and space.

The human consciousness is produced by social realities. In the words of Karl Marx, 'consciousness can never be anything else than conscious existence'.[74] He also says, 'Consciousness . . . is a social product'.[75] Theologically speaking, the human speech about God comes out of the consciousness shaped by the social context in a particular time. It is generated and mediated by the social factors which influence human thinking and course of life. It means social realities design theology.[76] The nature and content of theology is also decided by them. They are not swift phenomena but historical products. Theology, as subjective speech, is a social construct shaped by the societal realities which are historically rooted.

Theology as Expression of Religious Experience in History

The Exodus, a decisive historical event in the life of Israelites was the basis of their faith in God. Through this, they became ex-slaves and God's free people.[77] What is understood from the Exodus is that God placed the people of Israel in a historical movement, and they encountered God in that specific event. Thus the event became the site of experiencing God.[78] They met God in the historical event of liberation. They realized that divine freedom empowered them to experience liberation in the particular historical situation.[79] In fact, the Exodus was an experience of God in the history of the people of Israel. Their faith in God cannot be explained without this historical event. R.N. Yesudas says, 'Our histories are integral to our faith tradition. Faith has been developed through our histories.'[80] It means theology as an expression of faith, is not an intellectual exercise but an expression of the religious experiences of people in different historical stages of their lives. It comes out of their existential encounter with God. This encounter primarily happens in the concrete historical locations.[81] The religious experience is not a monopoly of priests and the prophets, but the experience of an entire community from common people to the ruler. Everyone is part of the religious experience of a community.[82]

The present religious experience (faith experience) is not separated from the past. It is built upon the religious experiences of the past. Therefore, the past religious experiences are integral component not only to develop new theologies but also to shape new religious experiences. The scope of past experiences is not limited to mold the present religious experiences, but extends in shaping the future, though not directly. It points to the fact that historical experiences are crucial in developing theologies, the expressions of religious experiences. A living theology will integrate the past, present and future. It will give the expression of past experience to make the present meaningful and the future hopeful. [83]

While the people of Israel developed their theology based on their encounter with God in various circumstances, the early Christians articulated their theology based on their experiences with Jesus. The histories of the encounter of both communities played a crucial role in shaping them in life and in faith. The people of Israel retold their histories throughout the generations. The early Christians also retold the stories of their encounter with Jesus Christ to strengthen their faith within the community and to bring more people into their faith experience from outside the community. Their stories gave hope not only to them but also to others, and helped them to sustain their communities. Therefore, the historical experiences of the Divine are one of the sources of theology.[84] In theological articulations, religious experiences are expressed in systematic form intelligible to the people concerned.

Liberation Theologies

Liberation theologies are experiential-theological expressions of faith emerged in different historical contexts. They are intentional dialogues between the faith and context which includes all dimensions of human life. Liberation theologies point to the fact that since human beings are culturally and historically conditioned, no single theological proposition can meaningfully articulate the tenets of Christian faith to the people of diverse identities. The contextual-liberation theologies developed out of the awareness that 'traditional approaches do not make sense within different cultural patterns and thought forms and of the incarnational nature of Christianity . . . Incarnation is a process of becoming particular and in and through the particular, the divinity could become visible, some way graspable and intelligible.[85] The 'particular' makes the Christian faith relevant in a context. The 'particular' may be culture, tradition, historical experience, or language. The expressions Asian, African and Latin American basically refer to the historical conditioning of the people in those regions. The understanding of God through the historical experiences can speak to the people more meaningfully in the present situation. Some of the liberation theologies are studied in this section.

Kazoh Kitamori's Theology of the Pain of God

Theology of the Pain of God was developed in Japan in the context of the painful human realities inflicted by the Second World War. The untold miseries of people in a particular period of human history in Japan contributed to the emergence of this theological articulation. It was not only a response to the pain of Japan in the Second World War, but also a theological interpretation of the Japanese understanding of pain due to the personal and community tragedies in history.[86] Kazoh Kitamori, the architect of the Theology of the Pain of God, in order to base his argument, interacts with Hegel. In his *Reason in History*, Hegel argues that since reason rules the world, history is rational.[87] Kitamori places this Hegelian view in a religious framework and argues that 'The providence of God rules the world; in our terminology, God completely embraces our reality . . . the primary issue in the theology of the pain of God: God embraces our reality.'[88] According to him, the Gospels teach us that God endures pain because God embraces human reality. The human realities are broken and painful realities.[89] God's act of embracing basically shows the historical involvement of God in human life. Human reality can imply the present and the past experiences of the people. Every present experience is historically rooted. God embraces the realities of entire humanity, not particular community. God's act of embracing of human realities can be understood from the histories of the respective peoples.

Kitamori developed his theological articulation with the help of both Biblical and Japanese resources. Biblically speaking, 'The Pain of God means that the love of God had conquered the wrath of God in the midst of the *historical* world deserving his wrath. Thus the pain of God must *necessarily* enter the historical plane as a person. This truth is recorded in Romans: 8:3. The pain of God could not have existed had not the Redeemer, the personification of God's pain, been a historical figure.'[90] The love of God journeyed *from* the pain of God *toward* the historical Jesus. The historical Jesus is only an indispensable element in the pain of God. He is not 'the' pain of God but an important component in the pain of God rooted in the love of God.[91] It means God's pain continues as long as God embraces the human reality.

The theology of the Pain of God places sin in the historical world, not in any ideational world. Sin happens in historical context, not in an abstract setting. In order to save humanity from the world of sin, God had to come to the historical world. In this process, the personification of the pain of God happened through the human flesh of this historical world. It took place in Jesus, a 'real man' a *historical* person.[92] In this historical personification, God wanted to communicate God's pain through human pain.[93] Thus, the pain of God became a historical reality.

In the theology of the Pain of God, Kitamori attempts to relate the pain of God with the Japanese understanding of *tsurasa* in Japanese tragedy/tragedies. In the Japanese way of thinking, a person of perceptiveness and acumen is one who understands *tsurasa.* A true Japanese identity is confirmed by an understanding of *tsurasa.*[94] *Tsurasa* is the fundamental attitude in Japanese experiences of tragedy. It is experienced or understood 'when one suffers and dies, or makes his beloved son suffer and die, for the sake of loving and making others live'.[95] It is an experience of owning the pain of others as one's own pain. Etymologically, the word 'pain' would generally be apt for the term *tsurasa.* Kitamori observes that pain, the main element of Japanese tragedy can appropriately interact with the pain of God. The Japanese mind understands the heart of God in pain better than others because the Japanese had experienced the pain and seen the painful hearts of fellow men and women.[96] Their minds are historically shaped by the *tsurasa* caused by the tragedies.

Kitamori emphasizes the importance of history or historical context in the formation of theology. He argues that Greek theology or liberal theology could not articulate the pain of God comprehensively. Since the Japanese had lived in the different periods of pain, particularly in the painful historical time of the Second World War, they can understand pain in a better way. That is, those who lived in the period of pain can best understand the pain of God. Therefore, the historical experiences of the pain of the Japanese are the medium to decode the eternal truth of the pain of God.[97] As God embraces human reality – past and present – so the painful historical struggles and experiences of people are the sources to interpret the pain of God in different locations.

Kitamori also shows the limitation of the understanding of the pain of God through *tsurasa* or pain in Japanese tragedy. *Tsurasa* is experienced in human suffering and death or when one sacrifices his/her son in order to save the life of another person. Unlike *tsurasa*, the pain of God is out of love toward the unlovable. Love is the basis of God's pain. The sacrifice of God's only son is because of God's love toward humanity. *Tsurasa* is experienced not because of loving the unworthy or unlovable or the enemy. Hence, it can speak about only one side of the pain of God.[98]

The theology of Pain of God teaches that 'we must speak about the things of God by using our human experience. The pain of God gives meaning and value to human suffering.'[99] The theology of the pain of God has articulated the pain of God through the painful historical experiences of the people of Japan. It encourages us to consider the past experiences of pain as the sites of theologizing. In the Indian context, as far as the subalterns are concerned, their experiences of pain are caused by the caste and patriarchy. Therefore, the experiences of subalterns both men and women form the historical location of pain. In the light of the pain of God, the pain of the subalterns is a valid source to understand the pain of God. The subalterns experienced not only the pain inflicted by the unjust social order and unequal gendering but also the pain because of their bold and sacrificial resistance against the oppressive historical forces. Their resistance was out of their love toward future generations. The theology of the pain of God motivates to locate God in the historical events which narrate the pain of the subalterns and to use human realities to decode divine realities. In this sense, the Upper Cloth Revolt, a historical experience of Nadars, is a source of theologizing. Indeed, it is a historical narration of the pain of Nadar women who fought caste and patriarchy. It also contains the painful experiences of men and women which can be theologically interpreted to widen the understanding of God's painful historical intervention in humanity, through the historical struggle of a particular community.

Gustavo Gutierrez's Theology of Liberation

Theology of Liberation is a theological reflection emerged out of the experiences of the poor in the unjust socio-economic situation in Latin America where the Christians constituted majority of the population. It was an outcome of the shared attempts to get rid of the unjust exploitative systems and to build a more humane society where people experience freedom from all kinds of oppression.[100] When Theology of Liberation was developed, the 'poor' person in Latin America was 'the oppressed one, the one marginated from society, the member of the proletariat struggling for his most basic rights; he is the exploited and plundered social class, the country struggling for its liberation.'[101] In the context of exploited life realities of the poor, the theology of liberation 'reflects on the experience and meaning of faith based on the commitment to abolish injustice and to build a new society. . .'.[102]

Gustavo Gutierrez, in the situation of unequal social and economic relationships, evokes the idea of charity to develop the theology of liberation. For him, charity is the centre of Christian life. The Biblical faith functions within the framework of charity. It means Biblical faith is an act of faith which sets out from a person as a commitment to God and to the neighbor. It is an action of commitment which intends to establish a right relationship with others.[103] St. Paul also views that Christian faith functions through charity. In this faith-charity mechanism, love is the gift given by a person to God and to the others. Love is the foundation of the praxis of Christian charity. The praxis of faith, charity, makes his/her presence active in history.[104] It also leads to the building up of the brotherhood/sisterhood and communion in history.[105] As a faith which works through charity, Christian faith demands at least action and commitment to the fellow beings in society. In this sense, theology is reflection, and a critical attitude to faith praxis.[106] The praxis of faith can put an end to the historical forces of oppression and begin new era in history. The histories of faith praxis can speak to the present situation of oppression or exploitation; be it social, economic, political, or religious. At the same time, human charity cannot be practised in vacuum. It is possible only in respective historical context. Since the commitment to fellow human beings leads to an action which is historical in nature; theology must be an expression which comes out of a critical attitude to charity, in the present and past context.

The human history helps the theology to fulfill its critical function or attitude. In the words of Congar, 'if the Church wishes to deal with the real questions of the modern world and to attempt to respond to them . . . it must open as it were a new chapter of theologico-pastoral epistemology. Instead of using only revelation and tradition as starting points, as classical theology has generally done, it must start with facts and questions derived from the world and from history.'[107] In relation to praxis, theology fulfills its prophetic function by interpreting the historical events with the aim of bringing out their powerful meaning. This is basically intended to make the Christians' commitment more unambiguous and revolutionary.[108]

In the Theology of Liberation, Gutierrez does not endorse the idea of two histories; history cannot be divided into the sacred and the profane. Christ, the Lord of History, is the final destiny of humanity. The redemptive work of Christ in history is for every existence. His work not only embraces the existence of all living beings but also leads them into their fullness. It means human history is incomplete without the history of salvation. Every human existence is caused by the salvific action of God. Therefore, historical destiny of human beings must be located in the salvific horizon.[109] Moreover, the liberating action of Christ is not limited in a particular time and space. It is a historical progression. Therefore, the struggle for establishing a just society is also a part of the salvation history.[110] It also implies that people's movements against injustice and inequality belong to the salvific or redemptive mission of God.

Sin, in the Theology of Liberation, is a socio-historical fact. It is basically the absence of love and brotherhood/sisterhood in the relationships between human beings. Sin manifests in history because of the lack of right relationship with God and fellow beings. The collective nature of sin is evident in the oppressive and exploitative structures and institutions like slavery. Sin, the fundamental alienation – from God and fellow beings – is the source of injustice and exploitation.[111] Christ, through his liberating action liberates human beings from sin. He is the liberator in human history. But only participation in the historical process of liberation inaugurated by Christ can show the present in the contemporary unequal relations.[112] As liberator, Christ makes human beings truly free and enables them to restore the communion with God, and consequently with fellow beings.[113] The liberation which comes through His work is multi-faceted: political liberation, the liberation of human beings throughout history and liberation from sin and admission into communion with God.[114] This liberation occurs in concrete historical situations. It manifests primarily in the rectification of social relationships strained by the oppressive social and economic mechanisms.

Human history is the site of human encounter with God. Historically, the encounter happened in Christ. It is a continuous process, and is being celebrated in the present as eschatological joy. The dynamic and continuous presence of God in human history is one of the Biblical promises. In the Old Testament, the Tent and Ark indicate the incessant companionship of God who also shared the historical realities of His people. Moreover, the Spirit of God is present among humanity to fulfill the salvific plan.[115] It means that God is present in the historical movements of people, and knowingly or unknowingly, they encounter God in historical situations.

According to Gutierrez, 'since God has become man, humanity, every man, history is the living temple of God'.[116] If a person is the living temple of God, one may meet God in his/her encounter with another fellow being. It points to the fact that fellow beings are sites of encountering and knowing God in history. The knowledge of God leads one to do justice to the poor and the oppressed.[117] 'To know Yahweh, . . . to love Yahweh, *is* to establish just relationships among men, it *is* to recognize the rights of the poor. The God of Biblical revelation is known through inter-human justice. When justice does not exist, God is not known; he is absent.'[118] Right relationships can be experienced in our historical existence. Theologizing should be an attempt to give critical reflection on the right relationships between human beings. The absence of just and right relationships has created histories/historical events of oppression in the world. Theology of Liberation attempts to bring out the theological response to the unequal social relationships which resulted in different forms of oppression and exploitation in the socio-political-economic context of Latin America. It is the result of the interaction of faith with historical realities. The contextual realities of the poor in Latin America are historically developed. Theology of liberation affirms that the historical oppression and exploitation can be eliminated through the praxis of Christian faith which reaches out to the fellow beings. This eventually creates liberating historical events in society. In line with Gustavo Gutierrez's liberation theology, it can be said that in the context of the unequal social relationships created by the caste system and patriarchy in India, the subaltern historical movements of resistance like the Upper Cloth Revolt stand as movements to establish social justice. Theologically, they are the movements of faith-praxis.

Gutierrez observes that expansion of the Kingdom of God is a historical process. It historically happens in the liberation of the people, particularly the oppressed. Though the culmination of the process of liberation is with the final coming of the Kingdom, the liberating events are the medium of the growth of the Kingdom of God in human history. It means a liberating historical event or movement is a sign of the growth of the Kingdom of God. It can also be called as salvific event. It does not mean that any historical liberating event is 'the' coming of the Kingdom or 'all' of salvation.[119] Thus, the historical events of people which give them liberation – partial or full – from inequality and injustice, can be interpreted as the realization of the Kingdom in particular context. The Upper Cloth Revolt is one of such events which mediated the liberation of Nadar women from the bondage of the socio-patriarchal prohibition on dress code. The Nadar women experienced liberation not only from caste restrictions but also from patriarchal designing of their dress code. The liberative element qualifies this movement to be identified as a sign of the growth of the Kingdom of God. The Theology of Liberation, theological articulation based on the historical experiences of people, considers history as one of the sources of developing new interpretations of Christian faith and looks at the historical movements from the perspective of liberation.

Black Theology

Black theology is born out of the historical experiences of the black people in the context of racial discrimiantion. It revolts against the spiritual and physical enslavement of black people. It endeavours to affirm blackness.[120] The essence, nature and purpose of Black theology can be summarized as 'a theology of the oppressed, by the oppressed, for the liberation of the oppressed'.[121] The historical experience of 'colour' is the point of departure for the Black theology.[122] It is the story of the struggle of black people for their liberation from the oppression of white colonizers and slave masters.[123] In the South African black context, Black theological expression bases itself on the historical experiences of oppression, fear, hunger, insult, and dehumanization. The process of Black theologizing starts with the search and analysis of black history before and after the arrival of white people. Then, it turns to Scripture. What is the judgment on the rich oppressor? What is the hope for the oppressed? What is the freedom for the poor and how can the poor throw off their oppressive chains? etc., are the questions asked of the Scripture and tradition in Black theologizing.[124]

Black theologizing in America too emphasizes the history of black people. James H. Cone says they did not come to America by their choice; they did not come to America to escape despotism, but were brought as slaves. Their life in America was shaped by the experiences of slavery. Therefore, Black theology understands the identity of black people in relation to its African heritage.[125] Cone argues that black history 'did not begin with the fifteenth century European enslavement of Africans. Our origins go much further back into the pages of known and "unknown" history. Known in the sense that we were there in the Egyptian Nile Valley; unknown in sense that the meaning of our personality is not dependent on the records of ancient history.'[126] This assertion is necessary to define identity, and to raise consciousness defend themselves against oppressors.[127] Sadly, slavery shaped black minds to forget their African past and internalize the values of their slave masters. They were even made to accept slavery as divinely ordained and self-hatred was the result.[128] Regarding the relation of Black history to Black theologizing James Cone says, 'Black theology places our past and present actions toward black liberation in a theological context, seeking to destroy alien gods and create value structures according to the God of black freedom.'[129]

Black people articulated new expressions of faith out of their painful historical realities. For the indigenous people of South Africa, Christ is black. As a Jew in the first century, he was colonized and oppressed like the blacks. In his ministry, he proclaimed good news to the captives and identified with the poor. Though he was captive under the Roman rule, he was also the liberator of the oppressed.

His oppressed identity corresponds to his black identity.[130] Black people also believe that the description of Jesus as Black Messiah is not the product of minds 'distorted' by their oppressed condition, but rather the only meaningful Christological statement in their life.[131] 'Jesus is the Black Christ' is an outcome of their encounter with Jesus who was despised, humiliated, and went through pain-pathos like the blacks.[132] Indeed, Black Jesus is the product of black history.

For the blacks, Jesus was a God who came in person to set the enslaved free. The Black people were the enslaved throughout many centuries in their own land and in America. Jesus came to make the first (the Oppressors) last and the last (the Victims) first: the liberator of the Black people.[133] The image of the liberator of a black poeple cannot be white. Only the Black Jesus can share the black existence.[134]

In Black theology, 'Freedom' is the relational image of God. Black people affirm that 'God is Freedom'. 'God is Freedom' is the freedom that leads one out of the chains of oppression into wholeness of life. God exists as wholeness of life amongst the people when dignity and the value of every human being irrespective of colour, is mutually affirmed and respected in love, justice, and truth.[135] The liberating activity of Yahweh in the Exodus (Ex. 19: 4-5) endorses the image of God as Freedom. In the Exodus, God freed the people of Israel from slavery. [136] 'God as freedom' reflects the longing of blacks to come out of the discriminated life realities which are historically created.

The Black theology rejects the understanding of salvation which does not embrace the social, political and economic dimensions of human existence.[137] For the blacks, salvation is basically liberation from earthly bondage-racism. It is freedom from oppression, exploitation and dehumanization due to their color.[138] It is a historical reality. They believe that though the Kingdom of God will ultimately be consummated in future, Christ's resurrection reveals that the blacks are not alone. God is with the blacks, and their liberation will be a reality in this world.[139] The Black theological reflection on salvation comes out of their faith affirmation in the historical context.

In their theologizing attempts, black people interpreted the Biblical stories in the light of their historical humiliation and subjugation. They reflected on faith in relation to their memories of enslavement and present life realities. Through their own stories, their history, the historical interventions of God in the life of people of Israel were interpreted to open a new future.[140] The subalterns in India also should read and interpret their stories/historical events in the relation to Biblical stories which narrate God's liberating intervention. In this direction, as a liberating story, the Upper Cloth Revolt can be read to construct a new theological expression. As the Black theology is resourced by the 'blackness' of blacks, so the subaltern theological expression can be developed from the subjugated experiences of subalterns due to caste system and patriarchy. The Upper Cloth Revolt, the outcome of the subjugation of the Nadars, particularly their women, can widen theological expression of subalterns in Indian context. Finally, the Black theological reflections are the product of black stories. This underlines the possibility of developing contextual/local theologies based on the historical events of the people in respective context. It places the Upper Cloth Revolt, which contains the stories of pain, resistance and anger of a community, particularly its women against their caste oppressors, in the space of theological articulation.

Eleasar S. Fernandez's Theology of Struggle

Towards a Theology of Struggle is an articulation of Christian faith in the light of the life realities of Filipinos under the long years of colonial rule. It is the theological expression of their resistance to the colonial rule. The Filipinos share the experiences of being colonized by multiple colonizers: the Spaniards, the North Americans, the Japanese and again by the North Americans.[141] Their wealth was looted and they became subservient subjects in their own country. The culture of violence was a normal reality in their society. Uninterrupted colonial rule and subjugated life made them accept their condition as the will of God. But they did not live in the culture of silence for long. The Filipinos gradually understood that their subjugated life was not ordained by God, but the product of history. They believed that since it was a product of history, it could be changed. Their historically muted voices began to be heard in different forms.[142]

Theology of Struggle is a reflection from the historical experiences of Filipino Christians. It is a faith expression of 'those who suffer and therefore struggle together with those who struggle and therefore suffer'.[143] Christianity and classical theology were instrumental in Western subjugation of the Filipinos. A theological revolution was needed to strengthen their nationalistic democratic struggle.

Eleazar S. Fernandez explains: 'My reading claims to be a reading from below – from the experience of those whose history has long been muted. It is a reading derived from the experience of those who are daily threatened by another kind of trinity: the absence of breakfast, lunch and dinner.'[144] It implies that theological reading must come from the historical experiences of the people. He also observes that an authentic Filipino history can be written from the perspective of those who have realized their subjugated condition and have begun to struggle for liberation. Their history is a history of struggle. It is a struggle to own a nation which embodies the hopes and aspirations of the Filipinos. If the history of Filipinos is the history of struggle, then theology must be theology of struggle. They cannot think of a theological expression outside the history of struggle.[145]

Since, Theology of Struggle is born of the history of struggle; it has no existence apart from struggle. It is shaped by the history of struggle, and can be aptly understood only in terms of struggle. It is completely rooted in the experience of struggle and aspirations of Filipinos.[146]

Theology of Struggle endorses the words of Edicio de la Torre: 'Christ must be a Filipino if Filipinos are to be Christians'.[147] In line with this expression, Theology of Struggle argues that the image of God also must be Filipino. God in the image of their conquerors and their Filipino cohorts is not relevant and meaningful to the struggling Filipinos. Jesus is a struggling Filipino. They reject the

Christ of conquerors, and understand Him through their history of struggle, popular culture, and religiosity.[148]

His identification causes Jesus to suffer with them. The Filipinos understand 'suffering' in two ways. First, suffering is understood in terms of *kapalaran*, fatalism. According to *kapalaran*, suffering is predestined. Second, suffering is viewed in relation to *malasakit* (willingness to suffer for others or for a cause) and *pakikiramay* (vicarious suffering). Jesus can be best interpreted through *malasakit.* Jesus as *malasakit* is the apt image of Jesus for the suffering and struggling Filipino.[149] *Malasakit* is the heart of Jesus' life and work. His life, death and resurrection authentically proved it. He lived and suffered for others. He also stood for the cause of others.[150] 'Jesus' suffering is not a passive suffering, but a struggling suffering, encouraging others to do the same.'[151] Theological interpretation of struggle and Jesus as *malasakit* emerged out of the historical experiences of Filipinos.

Minjung Theology

Minjung theology is an attempt to understand and interpret the Christian faith in the light of the past and present realities of the *Minjung* in Korea. The term *Minjung* is translated in English as 'people.' But theology defines *Minjung* as those who are weak and powerless because of their class, race, status, or religion. As clarified by Young-Bock, those who experience political oppression, economic deprivation, and exploitation, social alienation, cultural or religious discrimination are the *Minjung.*[152] As a new theological development, *Minjung* theology was surfaced in 1970s in the context of the struggle of *Minjung* for their just and basic rights in Korea. The proponents of this theology reflected on the historical experiences of the *Minjung*, their contemporary realities of suffering and struggle and their aspirations and hopes.[153] By a re-reading of the Bible, theologians discovered that the Gospel is intended to affirm the life of the poor. They ultimately inherit the Kingdom of God as subjects. The feelings, different perceptions and perspectives shaped by the pain in the body of the poor are the subject of *Minjung* theology.[154]

Minjung theological expression is based on the exploited and discriminated condition of *Minjung,* which is historically formed. Their history is a history of suffering. They carry the burdens of the time to sustain the societies throughout the centuries. They sustain society through their work in the factories and agricultural fields and by rendering services in different capacities. It is their suffering which created new chapters in history. It means they sustain not only society but also 'history.' The socio-cultural-political dynamism of social life is completely dependent on the suffering and sacrifice of the *Minjung*. In fact, their suffering is the foundation of the society. History cannot be understood without them as subjects. Their stories are the flesh and blood of history.[155] The *Minjung* are the real subjects and the makers of the history of Korea. *Minjung* theology reflects on the historical experiences of *Minjung*.

The *Minjung* historical experiences show that the economy of Chosun Dynasty (1392-1910) was sustained by the sweat and blood of the *Minjung*. Young innocent Korean girls were forcibly taken for the entertainment of Japanese soldiers during the Second World War. Their experiences are part of *Minjung* stories. The painful stories of the war victims, their widows, and the members of families separated in the Korean War and the division of people because of the Cold War are stories of *Minjung* experiences. The *Minjung* in thousands were taken to Hiroshima and Nagasaki to work in the factories which produced war equipment for Japan. They became the historical victims of the atomic bomb. Even before the tragedy occurred they were living and working in inhuman conditions of the factories and slums. They had to face discrimination in the emergency situation. When atom bombs were dropped, the Japanese victims were evacuated first from the places of devastation and were given care.[156] These historical realities are the site of *Minjung* theologizing.

The *Minjung* theology understands the Bible as the paradigmatic story of *Minjung*. For the *Minjung*, the Bible depicts their social biography or the life history more meaningfully than any other narration. Biblical stories correspond to the histories of *Minjung* in different periods. Like these, individual *Minjung* stories are interlinked with the experiences of an entire community. For them, their stories also form the site for God's liberating action in history. They understand the visions of prophets and messianic vision in the light of their social biography which was shaped by agonies and wounds inflicted upon them by the historical forces of oppression and exploitation.[157] From their reading of the Bible they discovered that 'The Bible is a *Minjung* book'.[158]

Minjung theological reflections are centered on the pain experienced by the bodies of *Minjung*. The *Minjung* body experiences the pain caused by historical situations. Unlike the intellectuals and rulers who experience history in their heads, the *Minjung* experience history in their bodies. The workers, farmers and slaves, the main components of *Minjung* category, bear the pain of maintaining society. Their bodies were broken and bled when the Korean society had gone through different historical stages. Their society was built on the pain of their bodies.[159]

The *Minjung* identify their life with the life of Hebrews under Pharaoh. Like the people of Israel, they had to toil and bear the pain in their bodies under the oppressive socio-political systems. For them, the embodiment of God in Christ's incarnation and suffering took place among the *Minjung*. The suffering of *Minjung* and Christ points to a bodily solidarity between God and the *Minjung*. The *Minjung* make their Christological statement based on Philippians 2: 5-8. Christ became *Minjung*, a servant and bore the burden of the whole world. What the *Minjung* did for the Korean society, Jesus Christ did for the entire world. The movement of *Minjung* in history is expressed through the vision of Prophet Ezekiel in Chapter 37. As the *Minjung* of Israel moved against the powers of Babylonian and Assyrian power, the *Minjung* moved at the bottom of history to sustain the Korean society. Their movement was the movement of suffering, and endured the pain of injuries in bodies personally and collectively.[160] The suffering movement of the *Minjung* is the 'the manifestation of the Messianic movement of the *Minjung*, and it is not dictated by abstract historical dialectics or laws but by their bodily experiences.'[161]

For the *Minjung* who are alienated socially, exploited economically, and oppressed politically in Korea, God and Jesus are the God of *Minjung* and Jesus of *Minjung*. They affirm that God and Jesus are primarily on their side when they are oppressed or exploited.

Jesus is portrayed as a true man and true God and the Messiah who liberates them from their oppressors.[162] Since the classical Christological titles are unintelligible to the *Minjung*, they called Jesus *Minjung*. For the ordinary workers, Jesus is none other than the worker, the son of a carpenter. As a worker and son of a worker He can understand and embrace the painful realities of workers.[163] Ahn Byung-Mu interprets Matt 25: 31-46 that 'Christ exists among people who are in prison, poorly clothed, starving, poor or captive. These people are the *Minjung* and therefore Christ is *Minjung*.'[164] The *Minjung* theological reflections basically developed out of the *Minjung* history of suffering throughout the centuries. The existential historical realities of *Minjung* have been theologically interpreted in the *Minjung* theologizing. In India, the subalterns experienced the pain of sustaining the society as the *Minjung* did in Korea. Their bodies were broken to build the society controlled by the upper caste elites. The worst thing was that their bodies also had to bear the pain to 'sustain' the caste-based social order. With their wounded bodies they served the dehumanized society. Still it continues in different forms. The Nadars, one of the subaltern communities in Travancore, not only experienced the burden of caste rules but also resisted against it. Their resistance developed into the form of a revolt known as Upper Cloth Revolt. The memoirs of this subaltern movement can be theologically articulated as it was done with the *Minjung*. The *Minjung* Theology brings out the principle that social biography of the people can be the site of developing new theological formulations. It contains the historical experiences of pain and subjugation endured by the subalterns in a particular context. The Upper Cloth Revolt is the social biography of Nadars, particularly their women, in a caste-ridden patriarchal society.

Dalit Theology

Dalits, people who were categorized as 'impure' or 'outcastes' in the hierarchy of the caste system, were denied basic human rights, and as landless groups were forced to do cheap labour. They continue to experience discrimination in different forms because of their caste identity.[165] Dalit theology articulates the life-stories of Dalits with liberation from the bondage of caste discrimination and oppression as the focal point of theologizing.[166] Dalit theologizing is built on historical experience. Arvind P. Nirmal observes that Dalit theology is based on a painful history. It is the story of their sufferings and of their *pathos*. The history of Dalit *pathos* shapes the Dalit expression of Christian faith.[167] The importance of history in Dalit Theology is expressed by Sunder Clarke in this way, 'It cannot be an armchair theology or a verandah theology or a shadow theology but it will have to be a theology worked out from the history of a suffering at the grass-roots level.'[168] V. Devasahayam also views that Dalit theology primarily focuses on the historical life realities and experiences of Dalits in caste society.[169]

According to James Massey, knowing the history of Dalits is one of the requirements to articulate Dalit theology.[170] The Dalit's history of oppression is more than 3500 years old.[171] Therefore, the people who write Dalit theology should also go beyond the history of oppression and attempt to understand who the Dalits were before the institution of caste came into existence. This means a re-construction of Dalit history. The reconstruction can be done with the help of the oral traditions of Dalits and to an extent the written sources of their oppressors.[172] The reconstruction can reveal Dalits as the first dwellers or the indigenous people of India. They were once free human beings, and lived without any oppression and discrimination. They possessed land and natural resources. But with the arrival of Aryans and the institution of caste, they became non-persons and lost their freedom, dignity and identity. The original identity of Dalits can motivate the Dalits to counter the identity imposed on them by the caste people.[173]

The point of departure for Dalit theology is 'Dalitness,' the essence of Dalit history and identity. This 'Dalitness' is shaped by the historical and present experiences of Dalits under the caste system. Their history is a history of Dalitness – a history of exclusion, marginalization, and discrimination. The operation of caste wounded the Dalit psyche and kept them in a state of humiliating powerlessness. Their Dalitness includes loss of identity, a broken psyche, an exploited body. They experience Dalitness equally in the Church and in society.[174]

In the hermeneutical process, the Dalit world and the Biblical world are brought together in dialogical form. Here, the Dalit historical realties of oppression and discrimination interact with Biblical stories. The Dalit heritage – their popular stories, legends, songs, proverbs, folklore and traditions – is placed along with Biblical texts and interpret the text in the light of Dalit heritage. Thus, the Biblical texts can be made meaningful to the Dalit context. Dalit hermeneutics also attempts to place the assertive struggles of the Dalits and the stories of Biblical characters intertextually.[175] It gives theological meaning to Dalit movements.

In Dalit theology, God is interpreted in relation to the Dalit realities – past and present. It defines God as Dalit God in the light of the nature of the traditional jobs imposed upon the Dalits. Biblical God is interpreted as the Self-existent who does not create others to do servile work but does servile work himself. The servile work was and is the lot of Dalits in Indian society. In theology, Christ is identified as Dalit. Jesus is the prototype. As Son of Man and Dalit, He underwent rejection, mockery, contempt, suffering, and finally crucifixion. His Dalitness is best symbolized by the experiences on the cross. Jesus cried from the cross, 'My God, My God, why hast thou forsaken me?' The Nazareth manifesto of Jesus is really a manifesto for the Dalits who long to liberate themselves from the historical clutches of subjugation. Jesus' approach to publicans, tax collectors, and Samaritans shows his love and care for the downtrodden. The Holy Spirit is interpreted as a life-giver and empowerer who is on the side of the Dalits for their liberation.[176] According to V. Devasahayam, 'Dalits are the historical continuation of the suffering son of Man, the crucified one, whom the sinful caste system robs of humanhood.'[177] God is understood as Dalit and Jesus is addressed as Dalit, and this directly points to the essence of Dalit historical reality. The resistance of Dalits against caste inequalities is the work of the Holy Spirit. The Holy Spirit empowers the Dalits to assert their identity.

Dalit theology advocates the total salvation of Dalits and their oppressors. It primarily focuses on the liberation of Dalits from their earthly bondage, the bondage of caste and its oppressive structures.

The oppressors of Dalits also need to be liberated. Dalit theologizing can facilitate the process. On the one hand, it can enable the Dalits to resist the historical forces of caste in their journey towards whole salvation; on the other hand, it can bring changes in the minds of the oppressors.[178] The understanding of salvation is rooted in the historical relationship of Dalits and their oppressors. The condition of Dalits is because of the oppressive mentality of caste people in the Church and society and there should be liberation for both. Dalit theology makes the *pathos* of the Nadars in Upper Cloth Revolt as the point of departure for new theological articulation. The historical *pathos* of Nadar women caused by caste oppression and patriarchal culture occupies an important place in this theological expression. Dalit theology also informs us that the struggle involved in the Upper Cloth Revolt is primarily divinely inspired because it was fought against dehumanizing social restrictions which denied freedom to human beings.

Tribal Theology

Another Indian liberation theology, tribal theology, emerged out of the interaction between the tribal context and the Gospel. It seeks to reflect on the past and present experiences of the various tribes, and aims to liberate them from an inferiority complex, economic oppression, and social discrimination. It attempts to re-discover the theological value of liberative elements in tribal culture and to re-interpret the Bible and Christian doctrines in the light of their pertinent issues such as alienation of land and culture, struggle for identity, etc.[179] The vision, aspirations and the struggles of Tribals have been theologically articulated to enable them to challenge all forms of alienation in their land.[180] Their myths, stories, songs, experiences of suffering and struggle, cultural practices and relationship with land, are important sources of tribal theologizing.[181]

The history of tribal communities in India is a history of the suffering of alienation, discrimination, genocide, exploitation, and displacement. The Aryan invaders, the Muslim rulers, the British administrators, and the caste people of India have caused them alienation and oppression. They are culturally alienated, politically powerless, economically exploited and socially stigmatized.[182] It has been well-expressed that tribal 'cultural heritages are well preserved in books and museums, while the people themselves are treated with contempt.'[183] Nirmal Minz observes that like the Dalits, the *Adivasis* (Tribals) are indigenous people or the *Adi* community of ancient India. While the Aryan invaders subjugated the Dalits, *Adivasis* escaped Aryan subjugation by retreating to remote forests, and maintained their identity and distinct life-style.[184] Today, they are being displaced from their ancestral land, forest, and public places in the name of development and the protection of forest. They are displaced, but replaced by the caste people in their locations.[185] They have a history of struggle against the British and the landlords to prevent their land and culture from being alienated.[186]

In their attempts to affirm historical and cultural identity, some tribes reject the label 'tribal', which is often used in a derogatory sense by others. They wish to be called as Naga, Mizo, Khasi, Munda, Santali, etc. They argue that the names of their communities evoke their pride, confidence, and self-esteem, more than the generalized term 'tribal' which presents them as inferior, dependent, and passive.

Historical and contemporary experiences are prioritized in tribal theologizing. In the context of pejorative labels as tribals, such people identify with the Twelve Tribes of Israel whom God had chosen as His instrument to reveal Himself in history. They emphasize the tribal identity of the people of Israel and affirm that tribals are God's people. Tribal history is considered as the foundation of their faith in God. They place their history of alienation along with the historical experience of Israelites.[187]

Tribal theological reflections backed by the historical experiences are evident in the affirmation that Jesus is a displaced *Adivasi*. The experience of displacement led the *Adivasi* theologians to reflect Jesus as a displaced *Adivasi*. They argue that Jesus was born as a displaced person and represented a displaced community and thus shares the co-fate of many displaced *Adivasis*.[188] Nirmal Minz elaborates the point further that the displaced realities of *Adivasis* can be embraced and understood only by a displaced God. The cry of the *Adivasis* out of the pain of displacement made God displace Himself from heaven and came to this world as Jesus of Nazareth. He met the displaced ones. In His attempt to rehabilitate them, He became a suffering servant of God. In this way, He participates in the suffering and struggles of *Adivasis,* the weakest among the weak.[189]

Renthy Keitzar observes that Jesus becomes meaningful and appropriate to the Nagas if He is a Naga.[190] As a Naga, Jesus must be one who shares the present and past realities of Nagas, and the one who lives amongst the Nagas and speak their languages.[191] It implies that Jesus as Naga can emerge only from the historical existence of Nagas.

Jesus Christ is also interpreted as a 'suffering boy' in the Munda tribal context. In the Munda *Ashur Kahani* (Ashur traditional story) there is a story of a 'suffering boy' who was sent by God to liberate the people from the oppression of *Ashurs.* The 'suffering boy' came and became a sacrifice in the furnace of the *Ashurs.* But he came out of the furnace with a shining body and delivered the people.[192] In theologizing, the Pauline concept of reconciliation is interpreted in the light of *Ao* Nagas' practice of *Aksu.* In the custom, pigs are given as present between the persons or the clans or the villages as a symbol of restoring peace and friendship.[193] *Alhou*, whom the Semas worshipped and offered sacrifices, is identified with *logos.*[194] In these theological expressions, they used their past customs and oral history. Tribal theologizing like other theological ventures, is centred on the experiences of people who are historically rooted. Here, the past experiences interact with the elements of Christian faith. As the past experiences served to bring out Tribal theological reflections, the historical experiences of Nadar men and women centered on Upper Cloth Revolt can give birth to new theological expressions.

Indian Feminist Theology

Indian feminist theology is a contextual theological reflection on the historical and contemporary experiences of women in the Church and in society. The oppressed life realities of women in the patriarchal and caste-ridden social context are the locus of Indian feminist theologizing.[195] Indian women in general have a history of devaluation and oppression. Their inferior status has been historically assigned and operated within the framework of religious beliefs and patriarchal cultural values.[196] In feminist theologizing, an attempt is made to correct the traditional theology which overlooked the historical existence and the life of women. It critically analyses the condition of women and reads history and the religious texts from their perspective.[197] The point of departure for Indian feminist theologizing is women's historical experiences of devaluation and oppression which makes them valueless, faceless, and voiceless. A majority of Indian women face this reality though it varies from community to community. The women of high-caste origin are devalued less compared to the subjugated life of Dalit or tribal women.[198] Prasanna Kumari observes that Indian feminist theology is mainly drawn from historically discriminated, silenced, excluded, and subjugated reality of Indian women.[199]

The history of women's suffering and struggle plays an important place in Indian feminist theology. According to Gabriele Dietrich, 'We have to unearth such fragments of history which have remained invisible through the glasses tainted by patriarchy. We recapture the dimension of the resurrection for past sufferings and defeats and open up a new path into the future.'[200] This implies that recapturing the past is essential for developing feminist theological expressions.

Indian feminist theological methodology is informed not only by the stories of women in general but also by the experiences of Dalit and tribal women.[201] The stories of Dalit women are the stories of thrice alienation and oppression on the basis of class, caste, and gender. They bear the pain of being Dalit among the Dalits.[202] They constitute half the Indian Church. Therefore, any theological expression, particularly the feminist theology, which does not address and embrace their question, is unwholesome.[203] Birth in a Dalit community is the worst misfortune for a woman in Indian society. She is treated as 'non-person' and is deprived of freedom and dignity enjoyed by other women. Her life is justified by serving men and upper castes. Her womanhood is surpassed by her Dalitness. Her identity is primarily defined in terms of her Dalitness, not in terms of her gender. Her Dalitness is the root of her alienation and devaluation. The bodies of Dalit women bear the pain inflicted by the atrocities of upper caste men and their own men. Dalit women come across molestation, rape and death more than the women of non-Dalit origin. Often, they are subjugated to abusive and demeaning language.[204]

Feminist theology in northeastern India attempts to liberate women from the bondage of traditional patriarchy and empower them to become equal partners with men in all aspects of life.[205] It critiques women's deprivation of inheritance rights and the tribal customary law which places women inferior to men.[206] It also exposes the institutional practices which keep women subjugated and deny their humanhood.[207] The historical experiences of north-eastern women give theological response to patriarchal domination in church and society. For the Naga women, their pre-Christian history is a history of sorrow inflicted by the practice of headhunting. When their men went hunting, the Naga women had to bear the burden of sustaining the family and the village. They had to plough, sow, glean, and reap in the fields. While their men were hunting heads for the honour of their respective tribes, the Naga women had to go through the pain and struggle to give birth to babies in the fields. Apart from these struggles, they severely experienced the 'sorrow' of losing their husbands and sons in the headhunting custom. While head hunting was an act of honour for Naga men, it was a source of sorrow for the Naga women as a wife, a mother and a sister.[208] The Naga women continue their experience of 'sorrow' in their post-Christian history too. The patriarchal norms, customs and practices which caused the sorrow of Naga women in the past have been working in the contemporary Church and society. Naga women are not given adequate space and participation in the ministry life of the Church. The negation of deserved opportunity is a relic of traditional history of headhunting in the Church. It is done to honour men over women.[209]

Indian feminist theologians, in the light of the historically subjugated and devalued life realities of women, use the Hindu concept of *Shakti*, the feminine principle to develop new theological formulations. They reflect on *Shakti* to empower women in their struggle against patriarchal oppression in the Church and society. It is the oppressed historical experiences which led women to evoke the *Shakti* principle to counter their imposed inferior identity. Aruna Gnanadason explains *Shakti* 'as the dynamic energy which is the source and substance of all things, pervading everything. Nature is an expression of *Shakti*, the feminine and creative principle of the cosmos; in conjunction with the masculine principle (*Purusha*), *Prakriti* creates the world.'[210] Stella Baltazar sees Jesus as an embodiment of *Shakti*. She says, 'The question for us is not to make Jesus become a woman. Rather, the transcended Christ can be the embodiment of the feminine principle, the *Shakti*, the energizer and vitalizer.'[211] The implied meaning in these assertions is that women embody the creative principle, not the principle of inferiority. If Jesus is the embodiment of *Shakti*, women cannot be denied of partaking in the ministry of Jesus in the Church.

In feminist theologizing, the Biblical stories are understood and interpreted in relation to the stories of women. The story of courageous women who led relentless struggle against the atrocities of the Indian Army in Manipur, brings alive the story of Shiprah and Puah (Ex 1: 15 ff) who disobeyed the diktat of Pharaoh. For a Dalit woman, Hagar, the slave woman, the concubine of Abraham, is her sister in the experience of abuse and struggle for life. The Dalit women who experience humiliation and abuse from upper caste men and women because of their 'Dalitness' reminds one of the story of Hagar who was used and thrown away because of her social position (Gen. 21: 14). For a peasant woman who was forced to work in the field and then in the home, the routine work feels that Martha was not justly treated when Jesus allowed Mary to sit and interact with him. It is observed that the three should have finished the work together and then sat together for talking (Luke 10: 38-42).[212] The Biblical stories are placed along with the stories of women for enabling women to swim against the currents of subjugation and devaluation.

The Dalit women learn from the Mary's Magnificat the Divine Promise of elevating the despised ones in the world. Dalit women are the most despised because of their caste and gender. Thus they are the site of the fulfilment of Divine Promise. From the story of Syro-Phoenician woman (Mk 7: 24-30), the Dalit women understand that God's care extends to the racially despised too. Since they are being despised more than any other women, they deserve God's care more in society. God's care will enable them to assert their lives in society.[213] The Dalit women remember the promise of Jesus that 'I came so that you may have life in the full' (John 10), in their broken and despised lives to end their oppression and subjugation. Their historical memories are not only the memories with scars and bruises in their body and psyche but also the memories of courage and of survival against the odds in the dehumanized society.[214] The above theological reflections are emerged from their historical realities.

Though there are attempts to develop a full-fledged feminist theology in India, a further development of feminist theology lies in interpreting the 'usable past'. The usable past refers to the histories which enable women to chart their way to the future. They are the stories about women's struggle and resistance, which would give the contemporary women courage to challenge the different forms of oppression in society. Such histories have to be interpreted to expand the horizons of feminist theologizing.[215] In India, the resistance of subaltern women against the restrictions of patriarchy and caste has resulted in historical events or movements. The Upper Cloth Revolt is only one such movement in which the agency of women played a vital role to bring about social change.

Liberation Theologies are the outcome of encountering God in the historical realities of the people, particularly the subalterns. They encourage us to consider the historical sufferings and struggles of people against life-negating forces in respective contexts as valid sources for new theological expressions. Therefore the experiences centred on the Upper Cloth Revolt, the historical movement of Nadars, particularly their women, against the oppressive restrictions of caste system and patriarchal culture, are potential sources for developing contextual theological articulations. The histories of subalterns have theological value in the contemporary context.

Conclusion

The scope of history is not limited to the known past, but extends to shape the present and influence the future. The present cannot be meaningfully unlocked without the past. The future cannot escape from the influence of past. The present human experiences/realities are historically rooted and shaped. Likewise, the future cannot be dreamed or planned without looking back to the past. It points to the fact that history plays an important role in moulding the present and future dimensions of human life, including the emergence of new ideologies and new interpretations of faith. Every person/community has history. It may be a history of triumph or a history of subjugation or a history of oppression. It does not mean that the history of every community is well documented or written. Previously, the histories of the dominant and privileged in society were the focus of traditional historical narration. The histories of subalterns in respective contexts were either unwritten or ignored in the attempts of historicizing process. In the Indian context, history was meant only the history of rulers and the high castes. The lower castes, the subalterns and the women, particularly the subalterns among them, were outside the traditional ambit of history.

When such biases were challenged, the monopoly of elite, particularly the hegemony of caste in the narration of histories, as were gender prejudices, the voices of subalterns began to be heard. It placed subalterns as the subject and narrator of their history. Their experiences of pain and struggle because of caste and patriarchy were written from their perspective. Thus the notion of 'the' history was broken and the idea of histories came into existence. The subalterns are no more outside history.

The histories of subalterns in India cannot be understood apart from the dynamism of caste. It is the caste which kept the subalterns outside the histories written by the dominant. The subalterns did not become the writers of their own histories because education was denied to them. Their histories are histories of oppression and subjugation because of the operation of caste in different forms. The historical experiences of subalterns have the marks and bruises inflicted by the caste. On the one hand, their histories are painful stories of forcible submission to the caste and on the other, they contain the brave stories of resistance against the same. It is to be noted that the histories of subaltern women are the experiences of the inter-connected activism of caste and patriarchy. They have the marks of oppressive caste system and male domination.

History and faith cannot be separated because faith is historical. Faith is the historical response of humans to Divine Revelation. Faith develops as a response to God's revelation in a particular period through historical events. God cannot engage with humanity in a vacuum. God meets human beings in concrete historical situations. The human beings are instrumental of God's action in history. It means God's action is not only historically 'divine' but also 'human'. It is historical because God acts in a historical environment. It is human because God explicitly acts through human beings. In other words, history is the product of divine and human encounter. In history God acts; human beings participate either positively or negatively in the action. The action and response are 'recorded' in different forms – written or oral. The participation of God in human history makes history an important source of theologizing. It helps to understand how people encountered God in their lives. Their experiences of encounter are one of the sources of new theologies. At the same time, theologizing is not a single episode but a process. The historical experiences or events can continue to make and shape the theological expressions.

In liberation theologizing, the Christian faith is interpreted in the light of the contextual realities of subalterns, which are rooted in historical experiences. In this process, the Christian faith is looked at through the eyes of subjugated people. The historical existence of oppressed and subjugated peoples and their contemporary realties are one of the important sources of liberation theologizing. If faith is expressed through historical events, it becomes more intelligible to the people. It works as a bond between the past and present experiences in terms of God's participation in particular historical context. It is not logical to substantiate God's action in history through one particular historical event of a community. The universal meaning of God's action in history can be comprehended only through local histories. The Upper Cloth Revolt is one of such local histories. It is a local history of a subaltern community and subaltern women. It is a source for a new theological expression because it is the story of God's action in the life of a community, particularly its women, in asserting themselves and reclaiming their dignity. The next chapter theologically articulates the Upper Cloth Revolt.

NOTES

1. G. Krishnan Nadar, *A Text Book of Historical Method and Historiography* (Kottayam: Learners' Book House, 1998), p. 1.
2. Ibid.
3. R.K. Majumdar and A.N. Srinivasa, *Historiography: Method of History* (Delhi: Surjeet Books, 1985), p. 3.
4. E.H. Carr, *What is History* (Harmondsworth: Penguin Books, 1961), p. 30.
5. G.R. Elton, *The Practice of History* (Glasgow: William Collins & Co., 1967), p. 20.
6. A. Cherian, 'The Selection of Research Students,' in *Historical Research in India,* ed. John Correia-Afonso (New Delhi: Munshiram Manoharlal, 1979), p. 9.
7. John C.B. Webster, *An Introduction to History* (New Delhi: Macmillan, 1981), p. 15.
8. James Massey, 'Historical Roots,' in *Indigenous People: Dalits*, ed. James Massey (Delhi: ISPCK, 1994), p. 3.
9. Quoted from B. Croce, *History as the Story of Liberty* (1941), in E.H. Carr, *What is History*, p. 21.
10. Ibid., p. 21.
11. Ibid., p. 22.
12. Ibid., pp. 26-30.
13. Webster, *An Introduction to History*, p. 13.
14. Ibid., pp. 23-4.
15. Vijayakumar, 'History of Christianity: Methodology for Research', in *Methodological Issues in Theological Discipline,* ed. Samson Prabhakar (Bangalore: SATHRI, 2002), p. 51.
16. G. Venkatesan, *A Study of Historiography* (Rajapalayam: V.C. Publications, 2005), p. 3.
17. Elton, *The Practice of History,* p. 16.
18. Will and Ariel Durant, *The Lessons of History* (New York: Simon and Schuster, 1968), p. 12.
19. Carr, *What is History,* p. 33.
20. Ibid., p. 35.
21. Vijayakumar, 'History of Christianity: Methodology for Research', pp. 48-53.
22. Burton Stein, *A History of India* (New Delhi: Oxford University Press, 1998), p. 35.

23. Quoted in B.D. Basu, *Rise of Christian Power in India* (Delhi: Low Price Publications, 2001), p. 1.
24. Ranajit Guha, 'On Some Aspects of the Historiography of Colonial India', in *Subaltern Studies,* vol. I, ed. Ranajit Guha (New Delhi: Oxford University Press, 1994), p. 1.
25. Ranajit Guha, 'Dominance without Hegemony and Its Historiography', in *Subaltern Studies,* vol. VI, ed. Ranajit Guha (New Delhi: Oxford University Press, 1989), p. 306.
26. Ibid., pp. 308-9.
27. Guha, 'On Some Aspects of the Historiography of Colonial India', pp. 1-3.
28. V.V. Thomas, *Understanding Subaltern History: Theoretical Tools* (Bangalore: BTESSC/SATHRI, 2006), p. xiv.
29. V.V. Thomas, *Dalit Pentecostalism* (Bangalore: ATC, 2008), pp. 13 & 385.
30. V.V. Thomas, 'Methodological Discourses in Theological Disciplines and Approaches in Historiography with Special Reference to the Marginalized in the Pentecostal Churches in India', in *Margins in Conversation: Methodological Discourses in Theological Disciplines*, ed. Joseph Prabhakar Dayam and P. Mohan Larbeer (Bangalore: BTESSC, 2012), p. 241.
31. Abraham Ayrookuzhiel, 'Dalit Challenges to Religious Systems: A People Ignored by Church History', *Indian Church History Review* vol. XXIII, no. 2 (December 1989), pp. 115-31 at 116-17.
32. K. Thanzauva, *Theology of Community: Tribal Theology in the Making* (Aizwal: AICS, 2004), pp. 11-18.
33. Kwok Pui lan, 'The Emergence of Asian Feminist Consciousness on Culture and Theology', in *Culture, Women and Theology,* ed. John S. Pobee (Delhi: ISPCK, 2004), pp. 65-75; Gabriele Dietrich, 'The Origins of the Bible Revisited-Reconstructing Women's History', in *Theology of Humanhood: Women's Perspectives*, ed. Aruna Gnanadason (Delhi: ISPCK, 1986), pp. 31-48; Mary Grey, *The Unheard Scream: The Struggles of Dalit Women in India* (New Delhi: CDS, 2004), pp. 73-87.
34. B.E. Bharathi Nuthalapati, 'A Survey of the Historiographical Shifts in the History of Christianity in India', in *Margins in Conversation: Methodological Discourses in Theological Disciplines,* ed. Joseph Prabhakar Dayam and P. Mohan Larbeer (Bangalore: BTESSC, 2012), pp. 226-7.
35. V.V. Thomas, *Understanding Subaltern History: Theoretical Tools*, p. 50.

36. C. Selvaraj, *Historiography with Special Reference to India* (Udayamarthandam: CSR Publications, 1996), pp. 142f.
37. Prathama Banerjee, 'Caste and History Writing', in *Dalit Assertion in Society, Literature and History,* ed. Imtiaz Ahmad and Shashi Bhushan Upadhyay (New Delhi: Orient BlackSwan, 2010), pp. 227-8.
38. Banerjee, 'Caste and History Writing', p. 229.
39. Nuthalapati, 'A Survey of the Historiographical Shifts in the History of Christianity in India', p. 221.
40. John C.B. Webster, *Social History of Christianity* (New Delhi: Oxford University Press, 2007), p. 3.
41. Ibid., pp. 12-17.
42. Ibid., p. 4.
43. John C.B. Webster, 'The History of Christianity in India: Aims and Methods', *ICHR* 13/2 (December 1979), pp. 87-122 at 89.
44. Webster, *Social History of Christianity,* p. 11.
45. John C.B. Webster, *The Dalit Christians, A History* (Delhi: ISPCK, 2009), p. xii.
46. James Massey, *Dalit Roots of Christianity, Theology and Spirituality* (New Delhi: CDS, 2008), pp. 35-6.
47. Ibid., pp. 39-42.
48. Herbert Butterfield, *Christianity and History* (London: Collins & Fontana Books, 1957), pp. 9-12.
49. Massey, *Dalit Roots of Christianity, Theology and Spirituality*, p. 42.
50. Massey, *Dalit Bible Commentary, Old Testament*, vol. 9, 1&2 *Chronicles* (New Delhi: Centre for Dalit/Subaltern Studies, 2012), pp. 133-9 & 144 f.
51. A.M. Mundadan, 'Hindu and Christian Views of History', in *History and Contemporary India*, ed. John C.B. Webster (Bombay: Asian Publishing House, 1971), pp. 83-91.
52. Mundadan, 'Hindu and Christian Views of History', p. 87.
53. Ibid., p. 90.
54. Butterfield, *Christianity and History*, p. 12.
55. Massey, *Dalit Roots of Christianity, Theology and Spirituality*, pp. 26-7. He also argues that '. . . the existing theologies, particularly the one that came with the western missionaries . . . is rooted in the Greek thought form, as well as in the Pietistic thinking of the West, that mainly focus on the affairs of the "other world" and personal holiness, and the other that was constructed by the so-called upper caste Indian Christian theologians . . . is rooted in the classical Hindu philosophical thought form, which does not give due importance to human history.'

James Massey, *Caste-Class Victims and Their Assertion for Justice* (New Delhi: Centre for Dalit/Subaltern Studies, 2013), p. 9.
56. James Massey, 'Christianity to be Renewed? Rethink Theology', in *Rethinking Theology in India*, ed. James Massey and T.K. John (New Delhi: Manohar and Centre for Dalit/Subaltern Studies, 2013), p. 73.
57. M.M. Thomas, 'Foreword', in R.H.S. Boyd, *An Introduction to Indian Christian Theology* (Delhi: ISPCK, 1991), p. v.
58. K.C. Abraham, 'Third World Theologies', *CTC Bulletin,* vol. XI, nos. 2 & 3 (May-December 1992), pp. 4-12 at 5.
59. James Massey, 'Ingredients for a Dalit Theology', in *Towards a Dalit Theology*, ed. M.E. Prabhakar (Delhi: ISPCK, 1988), p. 60.
60. Huang Poho, 'Foreword', in Wati Longchar, *Returning to Mother Earth* (Tainan: PTCA & Kolkata: SCEPTRE, 2012), pp. vii-viii.
61. Gustavo Gutierrez, *A Theology of Liberation* (New York: Orbis Books, 1973), p. 13
62. V. Devasahayam, 'Doing Theology: Basic Assumptions', in *Frontiers of Dalit Theology,* ed. V. Devasahayam (Delhi: ISPCK and Chennai: Gurukul, 1997), p. 271.
63. V. Devasahayam, 'Doing Theology: Basic Assumptions', p. 273.
64. Kazoh Kitamori, *Theology of the Pain of* God (London: SCM Press, 1966), p. 7.
65. Massey, 'Christianity to be Renewed? Rethink Theology', p. 26.
66. K.Thanzauva, *Theology of Community* (Aizwal: Mizo Theological Conference, 1997), p. 59.
67. Wati Longchar, 'Tribal Identity and Theology', in *Rethinking Theology in India*, ed. James Massey and T.K. John (New Delhi: Manohar and Centre for Dalit/Subaltern Studies, 2013), p. 114.
68. Yangkahao Vashum, 'Sources for Studying Tribal Theology', in *Tribal Theology: A Reader*, ed. Shimreingam Shimray (Johart: Eastern Theological College, 2003), p. 74.
69. James H. Cone, 'The Social Context of Theology', in *Doing Theology Today*, ed. C.S. Song (Madras: CLS, 1976), p. 17.
70. Cone, 'The Social Context of Theology', p. 18.
71. Quoted from Ludwig Feuerbach, *The Essence of Christianity,* trans. George Eliot (New York: Harper Torchbooks, 1957), p. xxxvii, in James H. Cone, 'The Social Context of Theology', p. 18.
72. Quoted from Ludwig Feuerbach, *The Essence of Christianity,* trans. George Eliot (New York: Harper Torchbooks, 1957), p. 11, in Cone, 'The Social Context of Theology', p. 18.
73. Cone, 'The Social Context of Theology', p. 19.

74. Quoted from Karl Marx and Frederick Engels, *The German Ideology,* edited with an introduction by C.J. Arthur (New York: International Publishers, 1970), p. 47, in Cone, 'The Social Context of Theology', p. 21.
75. Quoted from Karl Marx and Frederick Engels, *The German Ideology,* edited with an introduction by C.J. Arthur (New York: International Publishers, 1970), p. 52 in Cone, 'The Social Context of Theology', p. 22.
76. Cone, 'The Social Context of Theology', p. 21.
77. James H. Cone, 'Christian Faith and Political Praxis', in *Confronting Life: Theology out of the Context*, ed. M.P. Joseph (Delhi: ISPCK, 1995), p. 18.
78. Gerhard Sauter, 'How Can Theology Derive from Experiences?', in *Doing Theology Today*, ed. C.S. Song (Madras: CLS, 1976), p. 78.
79. Cone, 'Christian Faith and Political Praxis', p. 25.
80. Interview with R.N. Yesudas, Professor of History and former Director, Institute of Distance Education and Dean of Social Sciences, Kerala University, 2 May 2013.
81. Musimbi Kanyoro, 'The Meaning of the Story: Theology as Experience', in *Culture, Women and Theology*, ed. John S. Pobee (Delhi: ISPCK, 1994), p. 23.
82. Ibid., p. 23.
83. Ibid., p. 24.
84. Ibid., pp. 32-3.
85. Stephen B. Bevans, *Models of Contextual Theology* (New York: Orbis Books, 2002), pp. 10 & 12.
86. Kitamori, *Theology of the Pain of God*, p. 12.
87. Ibid., p. 27.
88. Ibid., p. 27.
89. Ibid., pp. 27-8.
90. Ibid., p. 34.
91. Ibid., p. 34.
92. Ibid., p. 35.
93. Ibid., p. 47.
94. Ibid., p. 135.
95. Ibid., p. 135.
96. Ibid., p. 136.
97. Ibid., p. 137.
98. Ibid., p. 138.
99. Ibid., p. 147.

100. Gustavo Gutierrez, *A Theology of Liberation*, pp. ix-xi.
101. Ibid., p. 301.
102. Ibid., p. 307.
103. Ibid., p. 6.
104. Ibid., p. 7
105. Ibid., p. 10.
106. Ibid., p. 11.
107. Ibid., p. 12.
108. Ibid., p. 13.
109. Ibid., p. 153.
110. Ibid., p. 168.
111. Ibid., p. 175.
112. Ibid., p. 176.
113. Ibid., p. 37.
114. Ibid., pp. 176 & 178.
115. Ibid., pp. 189-91 & 193.
116. Ibid., p. 194.
117. Ibid., p. 194.
118. Ibid., p. 195.
119. Ibid., p. 177.
120. Basil Moore, 'Preface', in *Black Theology, The South African Voice*, ed. Basil Moore (London: C. Hurst & Company, 1973), p. ix.
121. Ibid., p. ix.
122. Cone, 'The Social Context of Theology', p. 33.
123. Ibid., p. 34.
124. Basil Moore, 'What is Black Theology', in *Black Theology, The South African Voice*, ed. Basil Moore (London: C. Hurst & Company, 1973), pp. 6-7.
125. James H. Cone, 'Black Theology and Black Liberation', in *Black Theology, The South African Voice*, ed. Basil Moore (London: C. Hurst & Company, 1973), pp. 48-9.
126. Ibid., p. 50.
127. Ibid., p. 50.
128. Ibid., p. 49.
129. Ibid., p. 52.
130. Moore, 'What is Black Theology', p. 8.
131. James H. Cone, *A Black Theology of Liberation* (Mary Knoll: Orbis Books, 1986), p. 204.
132. Ibid., pp. 213-19.
133. Cone, 'The Social Context of Theology', p. 35.

134. Cone, 'Black Theology and Black Liberation', pp. 56-7.
135. Sabelo Ntwasa and Basil Moore, 'The Concept of God in Black Theology', in *Black Theology: The South African Voice*, ed. Basil Moore (London: C. Hurst & Company, 1973), p. 27.
136. Cone, 'Black Theology and Black Liberation', p. 54.
137. Ibid., p. 53.
138. Ibid., p. 54.
139. Ibid., p. 55.
140. Ibid., pp. 35-40.
141. Eleasar S. Fernandez, *Towards a Theology of Struggle* (New York: Orbis Books, 1994), p. 4.
142. Fernandez, *Towards a Theology of Struggle*, p. 1.
143. Ibid., p. 2.
144. Ibid., p. 7.
145. Ibid., p. 8.
146. Ibid., pp. 22, 25-7.
147. Quoted from Edicio de la Torre, *Touching Ground, Taking Root: Theological and Political Reflections on the Philippine Struggle* (Quezon City, Philippines: Socio-Pastoral Institute, 1986), in Eleasar S Fernandez, *Towards a Theology of Struggle*, p. 2.
148. Fernandez, *Towards a Theology of Struggle*, pp. 95, 100.
149. Ibid., p. 102.
150. Ibid., p. 103.
151. Ibid., p. 103.
152. Kim Young-Bock, *Messiah and Minjung, Christ's Solidarity with the People for New Life* (Hong Kong: CCA, 1992), pp. 7-8.
153. Ibid., p. 3.
154. Ibid., p. 4.
155. Ibid., p. 5.
156. Ibid., pp. 5-7.
157. Ibid., pp. 8-11.
158. Ibid. p. 17.
159. Ibid., p. 13.
160. Ibid., p. 13.
161. Ibid., p. 14.
162. Yim Tesoo, 'Interpretation of the Old Testament from the Perspective of Minjung Theology', *Journal of Tribal Studies*, vol. XIII, no. 2 (July-December 2008), pp. 1-20 at 8-9.
163. Kim Young-Bock, *Messiah and Minjung, Christ's Solidarity with the People for New Life*, p. 16.

164. Yim Taesoo, 'Reflection on Minjung Theology: Messianism and a New Understanding of Minjung-Messianism', in *Dalit and Minjung Theologies: A Dialogue*, ed. Samson Prabhakar and Jinkwan Kwon (Bangalore: BTESSC\SATHRI, 2006), p. 138.
165. M.E. Prabhakar, 'Introduction', in *Towards a Dalit Theology*, ed. M.E. Prabhakar (Delhi: ISPCK, 1989), p. 2.
166. M.E. Prabhakar, 'The Search for a Dalit Theology', in *Towards a Dalit Theology*, ed. M.E. Prabhakar (Delhi: ISPCK, 1989), p. 44.
167. Nirmal, 'A Dialogue with Dalit Literature', in *Towards a Dalit Theology*, ed. M.E. Prabhakar (Delhi: ISPCK, 1989), pp. 78-9.
168. Sunder Clarke, 'Dalit Movement: Need for a Theology', in *Towards a Dalit Theology*, ed. M.E. Prabhakar (Delhi: ISPCK, 1989), p. 32.
169. V. Devasahayam, 'Doing Theology: Basic Assumptions', in *Frontiers of Dalit Theology*, ed. V. Devasahayam (Delhi: ISPCK and Chennai: Gurukul, 1997), p. 273.
170. Massey, 'Ingredients for a Dalit Theology', pp. 340-1.
171. Massey, *Dalit Roots of Christianity, Theology and Spirituality*, p. 31.
172. James Massey, 'Vision, Nature and Method of Dalit Theology', in *Dalit-Tribal Theological Interface*, ed. James Massey and Shimreingam Shimray (Johart: TSC/WSC and New Delhi: CDS, 2007), p. 56.
173. Massey, 'Vision, Nature and Method of Dalit Theology', pp. 57-9 & 69.
174. Charles Singaram, 'Dalit Identity and Textual Tradition', in *Revisiting and Resignifying Methodology for Dalit Theology*, ed. James Massey and Indukur John Mohan Razu (New Delhi: CDS and Bangalore: UTC, 2008), p. 171.
175. Maria Arul Raja, 'Points of Convergence: Dalit World and Biblical World', *Jeevadhara*, vol. XLI, no. 241 (January 2011), pp. 45-55 at 47-50.
176. A.P. Nirmal, 'Towards a Christian Dalit Theology', in *A Reader in Dalit Theology*, ed. Arvind P. Nirmal (Madras: Gurukul/ UELCI, 1991), pp. 63-4 & 65-9.
177. Devasahayam, 'Doing Theology: Basic Assumptions', p. 277.
178. James Massey, *Introducing Dalit Theology* (New Delhi: Centre for Dalit Studies, 2004), p. 27.
179. A. Wati Longchar, *Tribal Theology* (Jorhat: Eastern Theological College, 2000), p. 25.
180. K. Thanzauva, 'Issues in Tribal Theology', in *Tribal Theology: A Reader*, ed. Shimreingam Shimray (Jorhat: Eastern Theological College, 2003), pp. 17-18.

181. A. Wati Longchar, 'As Assessment of the Tribal Theology: Trends and Challenges for Future', in *Tribal Theology on the Move*, ed. Shimreingam Shimray and Limatula Longkumer (Jorhat: Tribal/Women Study Centers, 2006), pp. 8-9.
182. Thanzauva, *Theology of Community*, p. 11.
183. Barnes L. Mawrie, 'Experience of the Tribal Historical, Political, Socio-Cultural Contexts', in *Dalit-Tribal Theological Interface*, ed. James Massey and Shimreingam Shimray (Jorhat: TSC/WSC and New Delhi: CDS, 2007), p. 84.
184. Nirmal Minz, 'Theology and the Struggle of Adivasis/Indigenous People of India', in *Rethinking Theology in India*, ed. James Massey and T.K. John (New Delhi: Manohar and Centre for Dalit/Subaltern Studies, 2013), pp. 121-2.
185. Minz, 'Theology and the Struggle of Adivasis/ Indigenous People of India', p. 132.
186. Ibid., pp. 134f.
187. Thanzauva, *Theology of Community*, pp. 6-8.
188. A.S. Hemrom, 'Towards a Program of Contextual and Adivasi Theology', *Religion and Society*, vol. 50, no. 3 (September 2005), pp. 87-96 at 93.
189. Minz, 'Theology and the Struggle of Adivasis/Indigenous People of India', p. 147.
190. Renthy Keitzar, 'Theology Today', *Journal of Tribal Studies*, vol. II, no. I (Jan.-June 1998), pp. 1-18 at 1.
191. Renthy Keitzar, *In Search of a Relevant Gospel Message* (Guwahati: CLC, 1995), p. 71.
192. Nirmal Minz, *Rise Up My People, And Claim the Promise* (Delhi: ISPCK, 1997), p. 89.
193. Longchar, *Tribal Theology*, pp. 106-9.
194. Inato Aye, 'The Logos Christology from Sema Perspective', in *Tribal Theology: A Reader*, ed. Shimreingam Shimray (Jorhat: Eastern Theological College, 2003), p. 198.
195. Shalini Mulackal, 'Women: Theology and Feminist Movements in India', in *Rethinking Theology in India*, ed. James Massey and T.K. John (New Delhi: Manohar and Centre for Dalit/Subaltern Studies, 2013), p. 153.
196. Mulackal, 'Women: Theology and Feminist Movements in India', pp. 156-7.
197. Ibid., pp. 164-5.
198. Ibid., p. 166.

199. Prasanna Kumari Samuel, *Dalit Women's Experiences: A Theological Imperative for Indian Feminist Theology* (Chennai: Gurukul, 2009), p. 3.
200. Gabriele Dietrich, 'The Origins of the Bible Revisited-Reconstructing Women's History', p. 34.
201. Aruna Gnanadason, 'Feminist Methodology: Indian Women's Experience', in *Confronting Life: Theology out of the Context*, ed. M.P. Joseph (Delhi: ISPCK, 1995), p. 187.
202. Ruth Manorama, 'Dalit Women: The Thrice Alienated', in *Towards a Dalit Theology*, ed. M.E. Prabhakar (Delhi: ISPCK, 1989), p. 146.
203. Manorama, 'Dalit Women: The Thrice Alienated', p. 149.
204. Bama, 'Dalit Christian Women Today: Their Struggles and Prospects for Future', *Jeevadhara*, vol. XLI, no. 241 (January 2011), pp. 35-44 at 35-7.
205. T. Vanlaltlani, 'Problems and Challenges of Doing and Teaching Feminist Theology in North East India', in *Tribal Theology on the Move*, ed. Shimreingam Shimray and Limatula Longkumer (Jorhat: Tribal/Women Study Centers, 2006), p. 76.
206. Ibid., p. 78.
207. Atula Tzudir, 'The Future of Feminist Theology', in *Tribal Theology on the Move*, ed. Shimreingam Shimray and Limatula Longkumer (Jorhat: Tribal/Women Study Centers, 2006), p. 86.
208. Eyingbeni Humtsoe, 'Women's Experience of "Sorrow" As a Source for Doing Theology from Naga Perspective', in *No More Sorrow in God's Garden of Justice*, ed. Limatula Longkumaer (Jorhat: Eastern Theological College, 2007), pp. 1-6.
209. Ibid., p. 6.
210. Kwok Pui-lan, *Introducing Asian Feminist Theology* (Cleveland: The Pilgrim Press, 2000), p. 95.
211. Ibid., p. 96.
212. Aruna Gnanadason, 'Feminist Methodology: Indian Women's Experience', pp. 182-3.
213. Mary Grey, *The Unheard Scream*, p. 79.
214. Ibid., p. 82.
215. Musimbi Kanyoro, 'The Meaning of the Story: Theology as Experience', p. 29.

CHAPTER 4

A Subaltern Theological Interpretation of Upper Cloth Revolt

Introduction

The introductory chapter of this volume has elaborated the importance of interpreting historical events from a subaltern theological perspective and the methodology employed in such process. It argued that the Upper Cloth Revolt is a significant historical event which can be theologically articulated; people of lower caste origin were subjected to numerous oppressive caste regulations which denied their freedom and dignity in society. The survey of liberation theologies in the previous chapter has opened scope for the theological interpretation of the Upper Cloth Revolt.

A historical event can be studied and reflected from diverse perspectives to understand its significance at different levels. It can be read sociologically, politically, historically, or anthropologically, to make it meaningful in a particular context. Each reading brings out new meaning and implication for the readers of the present. It is generally observed that no absolute meaning or one meaning can be drawn from a historical event: an event unlocks a plurality of meanings and implications. The Upper Cloth Revolt as a historical event can be read from different perspectives. The experiences of people involved in this historical occurrence can speak many things to the present context. In order to understand the meaning of the experiences of people, they should be interpreted. In the subaltern framework an attempt is made to interpret the event from a theological view point. A new theological expression is developed out of the experiences of the Nadars, particularly Nadar women, centered on the Upper Cloth Revolt. It is aimed to encourage the subaltern communities and subaltern women to assert their space in their own societies.

Upper Cloth: Social Symbol and 'Theological Interpretant'[1]

A 'symbol' is defined as 'a thing that represents or stands for something else, especially a material object representing something abstract'.[2] A symbol carries multiple implications corresponding to the different dimensions of a reality. It can stimulate thinking, ideas, emotions, passions, senses and meanings though they cannot be completely expressed through a symbol. A new meaning can always be drawn from a symbol if it is looked at from a different angle.[3] As a symbol, the upper cloth opens new horizons of meaning in terms of dignity, freedom, identity, and gender.

Travancore society was characterized by a number of restrictions and prohibitions on the dress code of people of low caste origin. Low-caste women were not permitted to wear the Upper Cloth. It was the exclusive privilege of upper-caste women.[4] In a caste ridden society the dress code conveyed social status. Forbidden the upper cloth, not only the women of low castes and outcastes, but also their respective communities were belittled. This restriction did not deter the Nadars from claiming the upper cloth. As a social symbol the upper cloth 'united' the Nadars. On the one hand, it represented a social reality and on the other hand it can be taken as a theological interpretant. In Upper Cloth Revolt, upper cloth and its use not only symbolized the status and privilege but also the courage and resistance of subaltern women.

Social Symbol as 'Theological Interpretant'

'An interpretant is a sign of some sort – an image, concept, symbol, doctrine, set of categories – whose very reality is to take some other sign, or part of itself, as characterizing a logical object in some respect.'[5] If an object or reality is not interpreted, it remains abstract. Interpretation is needed for both physical and metaphysical realities. An interpretant is required even to explain divine realities in concrete terms. As regards matters related to God, interpretants function not only in expounding the divinity but also in experiencing it.[6] It is observed that 'a well constructed, archeologically deep, experiential interpretant of God can result only from a process in which historical analysis and theological speculation interact with and correct one another'.[7] The upper cloth stands as a theological interpretant for Nadar men and women in their past journey of faith and their struggle for a dignified life. The revolt shows that the prohibited upper cloth was a reason to denounce injustice and inequality. Their internalization of Biblical faith resulted in defiance and breaking the prohibition on the dress code.[8] They had shown what Christian faith meant to them through this symbol and their assertive action. In this process, a social symbol became a theological interpretant. It was this social symbol in which they experienced the Divine. It is an object through which the Nadars of Travancore not only experienced the Divine but also resisted upper-caste hegemony.[9] It happened in the experiences of Nadars, particularly the women among them. The upper cloth as a theological interpretant prompted the subaltern communities to use social symbols, both 'negated' and 'attributed', to explicate and experience divine power in their fight for dignified human life. It is interesting to note that the upper cloth, an object used by women to cover themselves above the waist, became a 'theological interpretant' for a community to understand and experience God of their faith in the context of caste prejudices. The subalterns experience selfhood when they claim and use the symbols denied to them as a mark of freedom, justice, and equality bestowed by the Divine.

The Upper Cloth Revolt: Revolt against Caste

The Upper Cloth Revolt happened in a society where caste defined the dress code of people. Nadar men and women challenged the caste rules and asserted the equal value and dignity of human beings. By wearing an upper cloth in public, the Nadar women were revolting against the caste hierarchy and its mechanisms. It was primarily a revolt against caste which is 'marked not merely by inequality but is affected by a system of graded inequality'.[10] It proclaimed that 'You cannot build anything on the foundations of caste. You cannot build up a nation; you cannot build up a morality. Anything that you will build on the foundations of caste will crack and will never be a whole.'[11] As B.R. Ambedkar noted, the 'abolition of caste'[12] is the only remedy for the marginalization of subalterns. It is a positive change to strive for a casteless society. The Upper Cloth Revolt was one of the initial ventures in this direction. The Christian faith asserts the equality of human beings who are created in the image of God and caste has no place in the Christian community. It encourages the subalterns to question the hegemony of caste and attempts to uproot it from religious communities and society.

God's Visitation/Revelation

Historically, Biblical God is the one who shared His solidarity with people of marginal identities in society. This resulted in creating and rebuilding the identities of marginal people without a sense of self or power. Such people are the location/site of God's visitation.[13] It is implied that the marginalized in any society are where God is experienced. God reveals Himself to people who are enslaved[14] socially, politically, or economically. At the same time, those who received divine revelation, respond to the oppressive realities around. Divine revelation empowers the whole community.[15] When they express their resistance to the oppressive systems and structures and question their subalternized life, God's glory is revealed.[16] The Upper Cloth Revolt was the culmination of God's visitation/revelation in the life of the Nadars at a particular time. It was the 'Text of God's revelation'[17] which was experienced by Nadar men and women. The revolt shares historical continuity with the Exodus event.[18] Like the Exodus, the Upper Cloth Revolt as a historical event carries God's revelation.[19] In the revolt, Nadar women were the primary recipient of divine revelation. Their realization of 'who/what God is' and 'who and what they are' enabled them to claim freedom.

Social Liberation as Salvation

Salvation is generally understood and interpreted in the 'individual soul saving' sense in Christian tradition. But the Biblical understanding of salvation has to do with socio-political and economic aspects of human existence too. In the Old Testament, the root meaning of the word used to communicate 'salvation' is 'to be wide' or 'to be spacious' or 'to develop without hindrance', and salvation is meant as liberation from physical suffering and oppression. It is more structural and corporal than individual experience. In the New Testament, God in Christ meets human beings and liberates them from existential evils of this world.[20] So Biblical salvation is integral in nature, and denounces every sort of injustice and exploitation. It cannot be restricted to the spiritual or 'soul saving' realm alone.[21] It emphasizes the holistic development of people, both material and spiritual. For subalterns, this view of salvation is necessary to come out of their oppressive situations[22] and to experience freedom from the feeling of inferior status and hopelessness, and the restoration of self-respect.[23] From the subaltern point of view, social liberation is an experience of salvation because the liberation sought is not only from physical slavery but also from social stigma.[24] The Upper Cloth Revolt and consequent liberation was for Nadar women salvation offered in Jesus Christ. What Jesus offered is a dignified and liberated life in this world and the world to come. As subalterns, Nadar women's experience of salvation in the context of the prohibition on wearing upper cloth is no less than the permission to cover their bosoms, and their bold appearance with upper cloth in public places.[25] It was a starting point of their salvific experience in its fullness. The uniqueness of this story is subaltern women became an instrument of leading their community into a liberative experience, though not fully, in the caste-infected society.

The Growth of the Kingdom of God

The promise and expectation of the Kingdom of God is an integral element of Christian faith. Though its fulfillment is eschatological in nature, the present dimension of the Kingdom of God is also emphasized in the Scripture. The historical manifestation of the Kingdom, particularly in terms of social justice, is important for the victims of discrimination in society. For Gustavo Gutierrez, the struggle for a just society indicates the coming of the kingdom in this world.[26] He quotes Dom Antonio Fragoso, 'The struggle for justice is also a struggle for the Kingdom of God.'[27] The manifestation of this kingdom happens historically in the liberative process. The liberation of people from oppression and exploitation is a prerequisite for the birth of a new society, the Kingdom of God where no life-negating forces/systems are at work. Liberation comes through liberating historical events/movements which facilitate the growth of the Kingdom of God on this earth. At the same time, a liberating event does not denote full salvation as such, but an event which leads to total salvation.[28] The Nadars experienced the Kingdom of God in two ways: one, by struggling for justice because a 'struggle for justice is a struggle for the Kingdom' and the other by achieving liberation from dehumanizing restrictions. The bold attempt of the Nadar women to cover their bosoms with upper cloth facilitated this liberating event and experience. It should be noted that the subaltern movements, particularly subaltern women's initiatives which resisted the demons of caste and patriarchy, actually are audacious endeavors to enlarge the Kingdom of God which has been already inaugurated. They are the movements which aimed to liberate the subalterns – both men and women – from degraded conditions of caste and gender prejudices. The liberating historical events enlarge the Kingdom of God, which in turn enlarges the space of subalterns.

Historical Event as Eschatological Hope

People experience eschatological hope through liberating historical events. Though not fully, they proclaim the fulfillment of eschatological promises in history. Simultaneously, liberating historical events open up new possibilities which will lead to the complete fulfilment of eschatological hope in future.[29] A ray of hope in one historical event can contribute to the final realization of hope in human community. This 'eschatologization of history' can be understood only by those who have endured pain in life. Moreover, the hopes and aspirations of the oppressed widen the horizon of hope. The realization of eschatological hope through liberating historical events shows that eschatological hope cannot be removed from historical realities.[30] On the one hand, liberating historical events carry a ray of hope and on the other, they point to the anticipation of the complete blossoming of the hope. In the context of social iniquities and graded inequalities caused by caste and patriarchy, subaltern communities and subaltern women see the budding of hope in their liberating historical actions. The Upper Cloth Revolt was a foretaste of the reign of God because it strove to bring about a transformation in society. It opened new horizons of liberation for the subalterns in society.

Women as Agency of Social Resurrection

'Agency' can be defined as 'a thing or a person that acts to produce a particular result'.[31] Women's agency is understood as capacity to act and remove the inequities that disempower women.[32] Transformative action is carried out through human body. Therefore, the body is an essential element of human agency. It is capable for holistic change. It enables human beings to interfere and act in the existential realities. However, the body is socially constructed by the social traditions and systems.[33] In Upper Cloth Revolt, the Nadar women became an agency to remove a social inequity- restriction on covering the bosoms with upper cloth-through their socially constructed subaltern bodies. They have shown that subaltern bodies can become an agency to resist the social evils. In their transformative action, breaking the oppressive social law, they in fact experienced 'resurrection' from their 'diminished humanity',[34] the negation of dignified life. The restriction on upper cloth diminished their human dignity in society. Christian faith affirms the dignity of women. Like men, they are also bestowed with full dignity by God (Gen 1: 26-8). She is created in the image of God. Therefore, she is not 'something' but 'someone' with full humanity. She has selfhood, identity, freedom and self-knowledge. Her dignity is integral to her birth and existence.[35] Since she is created in the image of God; she has the power of free choice. She can make use of her power of free choices and actions to transform her diminished life.[36] In a society where the dignity of subaltern woman is defined by caste and patriarchy, negating her dignity is tantamount to social death. If 'resurrection is liberation from death',[37] restoring the dignity of Nadar women is an experience of resurrection from social death, their diminished humanity. The Upper Cloth Revolt shows that women are also the agency of social transformation, which is often credited to men.[38] In the context of experiencing 'diminished humanity', the subaltern women should be challenged to become agents of social resurrection. They become an agency of social resurrection when they attempt to question and overcome those powers, beliefs, prejudices, ideologies and structures which restrict their freedom, dignity and selfhood.

Upper Cloth Revolt: An Exodus Experience

There are similarities in the experiences of Nadars, particularly their women, in South Travancore with the experiences of the people of Israel in the exodus liberation event. The experience of the people of Israel centered on exodus liberation is given in the Deuteronomic creed found in Deuteronomy 26: 5-9

> my father was a wandering Aramean, and he went down into Egypt with a few people, and lived there and became a great nation, powerful and numerous. But the Egyptians ill-treated us and made us suffer, putting us to hard labour. Then we cried out to the Lord the God of our fathers, and the Lord heard our voice and saw our misery, toil and oppression. So the Lord brought us out of Egypt with a mighty hand and outstretched arm, with great terror, with miraculous signs and wonders. He brought us into this place and gave us this land, a land flowing with milk and honey. . . .[39]

It can be read in relation to the general social experiences of Nadars and the particular experiences of Nadar women in the Upper Cloth Revolt.

A few Nadar ancestors came to South Travancore from Tinnevelly (Tirunelveli) District in present Tamil Nadu.[40] They lived there as palmyra climbers/cultivators and agricultural labourers in the fields of the upper castes. Gradually, they began to improve their condition with the arrival of Christian faith among them. They and their children began to get education and enlightenment. Christian followers increased among them, and this was considered a threat to the social hegemony of upper-caste people.[41] They were ill-treated in different ways. They were treated as polluted people.[42] They had to pay various kinds of taxes and give free or forced labour.[43] Nadar women were not allowed to cover themselves above the waist. They could not dress or wear ornaments like the Nair women. They were sexually harassed and physically exploited.[44] But the cry of the Nadar men and women was heard by God, and strengthened them to fight the oppressive social prohibitions. The bold initiative of Nadar women to appear with the upper cloth resulted in a violent revolt between Nadars and the upper castes in South Travancore. God's 'mighty hand and outstretched arm' was with the Nadars, and so they could resist the powerful upper castes.[45] God's 'miraculous sign and wonder' came in the form of a royal proclamation permitting the Nadar women to clothe themselves as they sought fit.[46] Though the proclamation was with a simple restriction, in the caste ruled society of Travancore, it was metaphorically an Exodus in the Nadar life. The Nadar women appeared with upper cloths like the women of high castes in markets and public places.[47] It was an experience of freedom, justice, and recognition of identity. It was also the 'Exodus experience' of a subaltern community and subaltern women.

Subaltern Liberation: A Divine-Human Partnership

In the Exodus metaphor, the Upper Cloth Revolt is a model subaltern movement which embodied the Divine-Human partnership, an event of the liberation of subalterns.[48] In other words, it can be phrased as Divine-Human partnership, the oppressed became conscious of their oppressed condition and cried to God for liberation. Divine intervention followed.[49] In Upper Cloth Revolt the Nadars became conscious of their social condition, and the Nadar Christian women with the support of their men took the initiative backed by Christian faith, to question the restriction imposed upon them.[50] The Upper Cloth Revolt reminds us that Divine intervention takes the side of the oppressed against their oppressors. God's intervention in the life of subalterns is holistic action which touches every aspect of their lives. Its scope cannot be restricted to the religious space alone (Ex 3: 7-8).[51] The God of Exodus not only hears the cries of subalterns but also restores their dignity and places them in safe location/space.[52] In Upper Cloth Revolt, the God of Exodus is not only the God of men but also the God of women because they primarily experienced the liberating hand of God.[53] It is observed that

> Exodus, the revolutionary event in Bible, was prepared for and made possible by five courageous and daring women. A princess (Pharaoh's daughter) daring to care for and bring up an Israelite boy, condemned to death by her King; Moses' mother (Jochebed) and sister (Miriam) keeping the boy alive in defiance of the King's orders; and two Egyptian midwives (Shiphrah and Puah) who feared God and refused to kill the babies and saw themselves as servants of life rather than as dealers of death.[54]

The courage of these women re-echoed in Nadar women in Upper Cloth Revolt. If they had not taken the daring action of appearing with upper cloth, there would not have been an Upper Cloth Revolt, a subaltern liberating movement. It was basically made possible by Divine-Women partnership. It encourages the subalterns, particularly women to follow Divine-Human/Women partnership in their journey of struggle for liberation.

Upper Cloth Revolt: A Potential Liberative Event for Ritual and Festival

The religious festivals of 'Passover' and 'Unleavened Bread,' the ritual of the consecration of first-born male and the new calendar were started among the Israelites after the Exodus. The festivals, ritual and calendar are memorial of the liberation of Israelites from Egyptian slavery. They are integral to the Israelite religious life. They were instituted by Lord God through Moses basically to help Israelites remember their past and live together as a community.[55] By observing rituals and festivals, the historical experience of slavery and the liberation story of the community are transmitted from generation to generation.[56] Like the religious life of Israelites, historical memories are a dynamic force behind the Christian faith. They are centered on certain historical events. In the New Testament, the Christ event, fundamental to Christian faith,[57] is remembered through sacraments such as baptism and the Lord's Supper. In this sense, Upper Cloth Revolt is a potential historical event for creating a new festival or ritual. A festival or a ritual based on a historical event of social significance can help a community experience history. Subalterns should remind themselves of the stories of the struggles of their forebears, and of their continued struggle to experience life in its fullness.[58] New ritual or festival needs to be developed on the basis of Upper Cloth Revolt. A festival can be celebrated or a ritual can be observed on 26 July every year because the final proclamation on the use of upper cloth was issued on 26 July 1859. If not as a particular ritual or festival, the memory of the Upper Cloth Revolt can accompany in the observance of existing Christian rituals such as Lord's Supper and festivals like Easter. The memories of Upper Cloth Revolt in rituals/festivals will help the Nadars to experience history. It will embolden Nadar women to act for their advancement and for the empowerment of other subaltern women in society.

The Upper Cloth Revolt as a Spirit Movement

The subaltern movements which challenged caste hegemony or male domination in India are generally defined as social or reform movements. But a liberating subaltern historical event, in Christian sense, can be called a 'Spirit Movement'.[59] A.P. Nirmal, reflecting on Ezekiel 37: 1-14, states that 'the Holy Spirit revives these dry bones, gives them life, unifies them and makes an army out of them. For us Dalits then, the Spirit is a life-giver, unifier and empowerer for the liberation struggle of the Indian Dalits.'[60] It is the Spirit of God who empowers the subalterns to fight against the oppression of caste and makes a journey with them in their continued struggle for liberation. The nature of the engagement of the Spirit of God in the life of the subalterns shows that it is the spirit of rebellion and renewal.[61] The Spirit of God who communicated the justice of God through the prophets continues to work through the subalterns of India.[62] It can begin the work from anywhere in the social hierarchy, as with subalterns. The work of the Spirit of God will be an experience of empowerment and liberation for the subalterns, but it will be a great disturbance for the caste people.[63] Only the Spirit of God can lead the subalterns into 'all truth' (Jn 16: 13) of their subalternised life and possibility of resistance and empowerment. If the subalterns are motivated by the Spirit of God to resist oppression and to experience the empowerment, then their movements too are Spirit-led movements. Therefore, Upper Cloth Revolt is a Spirit Movement. The boldness of Nadar women to cover their bosoms is a gift of the Spirit of God. The same Spirit empowered their community to resist the evil forces in the consequent violent revolt perpetuated by the upper castes. In Upper Cloth Revolt, the work of the Spirit of God began with women. Their experience of the Spirit led the community to experience the same Spirit and to encounter the life-negating forces in society. The subaltern movements of resistance, particularly of women come into reality when they are genuinely led by the Spirit. They need to be considered as Spirit Movements. Wherever resistance to hegemony happens there the work of Spirit can be discerned.

A Liberative Struggle

The subaltern movements and resistances basically manifest the subjecthood of subalterns. When they are defined or named by others, that subjecthood is violated. The subalterns should be allowed to define their movements and resistive efforts: who they are and what they are doing. Otherwise, it is just another form of control over subalterns.[64] There is a common tendency among dominant writers to define the resistance of subalterns negatively. Elitist historical narratives describe the subaltern movements or events 'as law and order problems'[65] and devalue them. They fail to understand the 'politics of the people'.[66] The language of the dominant is not innocent or unbiased. The struggles of subalterns may be 'disturbance' for them but for the subalterns, they are struggles of liberation.[67] The dominant naming of the 'Upper Cloth Revolt' both by the natives and missionaries or British authorities as 'Disturbances in South Travancore'[68] or 'The Upper Cloth Disturbances'[69] or narrating the event as 'the disturbances reached their height'[70] or 'Disturbances'[71] or 'The Breast-Cloth Disturbance'[72] or 'dress disturbances'[73] are part of a project of considering the subaltern movements/events as 'law and order' problem or 'violent behavior' of low castes, which 'disturb' the social order. But the Nadars were defying a compelled and demeaning nudity.

The subaltern description of Upper Cloth Revolt as 'the Upper Cloth Revolts',[74] the 'Upper Cloth Riots',[75] 'The People's Revolt',[76] 'A Violent Social Protest'[77] shows that it was not a 'disturbance' as defined by the dominant but a liberative struggle which began with subaltern women against the social inequalities. In this struggle, the Nadar women were marching 'towards a new identity and a fresh destiny'.[78] Thus subaltern movements are emerged from the disgust and discontent with the social disabilities. Knowledge and consciousness contribute to the course of action.[79] The negative naming of subaltern movement by the dominant is an attempt to negate the fact that the subaltern struggle/movement for liberation begins with the conviction of subalterns that they are being oppressed and marginalized. Even if a subaltern movement/event is violent or leads to violent reaction, it is spontaneous.[80] For subalterns, the revolt is the only way to come out of their oppressive condition.[81] The broken life realities force them to perceive that their liberation can be accomplished by force. Therefore, they attempt to break their chains.[82] If subalterns try to break the chains of subjugation, then violence is an outcome because the dominant resist them. In Upper Cloth Revolt, violence was unleashed mainly by the caste people when the Nadars, particularly their women, attempted to break the demeaning custom of being bare-breasted. If at all the Nadars were involved in violence, it was part of their resistance.

Naming and defining is an essential element in the process of empowerment. The subaltern communities need to take initiative to purge the dominant definition of their movements if they are defined negatively. The subaltern naming of Upper Cloth Revolt reminds that women's movements/initiatives/perspectives cannot be considered as 'capricious, emotional and fickle'[83] but they are conscious efforts to get empowered and liberated. It stands as a reminder to the subaltern women to re-define themselves: who they are, what they can do, etc., by taking bold initiatives for their holistic advancement.

A Call for Participation in Liberative Initiatives

It is observed that 'Remembering is to accept the reality of something that happened but which leads to hope of a new life, of a different future, a new humanity.'[84] Remembering the past is a biblical and a theological act. God does not want people to forget their history. God commanded the people of Israel to transmit their past, the history of slavery and liberation, from generation to generation (Deuteronomy 6: 20-5). It is re-emphasized in 1 Cor. 1: 26-8. Remembrance of the past helps the people, particularly the subalterns to know their identity and the struggles of their ancestors, and strengthens them to face present challenges.[85] Though subaltern memories are subjugated memories, remembrance of those memories makes them dangerous and subversive to existing social orders.[86] By remembering the Upper Cloth Revolt; the Nadars not only go back to their roots, but also equip themselves to confront the forces of oppression in contemporary life. When they affirm their history, they fulfil the command of God to remember their past.

The attempts of Nadars to negate and forget their past history, particularly the Upper Cloth Revolt,[87] were a blot on a subaltern liberative event which challenged caste hegemony. Denying the past is tantamount to denying history and identity.[88] A Christian faith community should affirm its roots, identity and historical consciousness along with Christian consciousness.[89] The memory of the past is very important. If Nadars, particularly Christians among them, forget the experiences of their ancestors centered on Upper Cloth Revolt, they not only deny their history and their identity as a community of combat against societal inequities but also neglect the intervention of God in the struggles of their ancestors and the command of God to remember one's history.

Remembering the past should lead to participation in liberative initiatives. The experiences of past generations have the power to inspire the present community. If memories lead to liberative action, the community can claim that past generation has an influence on them. Memory or remembrance is the only connection between generations. The liberative action of one subaltern community does not end with its partial or full success, but continues in the liberative struggles of other subaltern communities. The Upper Cloth Revolt led to the beginning of the social advancement of Nadars and the liberation of Nadar women from the restriction on their dress in the Travancore society and benefited other subaltern women. The remembrance of Upper Cloth Revolt has to lead the Nadars to participate in the liberation struggles of other subaltern men and women in the contemporary society. The participation in liberative initiatives is an honour to the Nadar men and women who suffered a lot for a dignified life in society. Indeed, the Upper Cloth Revolt is a call to liberative action and symbol of hope for the subjugated communities.

Remembering the past, particularly the brave stories of their foremothers motivate the subaltern women to participate in the struggles of women, particularly for justice and equality in various spheres of social life.[90] The Upper Cloth Revolt is a 'usable past'[91] for a subaltern women to learn how to make use of their agency for new hope and a better tomorrow. The present generation of Nadar women also has to look back to the history of their foremothers and participate in the struggles of women in general and subaltern sisters in particular.

United Action: An Essential Element for Subaltern Movement/Advancement

The Upper Cloth Revolt underlines the need of the unity of subalterns beyond religious lines. United action alone can bring success to subaltern struggles. In the beginning of the nineteenth century, by virtue of their religious faith, the Nadar Christian women were allowed to cover themselves. When they modified their dress like upper caste women, they were strictly restricted to jackets called *kuppāyam*.[92] But they appeared in jackets and upper cloths. This led to a violent backlash, later known as Upper Cloth Revolt.[93] Also the orders/proclamations which permitted the Nadar Christian women to cover their chest are silent about the Nadar Hindu women. They were not permitted even to cover their bosoms. But they imitated their Christian sisters, which is evident in the proclamation of 1829[94] which strictly warned the Nadar Hindu women to keep away from covering the upper part of their bodies and in the proclamation of 1859[95] which permitted them to clothe themselves in the manner they chose.

Although there was minimal participation on the part of Nadar Hindus in the initial stages of the revolt started by the Nadar Christian women and men, they began to actively participate in the movement after the proclamation of 1829. Beyond religious lines, both Hindu and Christian Nadars stood together for the dignity and the right of their women. They were united physically, emotionally and ideologically.[96] Both the Nadar Hindu and Christian women asserted their agency by appearing in public in upper cloths. They supported each other in their united liberative action.[97] They suffered a lot for their united assertion. They were physically and emotionally attacked, and their houses and earnings were plundered and destroyed.[98]

The Upper Cloth Revolt invites the subaltern communities to unite beyond the religious barriers. The subalterns can overcome their subalternized conditions only through united action. It is to be noted that the unity is a biblical virtue.[99] In a pluralistic context characterized by the interplay of religion and caste, the religious fundamentalists and the upper caste often attempt to divide the subalterns on religious lines and thwart the struggles of the subalterns. They know that if subalterns are united, they can no longer exercise their religious and caste power and control the subalterns. Therefore, unity is very important for subaltern communities to achieve their goals of any sort. It is suggested that the energy of subalterns should be diverted to united actions against their common enemies.[100] They should not give room for the dominant to divide them in terms of religion, ideology, etc. For the subaltern women, in a patriarchal society where they are haunted by the caste-patriarchy-class blend, unity is required to fight against their subalternized life. Only through unified action, they can manifest their agency and challenge the hurdles in their journey of holistic advancement. The oppressors will know the strength of women if they raise their voice in unison. If the subaltern women are divided in opinion and outlook they cannot come forward as a force to transform their lives and the lives of others in society. The unity should be ideological and emotional.

Women as Mediators of Liberation

The Upper Cloth Revolt ended with the royal proclamation of 1859 which granted permission to Nadar women of any religious faith to wear clothes of whatever form. They appeared in jackets and upper cloths in public places. The result of the liberative struggle of Nadar women and their community had ramifications for the women of other subaltern communities. Another proclamation was issued in 1865. It specifically mentioned that it was being issued to get the benefits of the proclamation of 1859 to the women of other subaltern communities. The clauses of the proclamations of 1859 and 1865 are similar in content.[101] It is also to be noted that in the same year another proclamation was issued to stop the practice of removing the upper cloth by the Shudra[102] women as mark of respect in front of royal family members or higher officials in the palace or Brahmins. It was decreed that

> Whereas Shudra women, when in the presence of persons in high office, and when serving in the Temple or Palace, lower their upper garment as a mark of respect, this appears to His Highness (the sacred mind) exceedingly immodest. We have informed the aforesaid persons that this offensive custom is henceforth unnecessary. It is our will that all the native people wear garments in accordance with propriety, and this we now make known, when women in temples, in the Palace, and other places, shall cover the upper parts with the cloth, in accordance with this circular, we hereby order that the officials do not oppose their doing so.[103]

These proclamations prove the achievement of Upper Cloth Revolt in the life of women in other communities. The proclamation of 1865 which benefited the other subaltern women proves the influence of the Upper Cloth movement. Though there is no direct mention of the struggle of Nadar women or their given privilege as the basis for the proclamation which prohibited the custom of removing upper cloth by the Shudra women, the time and circumstance lead to the assumption that the struggle of Nadar women and men might have influenced the king and the royal administration to issue the proclamation. It is worth noting that it was Sudra men, mainly Nairs, who physically assaulted Nadar women and men and plundered their wealth during the years of the Upper Cloth Revolt.

What can be observed in the Upper Cloth Revolt is that a subaltern struggle has become a liberative struggle not only for the respective community but also for sister subaltern communities. The liberative action of Nadar women on a particular social restriction facilitated not only their liberation but also the liberation of women in other subaltern communities and even the women of upper caste. The subaltern women became mediators of liberation for other women. It reminds that assertion of women only can bring change in the lives of women in respective society. They only can sincerely initiate the struggle for the empowerment of women. As seen in Upper Cloth Revolt, men can support and express solidarity with women.

Inter-Religious Convergence for Subaltern Liberation

The result of upper cloth revolt has another dimension: religious. Though it was initiated by the Nadar Christian women, its advantage was shared not only by their sisters but also the women of other subaltern communities and the Shudra women of Hindu faith. It implies that power of liberative action and its effect cannot be restricted to one particular community or religious group. Divine liberation is beyond religious affiliation. God wants the oppressed or the subalterns to experience liberation irrespective of their religious persuasions. It is the subalterns who need the urgent intervention of God. At the same time, the liberative intervention of God demands the creative initiative on the side of subalterns.

Theology of *Ta<u>n</u><u>t</u>ēṭam*: A Subaltern Theological Expression of Upper Cloth Revolt

There are different meanings for the Malayalam word, *ta<u>n</u><u>t</u>ēṭam*. 'Courage', 'capacity', 'competency', 'arrogance', and 'pride', are a few of them. *ta<u>n</u><u>t</u>ēṭakkāran*, a derivative of *ta<u>n</u><u>t</u>ēṭam,* means 'courageous man', 'brave man', etc. 'Courageous woman' is referred as *ta<u>n</u><u>t</u>ēṭakkāri*. Generally, one who is 'clever', or 'courageous' or 'arrogant', is called *ta<u>n</u><u>t</u>ēṭi*.[104] The term, *ta<u>n</u><u>t</u>ēṭam* is used in negative and positive senses. It is common practice in patriarchal society that the term *taṉṯēṭam* is attributed to men in a positive sense, and to women with a negative connotation. If a man does a courageous thing, he is called *taṉṯēṭi*, and his action is considered a result of his *taṉṯēṭam*. However, a woman who is strong or courageous and takes a bold and positive initiative is addressed as *taṉṯēṭi* in the sense of 'arrogant'.[105] If her action is not in terms of existing traditions she is defined as 'uncontrollable', 'disobedient', or 'defiant'. In the feminist theological discourse, *taṉṯēṭam* is understood positively. For women, *taṉṯēṭam* is the 'power within' to face oppressive forces and to stand against the challenges of everyday life. Though it has a negative connotation in the eyes of society, *taṉṯēṭam* is positive energy.[106]

The term *taṉṯēṭam* has another etymological dimension which also has feminist theological implications. Etymologically, word *taṉṯēṭam* is made of two words: *taṉṯē,* means one's/his/her and *ēṭam*, means space/place/room. *taṉṯē* is one of the genitive case forms of *tān* which means oneself/he/she/it.[107] The implied meaning of *taṉṯēṭam* is one's space/his space/her space. 'Space' is defined as 'a continuous area or expanse which is free, available, or unoccupied'. It also refers to 'the freedom to live, think and develop in a way that suits one'.[108] The 'space' is also a suitable zone both mental and physical; and voluntarily and consciously created to obtain and enjoy certain benefits.[109] 'Space' facilitates the freedom and the free mobility of a person and enables her/him to do what s/he plans to execute. There are different levels and forms of space: physical, mental, economic, religious, socio-cultural and political.[110]

The public and domestic space of women was and is controlled and limited in different forms and ways. The religio-cultural and patriarchal traditions, customs and ideologies still restrict the space of women and control their mobility in society. Enabling women to reclaim their space is the task of Indian feminist theology.[111] The women's space (*taṉṯēṭam*) can be reclaimed by injecting *taṉṯēṭam* (courage) in them. It means that their space in social, political, economic, religious realms can be affirmed only by making them *taṉṯēṭakkārikal* or *taṉṯēṭikal* (courageous women) to say 'no' to the patriarchal norms which define the space of women.[112] *Taṉṯēṭam* leads to *taṉṯēṭam* (one's space). The Upper Cloth Revolt is the example of '*taṉṯēṭam* which leads to the creation of *taṉṯēṭam* (one's space)'. It requires to be theologically articulated so that the subaltern women whose life is doubly or tribily subalternized can be encouraged to be *taṉṯēṭakkārikal* or *taṉṯēṭikal* in their liberative struggles.

The Upper Cloth Revolt was initiated in a context which was characterized by the mechanism of caste and patriarchy to a great extent. The subaltern communities were denied free mobility and space. They were spaceless in various ways. They were made subservient in all aspects of social life. The subaltern women had gone through various social restrictions and humiliations. Most heinous was the prohibition on covering their bosoms and the use of upper cloth. It not only denied their dignity but also restricted their space, if not spaceless, in society. But the Nadar women broke the social restriction and came out of their restricted 'space' and appeared with upper cloths in public space. It was the *taṉṯēṭam* of Nadar women which enabled them to cover their bosoms with upper cloths and appear in public with dignity restored. Their *taṉṯēṭam* led to reclaim their *taṉṯēṭam* (their space), the freedom to cover their bosoms like upper caste women. They became *taṉṯēṭakkārikal* or *taṉṯēṭikal* in their assertion to remove the restriction on their dress code. With this, they created *taṉṯēṭam* (their space) in the larger social space. They asserted that they were no more 'objects' but subjects who have *taṉṯēṭam* to create space and face the challenges. It is to be noted that violating royal proclamations and opposing upper caste men who virtually functioned as rulers is not an easy thing in those days. It needs *taṉṯēṭam*. The subaltern women need this *taṉṯēṭam* to come out of their 'enslaved mind-set'[113] to reclaim their space in today's world. The interpretation of Upper Cloth Revolt as theology of *taṉṯēṭam* can inculcate *taṉṯēṭam* in the lives of women, particularly the subaltern women who are struggling to create their space in society and in the religious communities.

God as *Taṉṯēṭam*

The experiences of Nadar women in Upper Cloth Revolt can interpret the Biblical God as God of *taṉṯēṭam*. It is God who gave them the *taṉṯēṭam* to break an oppressive social custom. The God of *taṉṯēṭam* enabled them to reclaim/create their *taṉṯēṭam* (their space) in society. Since the initiative which led to the Upper Cloth Revolt was taken by the Nadar Christian women, it can be said that they received *ta<u>n</u><u>t</u>ēṭam* from God. God is the source of their *ta<u>n</u><u>t</u>ēṭam.* Therefore, God who made the Nadar women courageous is none other than God of *ta<u>n</u><u>t</u>ēṭam.* The same God came to them as *ta<u>n</u><u>t</u>ēṭam.* Subaltern women encounter 'God as energizing, creating and re-building as . . . *ta<u>n</u><u>t</u>ēṭam*'.[114] It can be understood as the power of God which arouses a different power in women to challenge the powers of dominance.[115] If the Biblical God can be understood as freedom, love and justice,[116] the same God can be interpreted as God of *ta<u>n</u><u>t</u>ēṭam* in the light of the experiences of Nadar women in Upper Cloth Revolt.

The work of the God of *ta<u>n</u><u>t</u>ēṭam* can be seen in the life of five courageous women who protected the life of Moses against the orders of the King. It was the *ta<u>n</u><u>t</u>ēṭam* of Pharaoh's daughter, the princess; Jochebed, Moses' mother; Miriam, his sister and Shiphrah and Puah, two Egyptian midwives who initiated the liberative process of Exodus event in the Bible.[117] They manifested their *ta<u>n</u><u>t</u>ēṭam* by disobeying the order of the King to kill all Israelite boys. In fact, the God of *ta<u>n</u><u>t</u>ēṭam* worked through them. When Hagar was sent out of Abraham's home, it was God of *ta<u>n</u><u>t</u>ēṭam* who gave her *ta<u>n</u><u>t</u>ēṭam* to face the life and death struggle in the desert of Beersheba.[118] In the patriarchal social setting, the demand of the daughters of Zelophehad to get their inheritance (Numbers 27: 1-8 and 36: 2-12), the performance of Deborah as warrior, judge and prophetess (Judges 4: 4 ff) and the audacity of Jael who killed Sisera, the oppressor of the Israelites (Judges 4: 17-22 and 5: 24-7), the daring decision of Mary, the mother of Jesus to accept the message of the angel in spite of its consequences and the boldness of Priscilla, Junia, Phoebe and Lydia, the co-workers of Paul to stand for faith[119] show the manifestation of their *ta<u>n</u><u>t</u>ēṭam.* It is God who gave them *ta<u>n</u><u>t</u>ēṭam* to demand their rights; to rule the nation; to destroy the enemies; to take bold decisions and initiatives and to witness the faith. Their *ta<u>n</u><u>t</u>ēṭam* helped them to create their *ta<u>n</u><u>t</u>ēṭam* (one's space) in a context where they were expected to live in a restricted space. The God who functioned as God of *ta<u>n</u><u>t</u>ēṭam* in the lives of the women in Biblical stories and in the lives of Nadar women in the event of Upper Cloth Revolt continues to work in the lives of subaltern women who are involved in the struggles of liberation. Those who have *taṉṯēṭam* only can participate in the struggles against the powers of dominance. God of *taṉṯēṭam* is in their movements to create space for them in the respective societies. In short, God as *taṉṯēṭam* implies two things: God who gives the subalterns *taṉṯēṭam* and God who creates *taṉṯēṭam* (space) for the subalterns.

Jesus as *Taṉṯēṭi/Taṉṯēṭakkāran*

The courageous actions of Nadar women against patriarchal norms can define Jesus who crossed patriarchal borders, as *taṉṯēṭi/ taṉṯēṭakkāran* (a courageous person). In his actions and words, Jesus stood against the patriarchal prejudices and affirmed the dignity and equality of women. Normally, a man in a patriarchal society does not show *taṉṯēṭam* to support the cause of subaltern women sincerely. But Jesus showed his *taṉṯēṭam* to express his views regarding the status and personhood of women. In this regard, Jesus can be called *taṉṯēṭi / taṉṯēṭakkāran*. As Christians, the Nadar women were influenced by the life and ministry of Jesus.

In the patriarchal Jewish society, Jesus did not consider women inferior, but affirmed the full humanhood of women.[120] He loved and respected women in society where they were disrespected and considered as objects.[121] He went against the traditions of Jewish-Greco-Roman society and upheld a more humane and liberal approach to the issues of women.[122] Jesus' courageous position shows His *taṉṯēṭam* to break the patriarchal restrictions and to create space for women. When Jesus healed a woman who was crippled for eighteen years, violating the Sabbath law (Luke 13: 10-17), accepted the anointment of a sinful woman against the social customs (Luke 7: 36f);[123] interacted with a Samaritan woman (John 4: 4 ff)[124] and affirmed the life and dignity of a woman accused of adultery (John 7: 53-8:11)[125] Jesus was actually showing His *taṉṯēṭam* and helping those women to claim and restore their *taṉṯēṭam* (one's space) in the patriarchal society. Jesus not only provided a space for women but also helped them to expand their mental and physical spaces. He encouraged women to transgress the traditional space allotted to them.[126] It is to be noted that Jesus always attempted to give space to the subalterns (Luke 14: 12ff).[127]

The interpretation of Jesus as *ta<u>n</u><u>t</u>ēṭi/ta<u>n</u><u>t</u>ēṭakkāran* in the light of the experiences centered on Upper Cloth Revolt encourages subaltern women to follow the footsteps of Jesus and become *ta<u>n</u><u>t</u>ēṭakkārikal* or *ta<u>n</u><u>t</u>ēṭikal* (courageous women). They have to show their *ta<u>n</u><u>t</u>ēṭam* as Jesus had shown to affirm the dignity and status of women. When subaltern women question any restriction or remove any obstacle in their way to freedom, they imitate Jesus who strengthened women to create and expand their space (*ta<u>n</u><u>t</u>ēṭam*). If they participate in the liberative struggles, they evoke the *ta<u>n</u><u>t</u>ēṭam* of Jesus who intentionally engaged in the lives of women. The *ta<u>n</u><u>t</u>ēṭam* of Jesus is revealed in *ta<u>n</u><u>t</u>ēṭakkārikal* or *ta<u>n</u><u>t</u>ēṭikal* who attempt to go beyond conventional space and assert freedom and gender equality in different spheres of life.

The Holy Spirit as the Spirit of *Ta<u>n</u><u>t</u>ēṭam*

The Holy Spirit can be interpreted as the Spirit of *ta<u>n</u><u>t</u>ēṭam*. It is observed that any dehumanizing practice/tradition is against the innovative work of the Holy Spirit who re-creates and renews everything.[128] What the Nadar women needed was *ta<u>n</u><u>t</u>ēṭam* to break a social practice created and maintained by caste and patriarchy. Therefore, the Holy Spirit can be interpreted as the Spirit of *ta<u>n</u><u>t</u>ēṭam*.

The Holy Spirit as Spirit of *ta<u>n</u><u>t</u>ēṭam* can be read along with the understanding of Holy Spirit as *Shakti*. Indian Feminist theologians use Hindu concept of *Shakti* to interpret the Holy Spirit. Sanskrit word *Shakti* means 'power'. In terms of *Shakti*, Holy Spirit is interpreted as power or energy.[129] The Spirit of *ta<u>n</u><u>t</u>ēṭam* instils 'power' to the subaltern women to claim their *ta<u>n</u><u>t</u>ēṭam* (one's space). They are energized by the power of the Spirit of *ta<u>n</u><u>t</u>ēṭam* to overcome the patriarchal hurdles in their journey of liberative struggle. The Spirit of *ta<u>n</u><u>t</u>ēṭam* makes subaltern women courageous in resisting dehumanizing realities. It is the power of the Spirit of *ta<u>n</u><u>t</u>ēṭam* which enables the subaltern women to transcend self-pity and express solidarity[130] with one another.

The Holy Spirit is the Spirit of *tan̲t̲ēṭam* because the Spirit of God also functions as the empowerer of the subalterns in their struggle for liberation.[131] It empowers subaltern women to rebel and raise voice against oppression and devaluation.[132] The work of the Spirit of *tan̲t̲ēṭam* can be experienced wherever the process of empowerment and liberation is going on.[133] For subaltern women, the liberative processes can be initiated only with the help of the spirit of *tan̲t̲ēṭam* as happened in the Upper Cloth Revolt.

The Biblical Models of *Tan̲t̲ēṭam* for Subaltern Women

Shiphrah and Puah

Shiphrah and Puah were the two midwives who defied the order of the mighty Pharaoh and allowed the Israelite newborn male babies to live (Exodus 1: 15ff).[134] They were courageous to reject the orders of the Pharaoh.[135] They refused to kill babies in spite of knowing the consequences. They were confident that their daring act was right.[136] The brave action of Shiphrah and Puah actually manifests their *tan̲t̲ēṭam.* They defied the king because they 'feared God' (v 17).[137] Their *tan̲t̲ēṭam* came from God who is God of *tan̲t̲ēṭam.* They became *tan̲t̲ēṭakkārikal* or *tan̲t̲ēṭikal* through their bold action. The *tan̲t̲ēṭam* of Shiphrah and Puah is also reflected in the *tan̲t̲ēṭam* of Nadar women in the Upper Cloth Revolt. Like Shiphrah and Puah, the Nadar women also defied the dress conventions of the Travancore realm. The subaltern women of today are invited to attain *tan̲t̲ēṭam* from the stories of Shiphrah and Puah and the experiences of Nadar women in the Upper Cloth Revolt. They need to be empowered themselves to disobey the life-negating powers to claim their space in society.

Ruth

Ruth, a Moabitess, was married to an Israelite. After the death of her husband, she and Naomi, her mother-in-law, came to Bethlehem, in Judah, the land of her husband. Though she was a foreigner, Ruth took initiative to go out to find out resources for her and her mother-in-law's livelihood. Her foreign birth did not deter her from taking initiative in Israelite society. She went to glean in the field during the barley harvest. On the one hand, Ruth was courageous to take initiative; on the other hand, though she was a widow, she asserted her right of livelihood in society. By going out for gleaning in the field, she was claiming her space in the society as a widow of an Israelite man (Ruth 2: 1-23).[138] Her initiative brought her legitimate right as per the customs of the Israelite society. She was redeemed by her kinsman-redeemer (4: 1-12).[139] It was the *ta<u>ṉṯ</u>ēṭam* of Ruth that helped her to take initiative to go to the field of an Israelite in spite her non-Israelite identity. At the same time, she had *taṉṯēṭam* to assert her right as a widow of an Israelite man. She did not depend on others for livelihood. She ventured out and claimed her right. Her courageous step gave her and her mother-in-law *taṉṯēṭam* (one's space) in the Israelite society.

In the Upper Cloth Revolt, the *taṉṯēṭam* of Nadar women enabled them to take initiative and assert their right to cover their bosoms like upper caste women. They affirmed their womanhood and humanhood in their struggles. Like Ruth and the Nadar women in the Upper Cloth Revolt, the subaltern women of today must have *taṉṯēṭam* to take new initiative and to claim their right to live with full humanhood in society. Courage to take initiative and assertion of rights are very much needed for subaltern women to resist the challenges in the respective societies. Those who have *taṉṯēṭam* only can venture out and claim space in the male-dominated communities. *Taṉṯēṭam* motivates women, particularly subalterns, not to limit themselves within the space assigned to them. It stirs them up against the existing patriarchal control over women.

Queen Vashti

Vashti was Queen of King Xerxes. In the third year of his rule, King Xerxes gave a banquet for his officials and ministers. During the feast, he exhibited his wealth and grandeur. On the seventh day of the banquet, Queen Vashti was asked to appear and display her beauty before the king and nobles. But she refused to do so. Her refusal to obey the king's command cost her status as queen in the country (Esther 1: 1-2: 4). In this story, Queen Vashti displayed her courage instead of her beauty before the king and the nobles. She did not allow herself to be reduced as an object of 'sex' or 'display'.[140] In other words, she displayed her *taṉṯēṭam* and asserted her *taṉṯēṭam* (one' space) in the royal setting. In her action, Vashti proved her competency in thinking about her 'selfhood'. By disobeying the king, Vashti was questioning the oppressive patriarchal structure that objectified women and devalued their dignity and conscience. The action of Vashti was a resistance to the oppressive structure. Her open disobedience was feared by the royalty as a threat to preserve the patriarchal norms. Therefore, she was disposed from her position. It is common that a woman who opposes the oppressive structure/system is punished or silenced so that the power and domination of males can be maintained. Vashti had to pay the price for her assertive action of affirming her dignity and identity.[141] It is the *taṉṯēṭam* within her enabled Queen Vashti to assert her dignity and identity before the king and nobles who considered women as objects of pleasure. For her, human dignity and autonomy were more important than royal position. She did not allow the 'man' to decide her appearance before the king and nobles. The Nadar women in Upper Cloth Revolt exercised their *taṉṯēṭam* to cover their bosoms against the desire of upper caste men who wanted to keep the subaltern women bare-breasted. They refused to be sex objects. They challenged the sexual and caste mind of upper caste men. Though violence was unleashed to destroy their *taṉṯēṭam* and silence their voice, Nadar women continued their struggle. Like Queen Vashti they also disobeyed the royal proclamations which restricted their freedom of deciding their dress code. The subaltern women of today must have *taṉṯēṭam* to resist the root cause of their subalternization: sexual and casteist outlook of men. The diktats of men which question the dignity of women has to be countered with the energy of *taṉṯēṭam*. Subaltern women with *taṉṯēṭam* only can stand against the attempts of negating their legitimate *taṉṯēṭam* (one's space) and dignity in the religious and social communities.

Mahlah, Noah, Hoglah, Milcah and Tirzah

Mahlah, Noah, Hoglah, Milcah and Tirzah were daughters of Zelophehad. He died without sons. The tradition did not allow his daughters to have his inheritance. But his daughters did not want his name to disappear from the clan. They demanded their right of inheritance and property (Num. 27: 1-8 and 36: 2-12).[142] In the patriarchal Israelite society, demand of the daughters of Zelophehad is a courageous step to challenge the age-old cultural practice. They showed their courage (*ta̱ṉṯēṭam*) to break the silence and demand their right and won it. In their daring attempt, they were trying to end cultural subordination.[143] One can sense *ta̱ṉṯēṭam* in their attempt to ask for property among their father's relatives (Num. 27: 4) against the existing socio-cultural practice. One needs *ta̱ṉṯēṭam* to raise her voice and demand her right in a male-dominated community. The daughters of Zelophehad actually were claiming their *ta̱ṉṯēṭam* (one's space) within the community. The Nadar women in Upper Cloth Revolt were also affirming their *ta̱ṉṯēṭam* (one's space) through demanding their innate right to cover their bosoms with upper cloths. They demanded something which subaltern women accustomed not to be demanded and broken. They asserted the right which was contradictory to the customary practice of the time. The subaltern women have to courageously demand their *ta̱ṉṯēṭam* (one's space) in the socio-religious-political spheres. If they do not display their *ta̱ṉṯēṭam* in demanding equal space and legitimate rights such as right of inheritance, they will remain in the restricted space with less right within the respective communities.

The Body as a Site of *Ta̱ṉṯēṭam*

The body locates human existence in the world. Although the human presence transcends the body, it is through it that the human presence is known, located and experienced.[144] There is an inseparable unity of the body and the self. Whatever happens in the body, negative or positive, has an effect on the self.[145] Moreover, the human identity, personality and uniqueness are expressed through the body.[146]

In the context of caste, the subaltern bodies are primarily the site of sufferings[147] than the location of one's 'self' because his/her 'self' is subalternized and devalued. The nexus of patriarchal norms and caste restrictions/rules have made the body of woman, particularly the subaltern woman, as 'the site of inscription, oppression, exploitation and violence'.[148] Woman's body becomes the site of violence when she rejects or resists the socio-cultural customs and expectations of the male-dominated society.[149] The bodies of subaltern women carry the marks of violence and humiliation inflicted by upper caste men to subjugate the subaltern men or the community.[150] However, the experiences of Nadar women in the Upper Cloth Revolt prove that the subaltern women's bodies are not only the site of violence, abuse, subjugation[151] but also the site of *ta<u>n</u><u>t</u>ēṭam*. It is also site of 'new power, the basis to claim their dignity and agency'.[152] The bodies of Nadar women were tortured and degraded by the caste rules in the society. They had gone through violence, humiliation, suffering, and sexual harassment, their bodies being controlled by the men of high caste origin. But Nadar women did not allow this to continue. They appeared in public dressed in jackets and upper cloths. This was evidence of *ta<u>n</u><u>t</u>ēṭam* in the caste and male-dominated society of Travancore. They expressed their *ta<u>n</u><u>t</u>ēṭam* in and through their bodies.

The bodies of subaltern women become site of *ta<u>n</u><u>t</u>ēṭam* when they take bold steps against the oppressive customs and practices promoted by the ideologies of caste and patriarchy in the larger society and in the respective faith communities.

Characteristics of *Ta<u>n</u><u>t</u>ēṭam*

Resistance

'Subordinate groups can contest hegemonic social formations and threaten to unravel the strategies of domination'.[153] The resistance of women emerges as a conscious act. It is an attempt or ability to abolish or weaken the structures of power which control the lives of women.[154] It is a powerful response that comes from the inner beings of women.[155] The resistance of women can be seen in everyday life. It has distinctive socio-political-moral agenda. It is a deliberate expression of power relations.[156] Those who have *taṉṟēṭam* resist the powers of subjugation and objectification. Therefore, it is essential for the subaltern women to develop *taṉṟēṭam* within themselves to put up resistance.

Empowerment

For subaltern women, empowerment is a journey from a 'victimhood mentality' to 'a state of active resistance' against the painful experiences of humiliation and discrimination inflicted by the caste and gender prejudices.[157] The empowerment of subaltern women is not without conflicts and confrontations: physical or ideological. Their empowerment includes developing critical thinking, innate talents and abilities to initiate the process of equipping themselves to control over all aspects of their lives. It produces or increases their self-confidence to face the challenges in private and public spaces, and strengthens their consciousness to confront the broken situations.[158] Empowerment comes where *taṉṟēṭam* is manifested.

Assertion

Assertion differs from other manifestations of resistance. It is actions by women that demand recognition of their claims or rights. A woman who is confident in behaviour and in expression of opinion, and claims her rights fearlessly can be called a 'assertive woman.'[159] One needs *taṉṟēṭam* to assert her right of any kind in the male-dominated society. The Nadar women in Upper Cloth Revolt asserted their right of covering their bosoms with upper cloths. Their assertion was an expression of *taṉṟēṭam.* The subaltern women should become assertive to secure their *taṉṟēṭam* (one's space) in the society. Asserting the rights means enlarging one's space. Those who have *taṉṟēṭam* automatically assert their space within and outside the community.

Autonomy

Autonomy is meant as 'freedom from external control or influence.'[160] It implies freedom from all kinds of restriction or control imposed from outside. An autonomous person is one who is independent in thinking, action, etc. For women, autonomy 'is freedom from biological and societal restrictions. Autonomy is self-determination which means being free to decide one's own destiny; being free to define one's social role and space; having freedom to make decisions concerning one's body.'[161] It is to be noted that women can respond, challenge, subvert, take initiatives and celebrate life in their own ways.[162] But in a socio-cultural context where men decide the freedom of women, one requires *taṉṯēṭam* to be autonomous. In Upper Cloth Revolt, the Nadar women took the decision (autonomy) on how to cover their bosoms against the socio-cultural restriction. The subaltern woman cannot decide her destiny or define her space or control her body without *taṉṯēṭam*. Autonomy is natural outcome of *taṉṯēṭam*. At the same time, autonomous thinking, decisions, actions expand the *taṉṯēṭam* (one's space) of subaltern women. In short, subaltern women who have *taṉṯēṭam* will resist dehumanizing tendencies and forces; assert their rights and privileges; act as autonomous beings and initiate the process of empowerment. They only can create and celebrate their *taṉṯēṭam* (one's space) in the respective societies.

Conclusion

The Upper Cloth Revolt, a liberative historical event of a subaltern community initiated by its women, is a source of developing new theological expression. In this theological articulation, the historical experiences of a community have emerged as its main source. The historical experiences of a subaltern community, particularly its women, in their liberating struggle can speak to the contemporary realities of other subaltern communities and women. The theological interpretation of the Upper Cloth Revolt acknowledges the potential of a subaltern historical movement/event to construct a new expression of faith. Theologizing is an attempt to articulate faith meaningfully in a context. It means that faith can be made meaningful through interpreting historical events. In the attempt of theologizing Upper Cloth Revolt, Christian faith is articulated in the light of the historical experiences of Nadar women and their community as a whole and vice-versa. In this endeavour, the various aspects of Christian faith are reflected through the subaltern eyes. The subaltern perspective facilitates to interpret the faith from below, in terms of the broken/subjugated realities of subalterns. The interpretation of faith based on the painful realities of people can evolve another meaning of faith, and help the subalterns understand the significance of faith in their efforts of resistance.

The subaltern theological expression of the Upper Cloth Revolt encourages bringing the subaltern realities and histories on to centre stage. The histories of people are sites of divine intervention, and must be articulated theologically. Not only historical events but also the subaltern social symbols or symbols of protest like the 'upper cloth' have theological significance. The social symbols of dignity and identity denied to the subalterns becomes symbols of theography when the subalterns attempt to claim and appropriate them in their lives. The theological value of those symbols should be retrieved. The movements of subaltern communities and subaltern women are the location of divine visitation. These movements also become instruments of experiencing liberation in a particular historical context. Since subaltern movements aim to blossom justice, equality, freedom and casteless society, they further the Kingdom of God inaugurated by Jesus Christ. The subaltern liberative movements of the past remain as symbol of hope for the present movements to continue their journey of struggle against oppressive systems like caste and patriarchy.

The Upper Cloth Revolt showed that subaltern women have the ability to challenge the social iniquities and assert their rights. The historical protest of Nadar women was a transformation from diminished human life to an experience of empowered and dignified life. A divine-human partnership can be sensed in this change of life. Human initiative and divine intervention are equally important for the liberation of subalterns.

The liberation struggles or movements of subaltern communities and subaltern women, in Christian language, can be termed as Spirit movements. The Spirit of God is behind the liberative struggles. Holy Spirit only can strengthen the subalterns to resist the oppressive forces in the caste-ridden society. Resisting the powers of dominance and hegemony needs the power of God. The remembrance of subaltern struggles and liberative action should motivate the liberated or advanced subaltern communities to participate in the struggles of other subaltern communities. The liberation of one subaltern community has to continue with the emancipation of other subaltern communities. At the same time, the subalterns should be aware of the politics of the dominant in naming and defining of subaltern movements. The subaltern movements are essentially liberative struggles because they ultimately stand for the holistic liberation of subalterns. But they are often described negatively in the narrations of the dominant.

The theology of *taṉṯēṭam* informs that subaltern women can take initiative to come out of their subalternised conditions. Therefore, the subaltern women of today have to manifest their *taṉṯēṭam* to create their space (*taṉṯēṭam*) in the socio-political-religious realms of societal life. If they are not taking bold initiatives, they will continuously remain in the restricted space allotted by caste and patriarchy. In the light of the experiences of Nadar women in Upper Cloth Revolt, it is clear that Biblical God is God of *taṉṯēṭam* who gives subaltern women courage to fight for their rights and have their own *taṉṯēṭam* (one's space). In their liberative struggle, Jesus shows how to take courageous steps to break the oppressive traditions and practices in the male-dominated society. Jesus as *taṉṯēṭi* motivates the subaltern women to cross the conventional space and re-define their *taṉṯēṭam* (one's space). The Sprit of *taṉṯēṭam* empowers the subaltern women in their struggle for dignity, selfhood and identity.

NOTES

1. Robert Cummings Neville, *Behind the Masks of God: An Essay Toward Comparative Theology* (Albany: State University of New York Press, 1991), p. 46.
2. Catherine Soanes and Angus Stevenson, *Oxford Dictionary of English,* 2nd edn., revd. (Oxford: Oxford University Press, 2005), p. 1787.
3. Francis Gonsalves, 'Body Symbols and Symbolic Bodies: Reaffirming Womanhood in the Church and Society', in *In Search of Space . . .* (New Delhi: Commission for Women, Catholic Bishops' Conference of India, 2008), p. 86.

4. C.M. Agur, *Church History of Travancore* (Madras: S.P.S. Press, 1903; New Delhi: Asian Educational Service, 1990), pp. xlvii, l, liii & lvii; *Madras Census 1891*, p. 224, cited by G.S. Ghurye, *Caste and Race in India* (London: Routledge and Kegan Paul, 1932; reprint of fifth edition, Bombay: Popular Prakashan, 1994), p. 13; *Selected Proclamations by the Sovereign from 1811-1939 AD* (Trivandrum: Government Press, 1937), pp. 301-2, 319-20 & 324-7; A. Sreedhara Menon, *A Survey of Kerala History* (Madras: S. Viswanathan, 1998), p. 393.
5. Neville, *Behind the Masks of God*, p. 46.
6. Ibid., p. 47.
7. Ibid., p. 49.
8. *LMS Report of the James Town Mission District for the Year 1859*, UTCA, p. 3; John Abbs, *Twenty-Two Years' Missionary Experience in Travancore* (London: John Snow & Co, 1870), pp. 161 & 224-5; P. Shungoonny Menon, *A History of Travancore from Earliest Times* (Madras: Higginbotham and Co., 1878), p. 507.
9. Sathianathan Clarke, *Dalits and Christianity, Subaltern Religion and Liberation Theology in India*, p. 3.
10. *Dr. Babasaheb Ambedkar Writings and Speeches,* vol. 1, Compiled by Vasant Moon (Bombay: Education Department, Government of Maharashtra, 1989), p. 167.
11. *Dr. Babasaheb Ambedkar Writings and Speeches,* vol. 1, p. 66.
12. Ibid., p. 41.
13. Felix Wilfred, *Margins: Site of Asian Theologies* (Delhi: ISPCK, 2008), pp. xvii-xviii.
14. Monodeep Daniel, *Dalit Bible Commentary, Old Testament*, vol. 18, *Ezekiel* (New Delhi: CDS, 2012), p. 30.
15. Mary Timothy Prokes, *Toward a Theology of the Body* (Edinburgh: T &T Clark, 1996), p. 77
16. Monodeep Daniel, *Dalit Bible Commentary, New Testament*, vol. 7, *The First and Second Letters of Paul to the Corinthians* (New Delhi: CDS, 2008), p. 124.
17. Chung Hyun Kyung, *Struggle to be the Sun Again* (New York: Orbis Books, 1990), p. 111.
18. John C.B. Webster, 'From Indian Church to Indian Theology: An Attempt at Theological Construction', in *A Reader in Dalit Theology*, ed. Arvind P. Nirmal, 1991; rpt. (Chennai: Gurukul, 2007), p. 120.
19. Gustavo Gutierrez, *A Theology of Liberation* (New York: Orbis Books, 1973), p. 154.

20. James H. Cone, 'Black Theology and Black Liberation', in *Black Theology, The South African Voice*, ed. Basil Moore (London: C. Hurst & Company, 1973), pp. 53-5; James Massey, *Dalit Bible Commentary, Old Testament*, vol. 9, 1811: *Chronicles* (New Delhi: CDS, 2012), pp. 138-9.
21. Gutierrez, *A Theology of Liberation*, p. 228.
22. James Massey, *Dalit Theology: History, Context, Text and Whole Salvation* (New Delhi: Manohar, 2014), p. 245; Israel Selvanayagam, *Samuel Amirtham's Living Theology* (Bangalore: BTESSC/SATHRI, 2007), p. 83; Massey, *Dalit Bible Commentary, Old Testament*, vol. 17, *Jeremiah, Lamentations, Baruch* (New Delhi: CDS, 2012), pp. 115-16.
23. Frantz Fanon, *The Wretched of the Earth,* tr. Constance Farrington (London: Penguin Books, 1990), pp. 57 & 74.
24. Monica Jyotsna Melanchthon, 'Dalit Readers of the Word: The Quest for Hermeneutics and Method', in *Frontiers in Dalit Hermeneutics*, ed. James Massey and Samson Prabhakar (Bangalore: BTESSC/SATHRI & New Delhi: CDS, 2005), p. 51.
25. *Selected Proclamations by the Sovereign from 1811-1939 AD* (Trivandrum: Government Press, 1937), pp. 301-2; Samuel Mateer, *Land of Charity* (London: John Snow & Co, 1871), p. 306; R.N. Yesudas, *The History of the London Missionary Society in Travancore 1806-1908* (Trivandrum: Kerala Historical Society, 1980), p. 196.
26. Gutierrez, *A Theology of Liberation*, p. 168.
27. Quoted in Gutierrez, ibid., p. 168.
28. Gutierrez, ibid., p. 177.
29. Ibid., pp. 167-8.
30. Eleasar S Fernandez, *Towards a Theology of Struggle* (New York: Orbis Books, 1994), pp. 43-6.
31. Soanes and Stevenson, *Oxford Dictionary of English,* p. 30.
32. Amartya Sen, *Development as Freedom* (Oxford: Oxford University Press, 1999), pp. 190-1.
33. Chris Shilling, *The Body and Social Theory* (London: Sage, 2003), pp. 4-9.
34. Shalini Mulackal, 'Living with Diminished Humanity: A Theological Critique', *Oriens Journal for Contextual Theology*, vol. 4 (2013), pp. 118-34 at 120.
35. Shalini Mulackal, 'Sexual Abuse and the Church: Some Moral Dilemmas', in *Gender Relations in the Church: A Call to Wholeness and Equal Discipleship*, ed. Astrid Lobo Gajiwala, Varghese Theckanath S.G. and

Raynah Braganza Passanha (Pune: Streevani & Hyderabad: Montfort Social Institute, 2012), p. 117.

36. Mulackal, 'Sexual Abuse and the Church: Some Moral Dilemmas', 120; Prasanna Kumari, 'God's Image and Women', in *Feminist Theology: Perspectives and Praxis* (Chennai: Gurukul, 1999), p. 382.
37. Raj Irudaya, *Dalit Bible Commentary, New Testament*, vol. 4, *The Gospel According to John* (New Delhi: CDS, 2009), p. 169.
38. V.V. Thomas, *Understanding Subaltern History: Theoretical Tools* (Bangalore: BTESSC/SATHRI, 2006), p. xix.
39. The Holy Bible, The New International Version, Deuteronomy 26: 5-9.
40. V. Nagam Aiya, *The Travancore State Manual*, vol. II (Trivandrum: Government Press, 1906), p. 393.
41. Ibid., vol. II, p. 398; T.K. Velu Pillai, *The Travancore State Manual*, vol. I (Trivandrum: Government of Travancore, 1940), p. 856.
42. Ghurye, *Caste and Race in India*, pp. 9-10; Mateer, *Land of Charity*, pp. 28-31.
43. Yesudas, *The History of the London Missionary Society in Travancore 1806-1908*, pp. 16-18; idem, *Native Life in Travancore* (London: W.H. Allen & Co., 1883), pp. 292-4; idem, *Land of Charity*, p. 41; Agur, *Church History of Travancore*, pp. 74 & xlviii; *Selected Proclamations by the Sovereign from 1811-1939 AD*, pp. 5-7; Robin Jeffrey, *The Decline of Nair Dominance* (New Delhi: Manohar, 1994), p. 52; D. Peter and Ivy Peter, *Liberation of the Oppressed: A Continuous Struggle* (Nagercoil: Kanyakumari Institute of Development Studies, 2009), pp. 31-3.
44. Mateer, *Land of Charity*, pp. 41 & 60; I.H. Hacker, *A Hundred Years in Travancore (1806-1906)* (London: H.R. Allenson, 1908), p. 14; J. Bhattacharya, *Hindu Castes and Sects* (1896), p. 259, cited by Ghurye, *Caste and Race in India*, pp. 12-13; D. Peter and Ivy Peter, *Liberation of the Oppressed: A Continuous Struggle*, p. 33; *Selected Proclamations by the Sovereign*, pp. 82-3; Mateer, *Native Life in Travancore*, pp. 206 and 340-1.
45. Letter from the Deputy Peishkar Shungoony Menon, in-charge of the Southern Division to the Dewan of Travancore, 4 January 1859, Bundle no. 29, Cover File no. 2115 of 1858, *Shanar Disturbances in South Travancore*, Archives Directorate, Trivandrum; Agur, *Church History of Travancore*, p. 933; V. Nagam Aiya, *The Travancore State Manual,* vol. 1 (Trivandrum: Government Press, 1906), p. 529.

46. *Selected Proclamations by the Sovereign*, pp. 301-2; Mateer, *Land of Charity*, p. 305; Agur, *Church History of Travancore*, p. 937.
47. Mateer, *Land of Charity*, p. 306; Yesudas, *The History of the London Missionary Society in Travancore 1806-1908*, p. 196.
48. Arvind P. Nirmal, 'Towards a Christian Dalit Theology', in *A Reader in Dalit Theology*, ed. Arvind P. Nirmal, 1991; rpt. (Chennai: Gurukul, 2007), pp. 60-2.
49. Massey, *Dalit Bible Commentary, Old Testament*, vol. 2, *Exodus* (New Delhi: CDS, 2010), p. 22.
50. V. Nagam Aiya, *The Travancore State Manual,* vol. I, p. 528; *LMS Report of the James Town Mission District for the Year 1859,* UTCA, p. 3.
51. Massey, *Dalit Bible Commentary, Old Testament*, vol. 5, *Judges* (New Delhi: CDS, 2012), pp. 84-5.
52. Kim Young-Bock, *Messiah and Minjung, Christ's Solidarity with the People for New Life* (Hong Kong: CCA, 1992), p. 333.
53. Shalini Mulackal, 'Living with Diminished Humanity: A Theological Critique', p. 131.
54. Theramma Prayikalam, *Manakaruth Spirituality of Fisherwomen: Inspiration and Challenge to Consecrated Women* (Delhi: Media House, 2011), p. 113.
55. Massey, *Dalit Bible Commentary, Old Testament,* vol. 2, *Exodus*, p. 27.
56. Ibid., pp. 91-2.
57. Leonard Fernando, 'Editorial: Living Hope', *Vidyajyoti Journal of Theological Reflection*, vol. 76, no. 11 (November 2012), pp. 1-3.
58. Indukuri John Mohan Razu, *Dalit Bible Commentary, Old Testament*, vol. 4, *Leviticus and Numbers* (New Delhi: CDS, 2011), p. 177.
59. Gustavo Gutierrez, *A Theology of Liberation*, p. 177.
60. Arvind P. Nirmal, 'Towards a Christian Dalit Theology', p. 69.
61. Bama, 'Dalit Christian Women Today: Their Struggles and Prospects for Future', *Jeevadhara,* vol. XLI, no. 241 (January 2011), pp. 35-44 at 44.
62. Young-Bock, *Messiah and Minjung, Christ's Solidarity with the People for New Life*, p. 342.
63. Massey, *Dalit Bible Commentary, New Testament*, vol. 5, *Acts of Apostles* (New Delhi: CDS, 2008), pp. 37-8.
64. Young-Bock, *Messiah and Minjung, Christ's Solidarity with the People for New Life*, pp. 330-1.
65. Ranajit Guha, 'On Some Aspects of the Historiography of Colonial

India', in *Subaltern Studies*, vol. I, ed. Ranajit Guha (New Delhi: Oxford University Press, 1994), p. 3.

66. Guha, 'On Some Aspects of the Historiography of Colonial India', p. 4.
67. V.V. Thomas, 'Methodological Discourses in Theological Disciplines and Approaches in Historiography with Special Reference to the Marginalized in the Pentecostal Churches in India', in *Margins in Conversation: Methodological Discourses in Theological Disciplines*, ed. Joseph Prabhakar Dayam and P. Mohan Larbeer (Bangalore: BTESSC, 2012), p. 255.
68. T.K. Velu Pillai, *The Travancore State Manual,* vol. II (Trivandrum: Government of Travancore, 1940), p. 583; V. Nagam Aiya, *The Travancore State Manual,* vol. I, pp. 525 & 528; The Dewan's Report to the Resident, 12 February 1859, no. 196 in *Copies of the Official Papers Sent from India Touching the Recent Disturbances in Travancore*, Box no. 15 (MF), UTCA, 8.
69. C.M. Agur, *Church History of Travancore*, p. 779; Samuel Mateer, *Land of Charity*, pp. 295 & 300; P. Shungoonny Menon, *A History of Travancore from Earliest Times*, p. 508.
70. Hacker, *A Hundred Years in Travancore (1806-1906)*, p. 48.
71. F. Baylis, *LMS Report of the Neyyor Mission District for the Year 1859,* UTCA, p. 3; Letter from Rev. F. Baylis to the Resident, 17 January 1859, Bundle no. 29, Cover File no. 2115 of 1858, *Shanar Disturbances in South Travancore*, Archives Directorate, Trivandrum; The Petition of Missionaries of the LMS to the King of Travancore, 7 February 1859, in *Copies of the Official Papers Sent from India Touching the Recent Disturbances in Travancore*, Box no. 15 (MF), UTCA, pp. 39-47; Letter from W. Cullen, the Resident to T. Pycroft, Chief Secretary to Government, Madras, 16 February 1859, no. 4 in *Copies of the Official Papers Sent from India Touching the Recent Disturbances in Travancore*, Box no. 7 (MF), UTCA, p. 7; G.A. Oddie, *Social Protest in India* (Columbia: South Asian Books and New Delhi: Manohar, 1978), p. 70.
72. Koji Kawashima, *Missionaries and a Hindu State: Travancore 1858-1936* (New Delhi: Oxford University Press, 1998), p. 60; Jeffrey, *The Decline of Nair Dominance*, p. 53.
73. Dick Kooiman, *Conversion and Social Equality in India* (New Delhi: Manohar, 1989), p. 154.
74. J.W. Gladstone, *Protestant Christianity and People's Movements in Kerala* (Trivandrum: Seminary Publications, 1984), p. 81.

75. John A. Jacob, *A History of the London Missionary Society in South Travancore,* 1956, rpt. (Nagarcoil: Diocesan Press, 1990), p. 68.
76. Yesudas, *A People's Revolt in Travancore*, p. 113.
77. Yesudas, *The History of London Missionary Society in Travancore 1806-1908*, p. 171.
78. T.K. John S.J, 'Introduction', in James Massey, *Dalit Bible Commentary, Old Testament*, vol. 2, *Exodus* (New Delhi: CDS, 2010), p. 11.
79. Ibid., p. 11; James Massey and T.K. John, 'Preface', in *Rethinking Theology in India*, ed. James Massey and T.K. John (New Delhi: Manohar and Centre for Dalit/Subaltern Studies, 2013), p. 9.
80. Guha, 'On Some Aspects of the Historiography of Colonial India', pp. 4-5.
81. Albert Memmi, *The Colonizer and the Colonized* (Boston: Beacon Press, 1965), pp. 127-8.
82. Fanon, *The Wretched of the Earth*, pp. 57-8.
83. Veena Das, 'Subaltern as Perspective', in *Subaltern Studies*, vol. VI, ed. Ranajit Guha (New Delhi: Oxford University Press, 1999), p. 321.
84. Mary (Joy) Philip, 'A Woman of Shabbat', in *Mission with the* Marginalized, ed. Samuel W. Meshack (Tiruvalla: CSS, 2007), p. 151.
85. James Massey, *Dalit Bible Commentary, Old Testament*, vol. 5, *Judges*, pp. 79-81.
86. Fernandez, *Towards a Theology of Struggle*, p. 49.
87. *The Telegraph,* 'Caste Correction' (Wednesday, 2 January 2013, Calcutta), p. 5.
88. Massey, *Dalit Bible Commentary, Old Testament*, vol. 2, *Exodus*, 27.
89. Arvind P. Nirmal, 'Towards a Christian Dalit Theology', p. 62.
90. Kwok Pui-lan, 'The Emergence of Asian Feminist Consciousness on Culture and Theology', in *Culture, Women and Theology*, ed. John S. Pobee (Delhi: ISPCK, 1994), p. 75.
91. Musimbi Kanyoro, 'The Meaning of the Story: Theology as Experience', in *Culture, Women and Theology*, ed. John S. Pobee (Delhi: ISPCK, 1994), p. 29.
92. Agur, *Church History of Travancore*, p. liii.
93. Ibid., p. 779; A. Sreedhara Menon, *A Survey of Kerala History*, p. 396.
94. *Neetu,* vol. 20, pt. 1 (Central Achieves, Thiruvananthapuram), pp. 48-50; *Selected Proclamations by the Sovereign*, pp. 224-7; Agur, *Church History of Travancore*, p. lvii.
95. *Selected Proclamations by the Sovereign*, pp. 301-2; Mateer, *Land of Charity*, 305; Agur, *Church History of Travancore*, p. 937.
96. Yesudas, *A People's Revolt in Travancore*, 136; Mateer, *Land of Charity*, p. 298.

97. Letter from W. Cullen, the Resident of Travancore and Cochin to T. Pycroft, Chief Secretary to Government, Madras, 13 January 1859, no. 4 in *Copies of the Official Papers Sent from India Touching the Recent Disturbances in Travancore*, Box no. 15 (MF), UTCA, p. 5; Order of T. Pycroft, Chief Secretary to Government, Madras, 27 January 1859, no. 75 in *Copies of the Official Papers Sent from India Touching the Recent Disturbances in Travancore*, Box no. 15 (MF), UTCA, 6; C.M. Agur, *Church History of Travancore*, p. 935.
98. Letter from Rev. E. Lewis to the Resident, 21 January 1859, Bundle no. 29, Cover File no. 2115 of 1858, *Shanar Disturbances in South Travancore*, Archives Directorate, Trivandrum.
99. Massey, *Dalit Bible Commentary, Old Testament*, vol. 5, *Judges*, p. 122.
100. A. Maria Arul Raja, *Dalit Bible Commentary, Old Testament,* vol. 1, *Genesis* (New Delhi: CDS, 2012), p. 29.
101. Mateer, *Land of Charity*, p. 305; *Selected Proclamations by the Sovereign*, no. 192, pp. 319-20.
102. The rank of Shudras in South India was next to the Brahmins. But they were considered as polluted in the caste order in North India. The Aryans or Brahmins conferred the title Shudra to the middle and higher classes of the Dravidians because in South India there were other classes which were equal to the servile Shudras of North India (Robert Caldwell, *A Comparative Grammar of the Dravidian Family of Languages* (London: Harrison, 1856; revd. edn., Madras: University of Madras, 1961), pp. 112-13).
103. Mateer, *Land of Charity*, p. 62.
104. B.C. Balakrishnan, ed., *Malayalam Lexicon*, vol. VI (Trivandrum: The University of Kerala, 1988), p. 113.
105. Kochurani Abraham, 'And She Was Made Straight: A Feminist Theological Engagement with the "Bent" lives of Indian Women', in *Margins in Conversation: Methodological Discourses in Theological Disciplines*, ed. Joseph Prabhakar Dayam and P. Mohan Larbeer (Bangalore: BTESSC, 2012), p. 131; Theramma Prayikalam, *Manakaruth Spirituality of Fisherwomen: Inspiration and Challenge to Consecrated Women*, p. 307.
106. Prayikalam, *Manakaruth Spirituality of Fisherwomen*, pp. 108, 152 & 165-6.
107. Balakrishnan, ed., *Malayalam Lexicon*, vol. VI, pp. 112-13 & 250; Suranad Kunjan Pillai, ed., *Malayalam Lexicon*, vol. II (Thiruvananthapuram: The University of Kerala, 2003), p. 272.

108. Soanes and Stevenson, *Oxford Dictionary of English,* 2nd edn., p. 1694.
109. Fernando Franco, Jyotsna Macwan and Suguna Ramanathan, eds., *The Silken Swing* (Calcutta: STREE, 2000), p. 97.
110. Metti Amirtham, *Women in India: Negotiating Body, Reclaiming Agency* (Delhi: ISPCK, 2011), p. 162.
111. Kochurani Abraham, 'And She Was Made Straight: A Feminist Theological Engagement with the "Bent" lives of Indian Women', pp. 126 and 130.
112. Ibid., p. 131.
113. A. Maria Arul Raja, *Dalit Bible Commentary, Old Testament*, vol. 1, *Genesis*, p. 91.
114. Prayikalam, *Manakaruth Spirituality of Fisherwomen: Inspiration and Challenge to Consecrated Women*, p. 165.
115. Chung Hyun Kyung, *Struggle to be the Sun Again* (New York: Orbis Books, 1990), p. 51.
116. Paulose Mar Paulose, *Swathanthryamanu Daivam* (Malayalam) (Ariyannur: Patabhedam, 1996), pp. 169-70.
117. Prayikalam, *Manakaruth Spirituality of Fisherwomen: Inspiration and Challenge to Consecrated Women*, p. 113.
118. Aruna Gnanadason, 'Feminist Methodology: Indian Women's Experience', in *Confronting Life: Theology out of the Context*, ed. M.P. Joseph (Delhi: ISPCK, 1995), pp. 182-3.
119. Anna Vareed Alexander, 'Through the Feminist Looking Glass: Images of Women', in The *Emerging Christian Women*, ed. Stella Faria, Anna Vareed Alexander and Jessie B. Tellis-Nayak (Indore: Satprakashan Sanchar Kendra and Pune: Ishvani, 1984), pp. 84-6.
120. Mulackal, 'Living with Diminished Humanity: A Theological Critique', p. 133.
121. Chung Hyun Kyung, *Struggle to be the Sun Again*, p. 54.
122. Evelyn Monteiro, 'Re-imaging Woman and Reshaping her Destiny, An Indian Feminist Reading of the Bent Body (Lk 13: 10-17)', in *Body and Sexuality: Theological-Pastoral Perspectives of Women in Asia,* ed. Agnes M. Brazal and Andrea Lizares (Manila: Ateneo De Manila University Press, 2007), p. 146.
123. Evelyn Monteiro, 'Re-imaging Woman and Reshaping her Destiny, An Indian Feminist Reading of the Bent Body (Lk 13: 10-17)', pp. 146-50.
124. Raj Irudaya, *Dalit Bible Commentary, New Testament*, vol. 4, *The Gospel According to John*, pp. 69-70.

125. Ibid., p. 99.
126. Amirtham, *Women in India: Negotiating Body, Reclaiming Agency*, p. 163.
127. Massey, *Dalit Bible Commentary, New Testament*, vol. 3, *The Gospel According to Luke* (New Delhi: CDS, 2007), p. 160.
128. Prayikalam, *Manakaruth Spirituality of Fisherwomen*, p. 167.
129. T. Mercy Rani, *Assailants of the Spirit and the Upholders of 'Sakti': An Indian Feminist Assessment of the Holy Spirit* (Bangalore: SATHRI, 2003), pp. 43 & 55-74.
130. Shalini Mulackal, 'Margin as a Site of Sacred Encounter', in *Revisiting and Resignifying Methodology for Dalit Theology*, ed. James Massey and Indukur John Mohan Razu (New Delhi: CDS and Bangalore: UTC, 2008), p. 227.
131. Nirmal, 'Towards a Christian Dalit Theology', p. 69.
132. Bama, 'Dalit Christian Women Today: Their Struggles and Prospects for Future', p. 44.
133. Massey, *Dalit Bible Commentary, New Testament*, vol. 5, *Acts of Apostles*, pp. 37-8.
134. Prayikalam, *Manakaruth Spirituality of Fisherwomen*, p. 113.
135. Evangeline Anderson-Rajkumar, 'New Eyes, New Reading, New Woman . . .', in *Feminist Hermeneutics*, ed. Lalrinawmi Ralte and Evangeline Anderson-Rajkumar (Delhi: IWTI/ISPCK, 2002), p. 107.
136. Prema Vakayil, 'Biblical Women: A Retrospect', *Oriens Journal for Contextual Theology*, vol. 4 (2013), pp. 104-17 at 110.
137. Gnanadason, 'Feminist Methodology: Indian Women's Experience', pp. 182-3.
138. Shalini Mulackal, *Dalit Bible Commentary, Old Testament*, vol. 6, *Ruth, Esther and Judith* (New Delhi: CDS, 2011), pp. 31-2.
139. Ibid., p. 37.
140. Anderson-Rajkumar, 'New Eyes, New Reading, New Woman . . .', p. 108.
141. Mulackal, *Dalit Bible Commentary, Old Testament*, vol. 6, *Ruth, Esther and Judith*, pp. 54-5.
142. Alexander, 'Through the Feminist Looking Glass: Images of Women', pp. 84-6.
143. Prasanna Kumari, 'God's Image and Women', in *Feminist Theology: Perspectives and Praxis,* ed. Prasanna Kumari (Chennai: Gurukul, 1999), p. 383.
144. Arthur Vogel, *Body Theology: God's Presence in Man's World* (New York: Harper & Row, 1973), p. 91.

145. Christine E. Gudorf, 'Body, Self and Sexual Identity: Reflections on the Current Evidence', in *Body and Sexuality: Theological-Pastoral Perspectives of Women in Asia,* ed. Agnes M. Brazal and Andrea Lizares (Manila: Ateneo De Manila University Press, 2007), p. 3.
146. Mulackal, 'Sexual Abuse and the Church: Some Moral Dilemmas', p. 122.
147. Y.T. Vinaya Raj, *Re-imagining Dalit Theology, Post Modern Readings* (Thiruvalla: CSS, 2008), p. 65.
148. Evangeline Anderson-Rajkumar, 'Significance of the "Body" in Feminist Theological Discourse', *Bangalore Theological Forum,* vol. XXXIII, no. 2 (December, 2001), pp. 80-98 at 89.
149. Kochurani Abraham, 'Women and Violence: A Feminist Socio-Theological Enquiry', in *Violence in Today's Context,* ed. Shalini Mulackal and Roy Lazar A. (Bangalore: Indian Theological Association & Asian Trading Corporation, 2012), p. 24.
150. A. Maria Arul Raja, *Dalit Bible Commentary, Old Testament*, vol. 1, *Genesis*, p. 38.
151. Anderson-Rajkumar, 'Significance of the "Body" in Feminist Theological Discourse', p. 83; Amirtham, *Women in India: Negotiating Body, Reclaiming Agency*, p. 164.
152. Felix Wilfred, *Asian Public Theology* (New Delhi: ISPCK, 2010), p. 83.
153. Quoted from Douglas Haynes and Gyan Praksah (eds), *Contesting Power: Resistance and Everyday Social Relations in South Asia* (Berkeley and LA: University of California Press, 1992), 3 in Padma Anagol, 'From the Symbolic to the Open: Women's Resistance in Colonial Maharashtra', in *Behind the Veil*, ed. Anindita Ghosh (Ranikhet: Permanent Black, 2007), p. 25.
154. Anagol, 'From the Symbolic to the Open: Women's Resistance in Colonial Maharashtra', p. 27.
155. Monica Jyotsna Melanchthon, 'Dalit Readers of the Word: The Quest for Hermeneutics and Method', in *Frontiers in Dalit Hermeneutics*, ed. James Massey and Samson Prabhakar (Bangalore: BTESSC/ SATHRI, and Delhi: CDSS, 2005), p. 62.
156. Anindita Ghosh, 'Introduction', in *Behind the Veil*, ed. Anindita Ghosh (Ranikhet: Permanent Black, 2007), pp. 5 & 16.
157. Bama, 'Dalit Christian Women Today: Their Struggles and Prospects for Future', p. 41.
158. Ibid., p. 42.

159. Amirtham, *Women in India: Negotiating Body, Reclaiming Agency*, pp. 44-5.
160. Soanes and Stevenson, *Oxford Dictionary of English,* 2nd edn., p. 108.
161. Amirtham, *Women in India: Negotiating Body, Reclaiming Agency*, p. 45.
162. Franco, Macwan and Ramanathan, eds., *The Silken Swing*, p. 126.

Conclusion

Memory of Subaltern History: New Pathways of Liberation

The social context of India is characterized by the caste system which continues its hold in the consciousness of the people unabated. The caste factor in its varied forms and disguises appears in the different realms of today's social life and subalterns are the most adversely affected people. The new *avatars* of caste overtly and covertly marginalize and exclude many subaltern communities from the mainstream. The intensity of caste consciousness even in present-day Indian society seems to be on the increase. The Indian Church is also not free from the bondage of caste. In fact, Indian sensibility is controlled by caste consciousness.

Caste has its grip not only on the structure of society which includes the Church but also in different issues of the people. Poverty, high rate of illiteracy, suicide of farmers, child and bonded labour, communal violence, have all been perpetuated by willful negligence of the ruling class. Even if subalterns protest, their voice goes unheard. The ruling class only hears the music of caste people and ignores the groaning of subalterns, the majority populace. The subalterns are always ignored in the political system even though they form the majority vote bank. An obstacle for subaltern growth, caste is nevertheless a ladder for the upper castes to reach prominent places. Those who are outside the caste system: Dalits, tribal people, backward communities, religious minorities, particularly from low-caste origin etc., the real subalterns, are at the receiving end.

In the present socio-economic and political scenario, the 'dalitness' of Dalits, 'tribalness' of tribes and the 'backwardness' of backward communities are being perpetuated. The political and cultural space for subalterns is still limited. A lack of educational and occupational opportunities thwarts the social and economic advancement of many subaltern communities. Various religious communities have their own subalterns within, who face discrimination and negation of equal opportunities and treatment. Subalterns who constitute the majority of the Indian Christians share the same experience as their brothers and sisters in other religious traditions. In this context, the morale of the subaltern communities needs to be enhanced to fight against their social disabilities and come out of their subalternised conditions. They are to be enabled to resist the powers which prevent their holistic advancement. They should be empowered to take initiatives to decide their destiny. The content of this volume should encourage the oppressed of various religious traditions to redefine and occupy their own space in society.

Subaltern women appear to be more vulnerable and subalternized within their respective communities and in the larger society. Their broken life-realities are witness to the inter-connected mechanism of caste consciousness, gender prejudices and exploitative class structures and systems. Their womanhood/subjecthood/selfhood has been subjugated and victimized in different ways through the centuries. Neither post-modern ideas nor technological development can change the outlook of patriarchal society towards subaltern women. Indeed, a subaltern woman continues to be the epitome of subalternity. Even now she is addressed and treated as an inferior individual. She is a historical victim without voice, power or respect. They face discrimination even within the faith community as low-caste women.

The historical victimhood of subaltern woman continues in the contemporary society. They are expected to be passive and obedient in family, in faith community and in the larger society. They have to be content with the given space within and outside their community. They should not cross the borders of their conventional space. It is to be noted that the space of the subaltern women remain unchanged in society. The social space of subaltern women is controlled and dictated by their men and men of high caste origin. Often, a space is occupied or filled by the upper-caste women in political, economic, educational spheres. But subaltern women have been made passive in such a way that they cannot assert their rights easily. Any resistance or self-assertion invites derogatory comments and physical assault. Women of lower-caste origin have far less 'space' than their counterparts in high castes. Subaltern women have to be assertive and courageous to challenge the forces which block their advancement. The experiences of Nadar women in the Upper Cloth Revolt gives impetus to the contemporary subaltern women to affirm their dignity and selfhood.

In this volume, an effort was made to bring to light the theological significance of Upper Cloth Revolt, a historical movement in South Travancore. As a subaltern movement this Revolt can speak to contemporary subaltern communities. I attempted to construct a new theological expression out of a historical event from the subaltern perspective. The liberating message is that subalterns do have the ability to counter the powers of oppression and marginalization. They are capable of breaking dehumanizing practices. Liberation comes from them alone. The journey of liberative struggle is always a painful, not conflict-free. Sometimes, it has to pay a high price in the form of violence, physical assault, arson, or vandalism. Though the subalterns face life-threatening situations in the journey of struggles, they continue their resistance against the process of subalternization. Christian subalterns believe that the power to resist the dominant in the context of feudal and caste systems comes from God who abhors any kind of oppression and subjugation. The Upper Cloth Revolt encourages the subalterns to initiate 'revolt' against the dehumanizing powers like caste. Revolt can be efforts of dismantling the oppressive outlook, defying the caste practices or cultural traditions which keep the subalterns passive and non-resistant, questioning the unjust treatment, taking new initiatives to empower respective community against the diktats of oppressors, etc. God of Biblical tradition does not discourage the attempts of social advancement through violating the unwritten or traditional customs and practices. Therefore, the subaltern communities who are in the margins of society have to make use of their potential and initiate movements of liberation which will expand their space in society.

The histories of subaltern communities and subaltern women

in India are generally stories of suffering, subjugation, humiliation and denial of humanhood. But it has been common that the subaltern communities who are relatively in a better position in the contemporary society hesitate to look into the painful stories of their forefathers and mothers whose resistance restored the dignity of their communities. Theological articulation of the Upper Cloth Revolt encourages subaltern communities and subaltern women to look back into their past and know their historical roots to understand the significance of their liberative past in contemporary society. It is important to note that looking back to the past is a Biblical mandate. The liberative past helps Christian subalterns to interpret their faith meaningfully. The exceptional stories of resistance and defiance against the dominant ruling class and caste open new horizons of hope for the communities who are still in the journey of struggle. Looking back to the past not only motivates a group to know their historical life and faith but also encourages involvement in the struggles of other communities. The liberative struggle of a subaltern community does not end with its partial or full liberation. It continues in the struggles of other communities. This is carried out by expressing solidarity with and participating in the movements of subalterns of the day. The Upper Cloth Revolt calls for the intentional engagement of Nadar men and women in the movements of other subaltern communities and subaltern women irrespective of religion. It is the social and theological mandate of liberated subalterns, particularly Christians, to engage with less privileged subalterns to straighten their bent life.

There are historical events which redefined the future of at least a few subaltern communities who had been subalternized for centuries. The Upper Cloth Revolt was one of such historical events/movements which enabled the Nadars, particularly its women, to assert their dignity, identity and selfhood. It was a decisive event in the life of a subaltern community which motivated them to search for a new space in the society controlled by caste and feudal elements. The nature and thrust of Upper Cloth Revolt shows that it is a potential source to develop a new theological discourse. The Christian faith element and the values behind the movement give momentum for the theological interpretation of this movement.

Theological articulation of Upper Cloth Revolt suggests that focus on the interpretation of liberating historical events can contribute to the emergence and development of new contextual/liberation theological discourses in the Indian Christian theologizing process. Therefore, subaltern histories of resistance and struggle need to be prioritized in future Christian theologizing. The contemporary significance of subaltern histories of resistance and suffering can be brought out through contextual interpretation. It implies that local histories can give birth to new local theologies. As neglected cultural ethos and traditions of subalterns have become interpretative tools of Christian faith in Indian liberation/contextual theologies so local liberative histories can become sources and means of interpreting the Christian faith. Interpretation of Christian faith in the light of the historical experiences of people involved in a historical event can challenge the people who are in similar situations to take bold steps towards empowerment.

India has witnessed many subaltern movements which attempted to transform society and liberate subalterns from the clutches of oppressive social structures and traditions. In a caste-ridden society where the subalterns are made voiceless and passive, subaltern movements of social emancipation are a matter of courage. Being defiant and to resist the oppressor is difficult in the social chemistry of caste hierarchy. But Divine Power gives strength to defy the diktats of oppressors. In this sense, the subaltern movements like Upper Cloth Revolt are Spirit movements: resistance to be understood not as human endeavour alone but as an initiative of the Spirit of God who leads the people to the truth of justice and righteousness.

There is a common perception that subaltern women cannot resist and raise their voice against the caste and patriarchal prejudices and practices which negate their dignity and selfhood. The Upper Cloth Revolt disproves this view and challenges the contemporary subaltern women to show their assertive power and counter the traditions and ideologies which block their upward mobility in society. In the light of the experiences of Nadar women in the Upper Cloth Revolt, it can be argued that the subaltern women can become agents of resistance and change in respective community and in the larger society. To get courage and motivation, the subaltern women should look back to their forerunners who exercised their agency in the midst of violent reactions from the casteist-patriarchal power centres. Stories of foremothers can give guidance to the contemporary subaltern women to combat the forces of oppression. They are the stories of challenging the oppressive outlook and sexist mentality of men. The dignity, selfhood and space of subaltern women can be reclaimed and protected only through their bold initiatives in the form of protest movements/struggles, questioning gender inequality in different realms of societal life, etc. It helps them to emerge as new historical subjects and occupy new spaces. The Upper Cloth Revolt also prompts subaltern women to shun their inferiority complex and overcome the barriers of empowerment.

Theological articulation of Upper Cloth Revolt argues that the historical experiences of subaltern women should be interpreted to motivate contemporary subaltern women who are still struggling to secure their space in society. The stories of resistance by the subaltern women in the past can engage with the broken realities of contemporary subaltern women. Therefore, feminist theologizing should focus on bringing out the significance of those stories. It will contribute to the further development of feminist Christian theologizing. Interpreting the Christian faith in the light of the historical experiences of subaltern women opens new horizons of engagement and gives new momentum for addressing the issues of women in the respective faith community and in the larger society. The stories of foremothers should be celebrated along with the biblical women. Their sacrifice and pathos for the dignified life is also the site of God's visitation. The movements of subaltern women are the space where God meets the oppressed among the oppressed. They are the movements which seek freedom from patriarchal domination and celebration of identity and subjecthood of women. Therefore, feminist Christian theologizing can be understood as faith seeking freedom, dignity, selfhood and gender equality.

The Upper Cloth Revolt was the liberation struggle of an oppressed group in the Travancore society in the nineteenth century. The peculiarity of this movement is that dignity of women defined the social status of a community and decided its future action of combat. The concern of women became an issue of the community.

Women broke a centuries-old custom which prohibited them to cover their bosom with upper cloths. They took the risk involved in the questioning of a social restriction supported by the administrative and social systems of the day. The hegemony of caste and patriarchal traditions was challenged in this subaltern movement. Neither a low-caste identity nor repressive mechanism stopped them from seeking a dignified life. The Upper Cloth Revolt teaches that empowerment of subaltern women becomes a reality if the respective community considers it as their concern, and advancement of women brings respect to the community as a whole. Moreover, the upward mobility of any subaltern community depends on how the community responds to the hurdles of its advancement. It is also to be noted that the socio-political-economic-educational empowerment of subaltern communities and subaltern women comes through self/community assertion.

Religious faith worked as a source of liberation rather than source of bondage. The egalitarian values and principles of Christianity influenced the Nadars, particularly women to fight. The Christian faith provided an ideology for a life envisioned without restrictions. The contextual application of faith led them to search new prospects of life in society. It means the subaltern communities and subaltern women should attempt to understand and interpret faith and its values in terms of their contextual realities. The secondary position of subaltern women in the Christian faith communities is against the ethos of Christian faith. They must challenge the tendencies of using the precepts and traditions of faith to restrict their ministerial and community roles.

The Upper Cloth Revolt narrates a story of man-woman partnership in addressing the issue of women. Both men and women struggled and suffered physically and mentally for protecting of the dignity of Nadar women. The Nadar men supported the attempts of Nadar women to liberate their bodies from the control of the iniquitous social law. They placed the dignity of their women over the livelihood depended upon their labour in the fields of upper caste people. The implied meaning is that men in the subaltern communities are accountable to extend moral and physical support to the efforts of subaltern women to build up their lives in the domestic and public spheres. The empowerment of women, particularly the subaltern women in today's society can be achieved through the women-men partnership. Therefore, there has to be a change in the outlook and pattern of thinking of the subaltern men towards their women. They are not inferior beings but equal beings in every sense.

Theologically, the historical movements of subaltern communities are sites of divine-human encounter. God's liberative intervention in human history is visible through human endeavours of combating the evil forces which negate the celebration of life in its fullness. In this sense, the subaltern movements are divine initiatives to establish just life in this world. By trying to reclaim justice and equality in the life of subalterns, they are building up the Kingdom of God on earth. The subaltern struggles and historical experiences in the past stand as a beacon to the attempts of removing social disabilities of subaltern communities and women today.

The Upper Cloth Revolt calls for the unity of subalterns to achieve their goal of holistic development. Unity is very much needed within a subaltern community which is on the path of liberative struggle. Since the subaltern revolt is directly or indirectly against the hegemony of caste people, who constitute majority of ruling class, there will be attempts to thwart the united attempts of subalterns to shake off the societal disabilities. Therefore, the subalterns need to be aware of the possibility of religious and ideological divisions within the community. Beyond religious and ideological lines, subalterns have to join together against the common enemies. There has to be convergence of different subaltern groups within a community to initiate the process of empowerment. It will help the subalterns to put up united resistance to the powers of disempowerment and claim legitimate rights and space in the society.

Theological articulation of Upper Cloth Revolt gives shape to a new theological expression for the advancement of subaltern women in society as well as in faith community. The subaltern women are still unreasonably lagging behind in empowerment and representation in various realms of societal life. Their space in the contemporary socio-political-religious-economic spheres of the society continues to be limited or restricted because of their caste and gender identities. In this scenario, theology of *ta<u>n</u>ṯēṭam* suggests that subaltern women must cultivate *tan̲t̲ēṭam* within themselves to create and enlarge their limited *tan̲t̲ēṭam* (one's space) in the public and domestic life. In the Upper Cloth Revolt, the Nadar women exercised their *tan̲t̲ēṭam* to reclaim their negated *tan̲t̲ēṭam* (one's space). In the light of their experiences, it can be articulated that creating *tan̲t̲ēṭam* within subaltern women and enabling them to claim their legitimate *tan̲t̲ēṭam* (one's space) is the task of feminist theological discourse. Cultivating *tan̲t̲ēṭam* can be meant to make subaltern women courageous to say 'no' to the ideologies, traditions, outlook, customs, mannerism, religious beliefs, laws which question their dignity and selfhood. The subaltern women can create their space only if they have *tan̲t̲ēṭam*. Education, employment, activities of conscientization can be used as means to develop *tan̲t̲ēṭam*. The memories of the experiences of subaltern women in the historical struggle like Upper Cloth Revolt can instill *tan̲t̲ēṭam* in the psyche of contemporary subaltern women to initiate movements to develop *tan̲t̲ēṭam* (one's space). The Upper Cloth Revolt affirms that the body of subaltern woman is no more the site of humiliation and submissiveness but the space where *tan̲t̲ēṭam* is manifested. Therefore, the subaltern women need to be encouraged to exercise *tan̲t̲ēṭam* in every aspect of life.

In the theology of *tan̲t̲ēṭam*, the Biblical God is understood as God of *tan̲t̲ēṭam* who makes the weak powerful by injecting *tan̲t̲ēṭam* in them. The God of *tan̲t̲ēṭam* creates space for the spaceless, and empowers them to resist the powers which restrict their *tan̲t̲ēṭam* (one's space). The Upper Cloth Revolt proves that God of *tan̲t̲ēṭam* is with the subaltern women in their journey of struggle. The presence of the God of *tan̲t̲ēṭam* who made the Nadar women courageous (*tan̲t̲ēṭikal*) to question the oppressive caste and patriarchal customs and traditions can be sensed in the movements of subaltern women. It is the God of *tan̲t̲ēṭam* who enables subaltern women to go beyond the conventional space and demand justice. Jesus as *tan̲t̲ēṭi* who challenged the gender biased outlook of man in the Jewish society inspires the subaltern women in their march towards new destiny. Jesus as *tan̲t̲ēṭi* encourages them to question the social systems, traditions, laws, and way of thinking which makes them subordinate to men. Holy Spirit is the Spirit of *tan̲t̲ēṭam* for the subaltern women.

It dwells among them as *shakti* which instigate them to assert their *ta<u>n</u><u>t</u>ēṭam* (one's space). In short, the subaltern women have to acquire and manifest *ta<u>n</u><u>t</u>ēṭam* to challenge their imposed disabilities, and thereby creating their *ta<u>n</u><u>t</u>ēṭam* (one's space) in society. Simultaneously, the *ta<u>n</u><u>t</u>ēṭam* (one's space) of subaltern communities can also be affirmed through exercising *ta<u>n</u><u>t</u>ēṭam* in the respective societies. Courageous actions/initiatives lead to empowerment and creation of *ta<u>n</u><u>t</u>ēṭam* (one's space) of the subaltern communities and subaltern women in India. Recollecting and interpreting the subaltern history break new pathways of liberation and provide energy to claim new space in societal life.

Bibliography

1. Primary Source

(a) Documents and Reports

Baylis, F. *LMS Report of the Neyyoor Mission District for the Year 1859.* UTCA, Bangalore.

Copies of the Official Papers Sent from India Touching the Recent Disturbances in Travancore. Box no. 15 (MF). UTCA, Bangalore.

Cox, John. *LMS Report of the Trivandrum and Quilon Mission Districts for the Year 1858.* UTCA, Bangalore.

Dennis, John J. *LMS Report of the Nagercoil Home Station for the Year 1859.* UTCA, Bangalore.

London Missionary Society Report. May 1819. UTCA, Bangalore.

______. May 1820. UTCA, Bangalore.

______. May 1821. UTCA, Bangalore.

______. May 1825. UTCA, Bangalore.

LMS Report of the James Town Mission District for the Year 1859. UTCA. Bangalore.

Lewis, E. *LMS Report of the Santhapuram Mission District for the Year 1859.* UTCA, Bangalore.

Mateer, Samuel. *LMS Report of the Pareychaley Mission District for the Year 1859.* UTCA, Bangalore.

Neetu, vol. 20, pt. 1. Central Archives, Thiruvananthapuram.

Shanar Disturbances in South Travancore. Bundle no. 29. Cover File no. 2115 of 1858. Archives Directorate, Trivandrum.

(b) Books

Abbs, John. *Twenty-Two Years' Missionary Experience in Travancore.* London: John Snow & Co., 1870.

Agur, C.M. *Church History of Travancore.* Madras: S.P.S. Press, 1903; New Delhi: Asian Educational Service, 1990.

Aiya, V. Nagam. *Travancore Census Report 1891*, vol. I. Madras: Addison & Co., 1894.

______. *The Travancore State Manual,* vols. I, II. Trivandrum: Government Press, 1906.

Hacker, I.H. *A Hundred Years in Travancore 1806-1906.* London: H.R. Allenson, 1908.

Keralolpatti. Mangalore: Stolz & Reuther, Basel Mission Press, 1898.

Mateer, Samuel. *The Land of Charity.* London: John Snow and Co., 1871.

______. *Native Life in Travancore.* London: W.H. Allen & Co., 1883.

Menon, P. Shungoonny. *A History of Travancore from Earliest Times.* Madras: Higginbotham and Co., 1878.

Mullens, Joseph. *Missions in South India.* London: W.H. Dalton, 1854.

Pillai, T.K. Velu. *The Travancore State Manual,* vols. I, II. Trivandrum: Government of Travancore, 1940.

Selected Proclamations by the Sovereign from 1811-1939 AD. Trivandrum: Government Press, 1937.

Thurston, Edgar. *Castes and Tribes of South India*, vols. V, VI. Madras: Government Press, 1909.

2. Secondary Sources

(a) Books

Amirtham, Metti. *Women in India: Negotiating Body, Reclaiming Agency.* Delhi: ISPCK, 2011.

Amin, Shahid and Dipesh Chakrabarty, eds. *Subaltern Studies,* vol. IX. New Delhi: Oxford University Press, 1996.

Andrews, C.F. *Handbook of English Church Expansion North India.* London: A.R. Mowbray & Co., 1908.

Arnold, David and David Hardiman, eds. *Subaltern Studies,* vol. VIII. New Delhi: Oxford University Press, 1994.

Basu, B.D. *Rise of Christian Power in India.* Delhi: Low Price Publications, 2001.

Bevans, Stephen B. *Models of Contextual Theology.* New York: Orbis Books, 2002.

Bhanu, Busi Sunil, Monodeep Daniel and Indukuri John Mohan Razu. *Dalit Bible Commentary: New Testament*, vol. 8, *Ephesians, Philippians, Colossians, Thessalonians and Hebrews.* New Delhi: CDS, 2009.

Bhadra, Gautam, Gyan Prakash and Susie Tharu, eds. *Subaltern Studies,* vol. X. New Delhi: Oxford University Press, 1999.

Butterfield, Herbert. *Christianity and History*. London: Collins & Fontana Books, 1957.

Caleb, Sunil M. et al., *Dalit Bible Commentary: New Testament*, vol. 9, *Timothy, Titus, Philemon, Peter, James, Jude and John*. New Delhi: CDS, 2008.

Caldwell, Robert. *A Comparative Grammar of the Dravidian Family of Languages*. London: Harrison, 1856; revd. edn. Madras: University of Madras, 1961.

Carr, E.H. *What is History*. Harmondsworth: Penguin Books, 1961.

Chakravarti, Uma. *Gendering Caste: Through a Feminist Lens*. Calcutta: Stree, 2006.

Chatterjee, Partha and Gyanendra Pandey, eds. *Subaltern Studies*, vol. VII. New Delhi: Oxford University Press, 1992.

Chatterjee, Partha and Pradeep Jeganathan, eds. *Subaltern Studies*, vol. XI. New Delhi: Permanent Black and Ravi Dayal Publisher, 2000.

Clarke, Sathianathan. *Dalits and Christianity: Subaltern Religion and Liberation Theology in India*. New Delhi: Oxford University Press, 1998.

Cone, James H. *A Black Theology of Liberation*. New York: Orbis Books, 1986.

Daniel, J.T.K. *The Biblical Faith and Its Impact on Church and Society*. Delhi: ISPCK, 2008.

Daniel, Monodeep. *Dalit Bible Commentary New Testament*, vol. 7: *The First and Second Letters of Paul to The Corinthians*. New Delhi: CDS, 2008.

______. *Dalit Bible Commentary New Testament*, vol. 1: *Gospel According to Mathew*. New Delhi: CDS, 2008.

______. *Dalit Bible Commentary Old Testament*, vol. 3: *Deutronomy*. New Delhi: CDS, 2010.

______. *Dalit Bible Commentary Old Testament*, vol. 18: *Ezekiel*. New Delhi: CDS, 2012.

Daniel, Monodeep and Yangkahao Vashum (eds.), *Towards Justice and Peace: A Subaltern Initiative*. Jorhat: ETC, Nagpur: CNI Desk on Dalit and Tribal Concerns and New Delhi: CDS, 2010.

Daniel, Monodeep and James Massey. *Dalit Bible Commentary: Old Testament*, vol. 5, *Joshua and Judges*. New Delhi: CDS, 2012.

Deka, Meeta. *Women's Agency and Social Change: Assam and Beyond*. New Delhi: Sage, 2013.

Dhas, G. Issac Arul. *Kumari Mannil Kristhavam* (in Tamil) *Christianity in Kanyakumari*. Nagercoil: n.p., 2010.

Dietrich, Gabriele. *New Things on Earth*. Delhi: ISPCK, 1999.

Dumont, Louis. *Homo Hierarchicus*. English Edition. New Delhi: Oxford University Press, 1999.

Durant, Will and Ariel. *The Lessons of History*. New York: Simon and Schuster, 1968.

Elton, G.R. *The Practice of History*. Glasgow: William Collins & Co., 1967.

Fanon, Frantz. *The Wretched of the Earth*. Translated by Constance Farrington. London: Penguin Books, 1990.

Fernandez, Eleazar S. *Toward a Theology of Struggle*. New York: Orbis Books, 1994.

Fernando, Leonard and G. Gispert-Sauch. *Christianity in India*. New Delhi: Penguin/ Viking, 2004.

Forrester, Duncan B. *Caste and Christianity*. London and Dublin: Curzon Press & NJ: Humanities Press Inc, 1979.

Franco, Fernando, Jyotsna Macwan and Suguna Ramanathan (eds.), *The Silken Swing*. Calcutta: Stree, 2000.

Freire, Paulo. *Pedagogy of the Oppressed*. London: Penguin Books, 1972.

Galanter, Marc. *Competing Equalities: Law and The Backward Classes in India*. New Delhi: Oxford University Press, 1984.

Ghurye, G.S. *Caste and Race in India*. London: Routledge and Kegan Paul, 1932; reprint of fifth edition. Bombay: Popular Prakashan, 1994.

Gladstone, J.W. *Protestant Christianity and People's Movements in Kerala*. Trivandrum: The Seminary Publications, KUTS, 1984.

Gnanadason, Joy. *A Forgotten History*. Madras: GLTC, 1994.

Gnanadason, Aruna, ed. *Towards a Theology of Humanhood: Women's Perspectives*. Delhi: ISPCK, 1986.

Gonsalves, Francis. 'Body Symbols and Symbolic Bodies: Reaffirming Womanhood in the Church and Society', in *In Search of Space . . .* New Delhi: Commission for Women, Catholic Bishops' Conference of India, 2008.

Goretti, Maria, Monodeep Daniel and A. Maria Arul Raja. *Dalit Bible Commentary: New Testament*, vol. 2: *Gospel According to Mark*. New Delhi: CDS, 2009.

Gramsci, Antonio. *Selections from the Prison Notebooks of Antonio Gramsci*. Edited and translated by Quintin Hoare and Geoffrey Nowell Smith. Chennai: Orient Longman, 1996.

Grant, John W. *God's People in India*. Madras: CLS, 1960.

Grey, Mary. *The Unheard Scream: The Struggles of Dalit Women in India*. New Delhi: CDS, 2004.

Guha, Ranajit, ed., *Subaltern Studies,* vol. I. New Delhi: Oxford University Press, 1982.

______. *Subaltern Studies,* vol. II. New Delhi: Oxford University Press, 1983.

______. *Subaltern Studies,* vol. III. New Delhi: Oxford University Press, 1984.

______. *Subaltern Studies,* vol. IV. New Delhi: Oxford University Press, 1985.

______. *Subaltern Studies,* vol. V. New Delhi: Oxford University Press, 1987.

______. *Subaltern Studies,* vol. VI. New Delhi: Oxford University Press, 1989.

Gutierrez, Gustavo. *A Theology of Liberation: History, Politics and Salvation.* New York: Orbis Books, 1973.

H.A. *Day Dawn in Travancore: A Brief Account of the Manners and Customs of the People and the Efforts that are being Made for their Improvement.* Kottayam: C.M.S Press, 1860.

Hardgrave Jr., Robert L. *The Nadars of Tamilnadu.* Berkeley and Los Angeles: University of California Press, 1969.

Immanuel, M. *The Dravidian Lineages: The Nadars Through the Ages.* Nagercoil: HRPT, 2002.

Irudaya, Raj. *Dalit Bible Commentary New Testament*, vol. 4: *Gospel According to John.* New Delhi: CDS, 2009.

Jacob, John A. *A History of the London Missionary Society in South Travancore 1806-1959.* Nagercoil: The Diocesan Press, 1990.

Jeffrey, Robin. *The Decline of Nair Dominance.* New Delhi: Manohar, 1994.

Kadankavil, Thomas, ed. *Religion and Politics from Subaltern Perspective.* Bangalore: Dharmaram Publications, 1999.

Kawashima, Koji. *Missionaries and a Hindu State: Travancore 1858-1936.* New Delhi: Oxford University Press, 1998.

Kent, Eliza F. *Converting Women.* New York: Oxford University Press, 2004.

Keay, F.E. *A History of the Syrian Church in India.* London, 1938; Madras: SPCK, 1951.

Keitzar, Renthy. *In Search of a Relevant Gospel Message.* Guwahati: CLC, 1995.

Kerketta, Christ Sumit Abhay. *Adivasi Theology: Towards a Relevant Christian Theology for the Jharkhandi Adivasis.* Ranchi: ATCR/GTC, 2009.

Kitamori, Kazoh. *Theology of the Pain of God.* London: SCM Press, 1966.

Kooiman, Dick. *Conversion and Social Equality in India*. New Delhi: Manohar, 1989.

Kumari, Presanna, ed. *Reader in Feminist Theology*. Madras: Gurukul Lutheran Theological College and Research Institute, 1993.

Kumari, Prasanna. *Dalit Women's Experiences: A Theological Imperative for Indian Feminist Theology*. Chennai: Gurukul Lutheran Theological College, 2009.

Kyung, Chung Hyun. *Struggle to be the Sun Again*. New York: Orbis Books, 1990.

Logan, William. *Malabar Manual*, vol. I. Madras: Government Press, 1887; rpt. Trivandrum: Charithram Publications, 1981.

Longchar, A Wati. *Tribal Theology*. Jorhart: Eastern Theological College, 2000.

Mahajan, V.D. *India Since 1526*. New Delhi: S. Chand and Company, 1991.

Majumdar, R.K. and A.N. Srivastava. *Historiography: Method of History*. Delhi: Surjeet Books, 1985.

Mar Paulose, Paulose. *Swathanthryamanu Daivam* (Malayalam). Ariyannur: Patabhedam, 1996.

Massey, James. *Towards Dalit Hermeneutics: Re-reading the Text, the History and the Literature*. Delhi: ISPCK, 1994.

______. *Dalits in India*. New Delhi: Manohar, 1995.

______. *Introducing Dalit Theology*. New Delhi: CDS, 2004.

______. *Dalit Bible Commentary, New Testament*, vol. 3: *Gospel According to Luke*. New Delhi: CDS, 2007.

______. *Dalit Roots of Christianity, Theology and Spirituality*. New Delhi: CDS, 2008.

______. *Dalit Bible Commentary, New Testament*, vol. 5: *Acts of Apostles*. New Delhi: CDS, 2008.

______. *Dalit Bible Commentary, Old Testament*, vol. 2: *Exodus*. New Delhi: Centre for Dalit/Subaltern Studies, 2010.

______. *Dalit Bible Commentary, Old Testament,* vol. 8, I & II: *Samuel*. New Delhi: CDS, 2011.

______. *Dalit Bible Commentary, Old Testament*, vol. 17: *Jeremiah, Lamentations and Baruch*. New Delhi: CDS, 2012.

______. *Dalit Bible Commentary, Old Testament*, vol. 10: *Ezra, Nehemiah & Tobit*. New Delhi: CDS, 2013.

______. *Caste-Class Victims and Their Assertion for Justice*. New Delhi: Centre for Dalit/Subaltern Studies, 2013.

———. *Dalit Theology: History, Context, Text and Whole Salvation.* New Delhi: Manohar, 2014.

Massey, James and I. John Mohan Razu. *Dalit Bible Commentary, Old Testament*, vol. 9: I & II: *Kings,* I & II: *Chronicles.* New Delhi: CDS, 2012.

Massey, James and Monodeep Daniel. *Dalit Bible Commentary New Testament*, vol. 6: *Romans and Galatians.* New Delhi: CDS, 2008.

Massey, James and T.K. John, eds. *Rethinking Theology in India.* New Delhi: Manohar and CDS, 2013.

Memmi, Albert. *The Colonizer and the Colonized.* Boston: Beacon Press, 1965.

Menon, A. Sreedhara. *A Survey of Kerala History.* Revised Edition 1996; rpt. Madras: S. Viswanathan, 1998.

———. *Social and Cultural History of Kerala.* New Delhi: Sterling, 1979.

Menon, K.P. Padmanabha. *History of Kerala*, vol. II. Ernakulam: Cochin Govt. Press, 1929.

———. *History of Kerala,* vol. III. Ernakulam: Cochin Govt. Press, 1937; New Delhi: Asian Educational Services, 2001.

Minz, Nirmal. *Rise Up My People, And Claim the Promise.* Delhi: ISPCK, 1997.

Moon, Vasant, comp. *Dr. Babasaheb Ambedkar: Writings and Speeches,* vol. 1. Bombay: Education Department, Government of Maharashtra, 1989.

———. *Dr. Babasaheb Ambedkar: Writings and Speeches,* vol. 3. Bombay: Education Department, Government of Maharashtra, 1987.

———. *Dr. Babasaheb Ambedkar: Writings and Speeches,* vol. 5. Bombay: Education Department, Government of Maharashtra, 1987.

———. *Dr. Babasaheb Ambedkar: Writings and Speeches,* vol. 7. Bombay: Education Department, Government of Maharashtra, 1990.

Mulackal, Shalini. *Dalit Bible Commentary, Old Testament*, vol. 6: *Esther, Ruth and Judith.* New Delhi: Centre for Dalit/Subaltern Studies, 2011.

Muller, F. Max, ed. *The Sacred Books of the East*, vol. 25. *The Laws of Manu.* Translated by G. Buhler. Oxford: Oxford University Press, 1886; Delhi: Motilal Banarsidass, 1988.

Nadar, G. Krishnan. *A Text Book of Historical Method and Historiography.* Kottayam: Learners Books House, 1998.

Nadar, Kochu Krishnan. *Nadar Charitram* (Malayalam). Travancore: S.B. Press, 1956.

Neville, Robert Cummings. *Behind the Masks of God: An Essay Toward Comparative Theology.* Albany: State University of New York Press, 1991.

Oddie, G.A. *Social Protest in India.* Columbia: South Asian Books and New Delhi: Manohar, 1978.

Oommen, T.K. *Protest and Change.* New Delhi: Sage, 1990.

Osuri, Goldie. *Religious Freedom in India.* London & New York: Routledge, 2013.

Ouwerkerk, Louise. *No Elephants for the Maharaja.* New Delhi: Manohar, 1994.

Peter, D. and Ivy Peter. *Liberation of the Oppressed: A Continuous Struggle.* Nagarcoil: Kanyakumari Institute of Development Studies, 2009.

Phule, Jotirao Govindrao. *Slavery.* Translated by P.G. Patil. Bombay: Education Department, Government of Maharashtra, 1991.

Pillai, Elamkulam P.N. Kunjan. *Studies in Kerala History.* Trivandrum: Valsa Printers, 1970.

Poitevin, Guy. *The Voice and the Will, Subaltern Agency: Forms and Motives.* New Delhi: Manohar, 2002.

Prayikalam, Theramma. *Manakaruth Spirituality of Fisherwomen: Inspiration and Challenge to Consecrated Women.* Delhi: Media House, 2011.

Prokes, Mary Timothy. *Toward a Theology of the Body.* Edinburgh: T&T Clark, 1996.

Pui-lan, Kwok. *Introducing Asian Feminist Theology.* Cleveland: The Pilgrim Press, 2000.

Raj, Y.T. Vinaya. *Re-imagining Dalit Theology, Post Modern Readings.* Thiruvalla: CSS, 2008.

Raja, A. Maria Arul. *Dalit Bible Commentary: Old Testament,* vol. 1: *Genesis.* New Delhi: CDS, 2012.

______. *Dalit Bible Commentary: New Testament,* vol. 10: *Revelation.* New Delhi: CDS, 2009.

______. *Dalit Bible Commentary: Old Testament,* vol. 11: *Job.* New Delhi: CDS, 2012.

Rajkumar, Peniel. *Dalit Theology and Dalit Liberation.* Burlington: Ashgate, 2010.

Rani, T. Mercy. *Assailants of the Spirit and the Upholders of 'Sakti': An Indian Feminist Assessment of the Holy Spirit.* Bangalore: Sathri, 2003.

Razu, I. John Mohan. *Dalit Bible Commentary: Old Testament,* vol. 4: *Leviticus and Numbers.* New Delhi: CDS, 2011.

______. *Dalit Bible Commentary, Old Testament,* vol. 7: I & II, *Maccabees.* New Delhi: CDS, 2012.

_____. *Dalit Bible Commentary, Old Testament*, vol. 13: *Proverbs & Ecclesiastes*. New Delhi: CDS, 2013.

Sastri, K.A. Nilakanta. *A History of South India*. Fourth Edition. Madras: Oxford University Press (1955), 1992.

Sastri, K.S. Ramaswami, ed. *The Tamils*, vol. III. New Delhi: Cosmo Publications, 2002.

Selvaraj, C. *Historiography with Special Reference to India*. Udayamarthandam: CSR Publications, 1996.

Selvanayagam, Israel. *Samuel Amirtham's Living Theology*. Bangalore: BTESSC/SATHRI, 2007.

Sen, Amartya. *Development as Freedom*. Oxford: Oxford University Press, 1999.

Shilling, Chris. *The Body and Social Theory*. London: Sage, 2003.

Singh, K.S., ed. *People of India: Tamilnadu*, vol. XL, Part Two. Madras: Anthropological Survey of India, 1997.

Srinivas, M.N. *Social Change in Modern India*. Berkeley and Los Angles: University of California Press, 1968.

Srinivas, M.N. *India: Social Structure*. Delhi: Hindustan Publishing Corporation, 1986.

Stein, Burton. *A History of India*. New Delhi: Oxford University Press, 1998.

Templeman, Dennis. *The Northern Nadars of Tamilnadu: An Indian Caste in the Process of Change*. New Delhi: Oxford University Press, 1996.

Thanzauva, K. *Theology of Community*. Aizwal: Mizo Theological Conference, 1997.

_____. *Theology of Community: Tribal Theology in the Making*. Aizwal: AICS, 2004.

The Hymns of the Rigveda. Translated by Ralph T.H. Griffith. 1889 (1st edn.), revd. edn. 1973. Edited by J.L. Shastri. Reprint. Delhi: Motilal Banarsidass, 1986.

Thomas, V.V. *Understanding Subaltern History: Theoretical Tools*. Bangalore: BTESSC/SATHRI, 2006.

_____. *Dalit Pentecostalism*. Bangalore: ATC, 2008.

Thumma, Anthoniraj. *Wisdom of the Week*. Delhi: ISPCK, 2000.

Venkatensan, G. *A Study of Historiography*. Rajapalayam: V.C. Publications, 2005.

Vogel, Arthur. *Body Theology: God's Presence in Man's World*. New York: Harper & Row, 1973.

Webster, John C.B. *An Introduction to History*. Delhi: MacMillan, 1981.

———. *Social History of Christianity*. New Delhi: Oxford University Press, 2007.

———. *The Dalit Christians: A History*. Delhi: ISPCK, 2009.

Wilfred, Felix. *Margins: Site of Asian Theologies*. Delhi: ISPCK, 2008.

———. *Asian Public Theology*. Delhi: ISPCK, 2010.

Wilson, K. *Dialectics of Consciousness*. Madras: Oneworld Educational Trust, 1993.

Yesudas, R.N. *A People's Revolt in Travancore*. Trivandrum: Kerala Historical Society, 1975.

———. *British Policy in Travancore 1805-1859*. Trivandrum: Kerala Historical Society, 1977.

———. *Col. John Munro in Travancore*. Trivandrum: Kerala Historical Society, 1977.

———. *The History of the London Missionary Society in Travancore 1806-1908*. Trivandrum: Kerala Historical Society, 1980.

Yong-Bock, Kim. *Messiah and Minjung, Christ's Solidarity with the People for New Life*. Hong Kong: Christian Conference of Asia, 1992.

(b) Articles

(I) ARTICLES IN BOOKS

Abraham, Kochurani. 'And She Was Made Straight: A Feminist Theological Engagement with the "Bent" Lives of Indian Women', in *Margins in Conversation: Methodological Discourses in Theological Disciplines*, ed. Joseph Prabhakar Dayam and P. Mohan Larbeer. Bangalore: BTESSC, 2012.

———. 'Women and Violence: A Feminist Socio-Theological Enquiry', in *Violence in Today's Context*, ed. Shalini Mulackal and Roy Lazar A. Bangalore: Indian Theological Association & Asian Trading Corporation, 2012.

Anagol, Padma. 'From the Symbolic to the Open: Women's Resistance in Colonial Maharashtra', in *Behind the Veil*, ed. Anandita Ghosh. Ranikhet: Permanent Black, 2007.

Anderson-Rajkumar, Evangeline. 'New Eyes, New Reading, New Woman . . .', in *Feminist Hermeneutics*, ed. Lalrinawmi Ralte and Evangeline Anderson-Rajkumar. Delhi: IWTI/ISPCK, 2002.

Aye, Inato. 'The Logos Christology from Sema Perspective', in *Tribal Theology: A Reader*, ed. Shimreingam Shimray. Jorhat: Eastern Theological College, 2003.

Banerjee, Prathama. 'Caste and History Writing', in *Dalit Assertion in Society, Literature and History,* ed. Imtiaz Ahmad and Shashi Bhushan Upadhyay. New Delhi: Orient BlackSwan, 2010.

Cherian, A. 'The Selection of Research Students', in *Historical Research in India,* ed. John Correia-Afonso. New Delhi: Munshiram Manoharlal, 1979.

Chakrabarthy, Dipesh. 'Invitation to a Dialogue', in *Subaltern Studies IV*, ed. Ranajit Guha. New Delhi: Oxford University Press, 1985.

Clarke, Sunder. 'Dalit Movement: Need for a Theology', in *Towards a Dalit Theology*, ed. M.E. Prabhakar. Delhi: ISPCK, 1989.

Clarke, Sathianathan. 'Dalit Theology: An Introductory and Interpretative Theological Exposition', in *Dalit Theology in the Twenty-first Century*, ed. Sathianathan Clarke, Deenabandhu Manchala and Philip Vinod Peacock. New Delhi: Oxford University Press, 2010.

Cone, James H. 'Black Theology and Black Liberation', in *Black Theology: The South African Voice*, ed. Basil Moore. London: C. Hurst & Company, 1973.

______. 'The Social Context of Theology', in *Doing Theology Today*, ed. C.S. Song. Madras: CLS, 1976.

______. 'Christian Faith and Political Praxis', in *Confronting Life: Theology out of the Context*, ed. M.P. Joseph. Delhi: ISPCK, 1995.

Das, Veena. 'Subaltern as Perspective', in *Subaltern Studies* VI, ed. Ranajit Guha. New Delhi: Oxford University Press, 1999.

Devasahayam, V. 'Doing Theology: Basic Assumptions', in *Frontiers of Dalit Theology,* ed. V. Devasahayam. New Delhi: ISPCK and Chennai: Gurukul, 1997.

Divekar, V.D. 'Introduction', in *Social Reform Movements in India: A Historical Perspective*, ed. V.D. Divekar. Bombay: Popular Prakashan, 1991.

Dietrich, Gabriele. 'The Origins of the Bible Revisted-Reconstructing Women's History', in *Theology of Humanhood: Women's Perspectives*, ed. Aruna Gnanadason. Delhi: ISPCK, 1986.

Dube, Leela. 'Caste and Women', in *Caste: Its Twentieth Century Avatar*, ed. M.N. Srinivas. New Delhi: Penguin Books, 1996.

Gnanadason, Aruna. 'Feminist Methodology: Indian Women's Experience', in *Confronting Life: Theology out of the Context*, ed. M.P. Joseph. Delhi: ISPCK, 1995.

______. 'We Will Pour Our Oilment on the Feet of the Church: The Ecumenical Movement and the Ordination of Women', in *Feminist*

Hermeneutics, ed. Lalrinawmi Ralte and Evangeline Anderson Rajkumar. New Delhi: ISPCK, 2002.

Guha, Ranajit. 'Dominance without Hegemony and Its Historiography', in *Subaltern Studies VI*, ed. Ranajit Guha. New Delhi: Oxford University Press, 1989.

______. 'On Some Aspects of the Historiography of Colonial India', in *Subaltern Studies*, vol. 1, ed. Ranajit Guha. New Delhi: Oxford University Press, 1994.

______. 'Preface', in *Subaltern Studies*, vol. 1, ed. Ranajit Guha. New Delhi: Oxford University Press, 1994.

Gudorf, Christine E. 'Body, Self and Sexual Identity: Reflections on the Current Evidence', in *Body and Sexuality: Theological-Pastoral Perspectives of Women in Asia,* ed. Agnes M. Brazal and Andrea Lizares. Manila: Ateneo De Manila University Press, 2007.

Humtsoe, Eyingbeni. 'Women's Experience of 'Sorrow' As a Source for Doing Theology from Naga Perspective', in *No More Sorrow in God's Garden of Justice*, ed. Limatula Longkumaer. Jorhat: Eastern Theological College, 2007.

John S.J, T.K. 'Introduction', in James Massey. *Dalit Bible Commentary, Old Testament*, vol. 2: *Exodus.* New Delhi: CDS, 2010.

Jogdand, P.G. 'Caste System in India: Dr. Ambedkar's Perspective', in *Dalit Assertion in Society, Literature and History,* ed. Imtiaz Ahmad and Shashi Bhushan Upadhyay. New Delhi: Orient BlackSwan, 2010.

(Joy) Philip, Mary. 'A Woman of Shabbat', in *Mission with the Marginalized*, ed. Samuel W. Meshack. Tiruvalla: CSS, 2007.

Kanyoro, Musimbi. 'The Meaning of the Story: Theology as Experience', in *Culture, Women and Theology*, ed. John S. Pobee. Delhi: ISPCK, 1994.

Kumari, Prasanna. 'God's Image and Women', in *Feminist Theology: Perspectives and Praxis,* ed. Prasanna Kumari. Chennai: Gurukul, 1999.

Longchar, A. Wati. 'As Assessment of the Tribal Theology: Trends and Challenges for Future', in *Tribal Theology on the Move*, ed. Shimreingam Shimray and Limatula Longkumer. Johart: Tribal/ Women Study Centres, 2006.

______. 'Tribal Identity and Theology', in *Rethinking Theology in India*, ed. James Massey and T.K. John. New Delhi: Manohar and Centre for Dalit/Subaltern Studies, 2013.

Manorama, Ruth. 'Dalit Women: The Thrice Alienated', in *Towards a Dalit Theology*, ed. M.E. Prabhakar. Delhi: ISPCK, 1989.

Massey, James. 'Ingredients for a Dalit Theology', in *Towards a Dalit Theology*, ed. M.E. Prabhakar. Delhi: ISPCK, 1989.

_____. 'Ingredients for a Dalit Theology', in *Indigenous People,* ed. James Massey. Delhi: ISPCK, 1994.

_____. 'Historical Roots', in *Indigenous People: Dalits*, ed. James Massey. Delhi: ISPCK, 1994.

_____. 'Subaltern People and the Rise of their Movements', in *A Vision of Mission in the New Millennium*, ed. Thomas Malipurathu and L. Stanislaus. Mumbai: St. Paul's, 2001.

_____. 'Vision, Nature and Method of Dalit Theology', in *Dalit-Tribal Theological Interface*, ed. James Massey and Shimreingam Shimray. Jorhat: TSC/WSC and New Delhi: CDS, 2007.

_____. 'Christianity to be Renewed? Rethink Theology', in *Rethinking Theology in India*, ed. James Massey and T.K. John. New Delhi: Manohar and Centre for Dalit/Subaltern Studies, 2013.

Massey, James and T.K. John. 'Preface', in *Rethinking Theology in India*, ed. James Massey and T.K. John. New Delhi: Manohar and Centre for Dalit/Subaltern Studies, 2013.

Mawrie, Barnes L. 'Experience of the Tribal Historical, Political, Socio-Cultural Contexts', in *Dalit-Tribal Theological Interface*, ed. James Massey and Shimreingam Shimray. Jorhat: TSC/WSC and New Delhi: CDS, 2007.

Melanchthon, Monica Jyotsna. 'Dalit Readers of the Word: The Quest for Hermeneutics and Method', in *Frontiers in Dalit Hermeneutics*, ed. James Massey and Samson Prabhakar. Bangalore: BTESSC/ SATHRI & Delhi: CDS, 2005.

Mies, Maria. 'Class Struggles and Women's Struggles in Rural India', in *Women: The Last Colony*, ed. Maria Mies et al. New Delhi: Kali for Women, 1988.

Minz, Nirmal. 'Theology and the Struggle of Adivasis/ Indigenous People of India', in *Rethinking Theology in India*, ed. James Massey and T.K. John. New Delhi: Manohar and Centre for Dalit/Subaltern Studies, 2013.

Monteiro, Evelyn. 'Re-imaging Woman and Reshaping her Destiny: An Indian Feminist Reading of the Bent Body (Lk 13: 10-17)', in *Body and Sexuality: Theological-Pastoral Perspectives of Women in Asia,* ed. Agnes M. Brazal and Andrea Lizares. Manila: Ateneo De Manila University Press, 2007.

Moore, Basil. 'Preface', in *Black Theology: The South African Voice*, ed. Basil Moore. London: C. Hurst & Company, 1973.

———. 'What is Black Theology', in *Black Theology: The South African Voice*, ed. Basil Moore. London: C. Hurst & Company, 1973.

Mulackal, Shalini. 'Margin as a Site of Sacred Encounter', in *Revisiting and Resignifying Methodology for Dalit Theology*, ed. James Massey and Indukur John Mohan Razu. New Delhi: CDS & Bangalore: UTC, 2008.

———. 'Sexual Abuse and the Church: Some Moral Dilemmas', in *Gender Relations in the Church: A Call to Wholeness and Equal Discipleship*, ed. Astrid Lobo Gajiwala, Varghese Theckanath S.G. and Raynah Braganza Passanha. Pune: Streevani & Hyderabad: Montfort Social Institute, 2012.

———. 'Women: Theology and Feminist Movements in India', in *Rethinking Theology in India*, ed. James Massey and T.K. John. New Delhi: Manohar and CDS, 2013.

———. 'Dalit Belief Systems and Rituals', in *Theology for a New Community*, ed. T.K. John and James Massey. New Delhi: Centre for Dalit/ Subaltern Studies, 2013.

Mundadan, A.M. 'Hindu and Christian Views of History', in *History and Contemporary India*, ed. John C.B. Webster. Bombay: Asian Publishing House, 1971.

Nirmal, Arvind P. 'A Dialogue with Dalit Literature', in *Towards a Dalit Theology*, ed. M.E. Prabhakar. Delhi: ISPCK, 1989.

———. 'Doing Theology from a Dalit Perspective', in *A Reader in Dalit Theology*, ed. Arvind P. Nirmal. Madras: Gurukul/UELCI, 1991.

———. 'Towards a Christian Dalit Theology', in *A Reader in Dalit Theology*, ed. Arvind P. Nirmal. Madras: Gurukul/ UELCI, 1991.

Nuthalapati, B.E. Bharathi. 'A Survey of the Historiographical Shifts in the History of Christianity in India', in *Margins in Conversation: Methodological Discourses in Theological Disciplines*, ed. Joseph Prabhakar Dayam and P. Mohan Larbeer. Bangalore: BTESSC, 2012.

Ntwasa, Sabelo and Basil Moore. 'The Concept of God in Black Theology', in *Black Theology, The South African Voice*, ed. Basil Moore. London: C. Hurst & Company, 1973.

Poho, Huang. 'Forward', in Wati Longchar, *Returning to Mother Earth*. Tainan: PTCA & Kolkata: Sceptre, 2012.

Prabhakar, M.E. 'The Search for a Dalit Theology', in *Towards a Dalit Theology*, ed. M.E. Prabhakar. Delhi: ISPCK, 1989.

———. 'Introduction', in *Towards a Dalit Theology*, ed. M.E. Prabhakar. Delhi: ISPCK, 1989.

Pui lan, Kwok. 'The Emergence of Asian Feminist Consciousness on Culture and Theology', in *Culture, Women and Theology,* ed. John S. Pobee. Delhi: ISPCK, 2004.

Rege, Sharmila. 'Caste and Gender: The Violence Against Women in India', in *Dalit Women in India: Issues and Perspectives*, ed. P.G. Jogdand. New Delhi: Gyan Publishing House & Pune: University of Pune, 1995.

Sauter, Gerhard. 'How Can Theology Derive from Experiences?' in *Doing Theology Today*, ed. C.S. Song. Madras: CLS, 1976.

Singaram, Charles. 'Dalit Identity and Textual Tradition', in *Revisiting and Resignifying Methodology for Dalit Theology*, ed. James Massey and Indukur John Mohan Razu. New Delhi: CDS and Bangalore: UTC, 2008.

Taesoo, Yim. 'Reflection on Minjung Theology: Messianism and a New Understanding of Minjung-Messianism', in *Dalit and Minjung Theologies: A Dialogue*, ed. Samson Prabhakar and Jinkwan Kwon. Bangalore: BTESSC/SATHRI, 2006.

Thanzauva, K. 'Issues in Tribal Theology', in *Tribal Theology: A Reader*, ed. Shimreingam Shimray. Jorhat: Eastern Theological College, 2003.

Thomas, M.M. 'Foreword', in R.H.S Boyd, *An Introduction to Indian Christian Theology*. Delhi: ISPCK, 1991.

Thomas, V.V. 'Methodological Discourses in Theological Disciplines and Approaches in Historiography with Special Reference to the Marginalized in the Pentecostal Churches in India', in *Margins in Conversation: Methodological Discourses in Theological Disciplines*, ed. Joseph Prabhakar Dayam and P. Mohan Larbeer. Bangalore: BTESSC, 2012.

Tzudir, Atula. 'The Future of Feminist Theology', in *Tribal Theology on the Move*, ed. Shimreingam Shimray and Limatula Longkumer. Jorhat: Tribal/Women Study Centers, 2006.

Vanlaltlani, T. 'Problems and Challenges of Doing and Teaching Feminist Theology in North East India', in *Tribal Theology on the Move*, ed. Shimreingam Shimray and Limatula Longkumer. Jorhat: Tribal/Women Study Centers, 2006.

Vareed Alexander, Anna. 'Through the Feminist Looking Glass: Images of Women', in *The Emerging Christian Women*, ed. Stella Faria, Anna Vareed Alexander and Jessie B. Tellis-Nayak. Indore: Satprakashan Sanchar Kendra and Pune: Ishvani, 1984.

Vashum, Yangkahao. 'Sources for Studying Tribal Theology', in *Tribal*

Theology: A Reader, ed. Shimreingam Shimray. Johart: Eastern Theological College, 2003.

Vijayakumar. 'History of Christianity: Methodology for Research', in *Methodological Issues in Theological Discipline,* ed. Samson Prabhakar. Bangalore: Sathri, 2002.

Webster, John C.B. 'From Indian Church to Indian Theology: An Attempt at Theological Construction', in *A Reader in Dalit Theology*, ed. Arvind P. Nirmal, 1991; rpt. Chennai: Gurukul, 2007.

(II) ARTICLES IN JOURNALS

Abraham, K.C. 'Third World Theologies', *CTC Bulletin*, vol. XI, nos. 2 & 3 (May-December 1992), pp. 4-12.

Amalorpavadass, D.S. 'Theological Reflections on Inculturation', *Indian Theological Studies* 29/3-4 (1990), pp. 217-72.

Anderson-Rajkumar, Evangeline. 'Significance of the "Body" in Feminist Theological Discourse', *Bangalore Theological Forum*, vol. xxxiii, no. 2 (December 2001), pp. 80-98.

Arul Raja, A. Maria. 'Points of Convergence: Dalit World and Biblical World', *Jeevadhara*, vol. XLI, no. 241 (January 2011), pp. 45-55.

Ayrookuzhiel, Abraham. 'Dalit Challenges to Religious Systems: A People Ignored by Church History', *Indian Church History Review*, vol. XXIII, no. 2 (December 1989), pp. 115-31.

Bama. 'Dalit Christian Women Today: Their Struggles and Prospects for Future', *Jeevadhara,* vol. XLI, no. 241 (January 2011), pp. 35-44.

Fernando, Leonard. 'Editorial: Living Hope', *Vidyajyoti Journal of Theological Reflection*, vol. 76, no. 11 (November 2012), pp. 1-3.

Hemrom, A.S. 'Towards a Program of Contextual and Adivasi Theology', *Religion and Society*, vol. 50, no. 3 (September 2005), pp. 87-96.

Keitzar, Renthy. 'Theology Today.' *Journal of Tribal Studies*, vol. II, no. I (January-June 1998), pp. 1-18.

Mulackal, Shalini. 'Living with Diminished Humanity: A Theological Critique', *Oriens Journal for Contextual Theology*, vol. 4 (2013), pp. 118-34.

Tesoo, Yim. 'Interpretation of the Old Testament from the Perspective of Minjung Theology', *Journal of Tribal Studies*, vol. XIII, no. 2 (July-December 2008), pp. 1-20.

Vakayil, Prema. 'Biblical Women: A Retrospect', *Oriens Journal for Contextual Theology*, vol. 4 (2013), pp. 104-17.

Webster, John C.B. 'The History of Christianity in India: Aims and Methods', ICHR 13/2 (December 1979), pp. 87-122.

Weil, Shalva. 'Symmetry between Christian and Jews in India: The Cnanite Christians and the Cochin Jews of Kerala', *Contributions to Indian Sociology,* vol. 16, no. 2 (1982), pp. 175-96.

3. Newspaper

The Telegraph (Calcutta), 2 January 2013.

4. Dictionary/Lexicon

Soanes, Catherine and Angus Stevenson, eds. *Concise Oxford English Dictionary, Indian Edition.* New Delhi: Oxford University Press, 2007.

Balakrishnan, B.C., ed. *Malayalam Lexicon,* vol. VI. Trivandrum: The University of Kerala, 1988.

Pillai, Suranad Kunjan, ed. *Malayalam Lexicon,* vol. II. Thiruvananthapuram: The University of Kerala, 2003.

5. Interview

Gladstone, J.W. Former Moderator of Church of South India and Professor of Church History and Former Principal of Kerala United Theological Seminary. Interview, 15 April 2013.

Yesudas, R.N. Professor of History and former Director, Institute of Distance Education and Dean of Social Sciences, University of Kerala. Interview, 2 May 2013.

6. Commission Report

Reservations for Backward Classes, Mandal Commission Report of the Backward Classes Commission, 1980. New Delhi: Akalank Publications, 1990.

7. The Bible

The Holy Bible, The New International Version.

Index